PRAISE FOR *ERASING THE FINISH LINE*

"Getting into college has become an endless series of jumping through hoops for teenagers, yet when they get to campus they don't often know their purpose for being there....In this timely and important book, Ana Homayoun gives students and families the blueprint they need to launch into a fulfilling life and engaging career. At a time when the skills needed to keep up in any job are churning at an ever faster pace, Homayoun provides us with a guide to the foundational skills that will help us succeed no matter what."

—Jeffrey Selingo, *New York Times* best-selling author of
Who Gets In and Why and *There Is Life After College*

"*Erasing the Finish Line* is the book I will recommend over and over in the coming years, a gift to parents, educators, and adolescents confused by the conflicting demands of achievement and fulfillment."

—Jessica Lahey, *New York Times* best-selling author of
The Gift of Failure and *The Addiction Inoculation*

"Ana Homayoun has given parents a blueprint for guiding *all* kids—not just the most advantaged—in the "how," not the "what," of authentic, lifelong success.... What matters most are the skills our kids use to make sense of [things to] take on life's challenges....This book will come as a relief for every parent who wants to help strengthen the bones of the building [and] not just its facade."

—Rachel Simmons, author of *Odd Girl Out* and *Enough As She Is*

"Eye-opening and compelling, this book has the answers that parents and educators need right now. We've been mismeasuring achievement and pushing kids toward the wrong goals. Homayoun shows us how to shift our mindsets and nurture the real skills children need to identify and fulfill their own aspirations."

—Jordan Shapiro, author of *Father Figure* and *The New Childhood*

"Goodbye to the false finish line! Ana Homayoun is stoking important conversations, and we can only hope parents, teachers, and counselors are listening. I love her empowering, open-minded approach to guiding young adults on their varied paths to adulthood."

—Mary Laura Philpott, author of *Bomb Shelter:*
Love, Time, and Other Explosives

"What's more important than any acceptance letter? *Self-acceptance....*This book is practical, extraordinarily empathetic, and a breath of fresh air, and it's just what the doctor ordered for anxious parents and anxious teens alike."

—Anya Kamenetz, author of *The Stolen Year* and *The Art of Screen Time*

"In an exponentially changing world, *Erasing the Finish Line* gives us new perspectives and frameworks for redefining success. Recognizing the range of barriers every individual faces and the scope of talent each [young adult] brings, this brilliant book helps students and parents prepare for a fulfilling future in which one can run [their] own race."

—Sanyin Siang, executive director at Duke University's
Coach K Center on Leadership and Ethics (COLE),
CEO Advisor, and author of *The Launch Book*

"In her thought-provoking book, Ana Homayoun fearlessly questions the prevailing mindset that a good life is simply a linear path from good grades to a good school and ultimately a good job....With unflinching conviction, Homayoun gives readers the insight and encouragement needed to dismantle this harmful fallacy. *Erasing the Finish Line* will resonate deeply with caring adults who believe that young people deserve the opportunity to self-define success and chart their own authentic path."

—Kyle Schwartz, author of I *Wish My Teacher*
Knew and I *Wish for Change*

"There is a 'door's always open' sensibility to *Erasing the Finish the Line.* Ana Homayoun seemed to be writing just to me, as if I were one of the thousands of parents who've walked into her office looking for sage guidance for my kids from *that* advisor to whom everyone wants to talk. She answers *your* questions yet, more importantly, encourages you to ask better questions about what your kids genuinely want and need. This book offers smart [and] practical advice that will help every parent reset household expectations for what success really means."

—Gregg Behr, coauthor, *When You Wonder,*
You're Learning: Mister Rogers' Enduring Lessons
for Raising Creative, Curious, Caring Kids

ERASING
THE
FINISH
LINE

ERASING THE FINISH LINE

The New Blueprint for Success Beyond Grades and College Admission

ANA HOMAYOUN

hachette
BOOKS

New York

Copyright © 2023 by Ana Homayoun

Cover design and illustration by Sara Pinsonault

Cover copyright © 2023 by Hachette Book Group, Inc.

Hachette Go, an imprint of Hachette Books

Hachette Book Group

1290 Avenue of the Americas

New York, NY 10104

HachetteGo.com

Facebook.com/HachetteGo

Instagram.com/HachetteGo

First Edition: August 2023

Hachette Books is a division of Hachette Book Group, Inc.

The Hachette Go and Hachette Books name and logos are trademarks of Hachette Book Group, Inc.

The Hachette Speakers Bureau provides a wide range of authors for speaking events. To find out more, visit hachettespeakersbureau.com or email HachetteSpeakers@hbgusa.com.

Hachette Go books may be purchased in bulk for business, educational, or promotional use. For information, please contact your local bookseller or email the Hachette Book Group Special Markets Department at Special.Markets@hbgusa.com.

The publisher is not responsible for websites (or their content) that are not owned by the publisher.

Print book interior design by Amy Quinn.

Library of Congress Cataloging-in-Publication Data

Name: Homayoun, Ana, author.

Title: Erasing the finish line: the new blueprint for success beyond grades and college admission / Ana Homayoun.

Description: New York: Hachette Go, 2023. | Includes bibliographical references and index.

Identifiers: LCCN 2023008682 | ISBN 9780306830693 (hardcover) | ISBN 9780306830709 (trade paperback) | ISBN 9780306830716 (ebook)

Subjects: LCSH: Education—Aims and objectives—United States. | Academic Achievement—United States. | Critical thinking—Study and teaching—United States.

Classification: LCC LA217.2 .H647 2023 | DDC 370.973—dc23/eng/20230405

LC record available at https://lccn.loc.gov/2023008682.

ISBNs: 9780306830693 (hardcover); 9780306830716 (ebook)

Printed in the United States of America

LSC-C

Printing 1, 2023

For Cameron

CONTENTS

AUTHOR'S NOTE   *ix*

INTRODUCTION   *xi*

HOW TO USE THIS BOOK   *xxi*

CHAPTER 1
**EXPANDING OUR VISION BEYOND
THE FAULTY FINISH LINE**   1

CHAPTER 2
**NAVIGATING THE WORLD WITH
NEW FOUNDATIONAL SKILLS**   11

PART ONE
DEVELOP A SYSTEM   19

CHAPTER 3
START AT THE BEGINNING   23

CHAPTER 4
DELIVERABLES   37

CHAPTER 5
LEARNING TAKES LONGER   47

PART TWO
DEVELOP CONNECTION   57

CHAPTER 6
FLOATING   61

CHAPTER 7
OPTIMISM AND OPENNESS   77

CHAPTER 8
LEVERS   85

PART THREE
DEVELOP PERSPECTIVE   95

CHAPTER 9
OPPORTUNITY AND ACCESS   97

CHAPTER 10
EXPANDING POSSIBILITIES   109

CHAPTER 11
ONLINE AND IRL (IN REAL LIFE)   117

PART FOUR
DEVELOP ACCEPTANCE   131

CHAPTER 12
DIFFERENT PATHWAYS   135

CHAPTER 13
LIVING WITH HEIGHTENED UNCERTAINTY   145

CHAPTER 14
THE NEVER-ENDING CHECKLIST OF TO-DOS   157

PART FIVE
DEVELOP A BLUEPRINT   173

CHAPTER 15
THE BLUEPRINT CAN PIVOT   177

CHAPTER 16
NEURODIVERSITY   187

CONCLUSION: NOTEBOOK CHECKS   199
ACKNOWLEDGMENTS   203
REFERENCES   207
NOTES   215
INDEX   223

AUTHOR'S NOTE

I'VE ALWAYS BELIEVED THAT NO ONE COMES INTO MY OFFICE, OR INTO my life, hoping to be in a book someday. For this work, I had the immense privilege of listening to the stories of individuals who shared their insights with a mix of indefatigable humor and hard-won wisdom. Some of the young adults within these pages first walked into my office years ago, and a few of their stories were shared in the pages of my previous works. Speaking with them years later and learning about their winding journeys in their own words, with the benefit of time and reflection, is something I consider to be an enormous gift. Given this, I have disguised details as needed. Where people are identified by first name, those names have been changed. In a few select instances, a composite character streamlined details while remaining true to the overall spirit of the story.

INTRODUCTION

IT'S A FEW DAYS BEFORE THE WINTER HOLIDAYS, AND I AM SCROLLING through Instagram. The videos are hard to miss: a high school senior, sitting at a computer, clicking away. Sometimes the student is alone, other times surrounded by a group of family and friends. There is an initial concentration—a squinting of the eyes and furrowing of the brow as they click through to find the email that will reveal the seemingly life-changing news. Then, eyes widen, followed by shrieks of revelation and unadulterated joy.

The child has been *accepted*.

Getting into college has become an insidious cultural norm, with bragging rights when students are admitted to schools, car stickers and sweatshirts and entire industries catering to the belief that this one decision can fundamentally alter the entire trajectory of a young person's life.

As an academic advisor, I have spent more than twenty years guiding thousands of kids and their families through the middle school, high school, and college years, including helping students and families navigate the college application process. I've seen the process play out up close year after year—so much has changed, so much remains unchanged, and the same painfully unhealthy focus on college acceptance remains.

Years ago I experienced it all myself. In the spring of my senior year of high school, several weeks after receiving the coveted "you've been accepted" package in the mail, my father and I took a red-eye flight from San Francisco to Durham, North Carolina, to visit Duke University's campus for the first time. Until then, I'd avoided visiting campuses in advance of my application process, citing cost concerns but actually not wanting to fall in love with a school only to be rejected. It was one of the many things I did as a teenager that I now encourage students *not* to do.

———

Standing in front of the school's iconic chapel, I decisively turned toward my father and declared, "This is it."

Despite my jet lag, I vividly remember walking into the Duke Store after our campus tour, overwhelmed by row upon row filled with piles of every Duke-branded item you never knew you needed. I watched in disbelief as my comically frugal immigrant father cheerfully added everything and anything to our shopping basket. You want a sweatshirt? A hat? A keychain? *No problem.* How about that car blanket? Scarf? *Add it to the pile!* Never before and never since have I seen him spend money so willfully. I could see the happiness and enthusiasm in his eyes, and it made me happy. He was so proud of me. I was relieved. I had been accepted. His work was done. My work was done. (Spoiler alert: no one's work was done.)

There's nothing wrong with the feelings of elation that result from achieving something that feels hard earned. At my high school, I sensed the grudging approval of some of my classmates, some of whom were impressed, others who couldn't hide their jealousy. "*You* got into Duke?!" the girl in my Calculus BC class asked me as she whipped around and tried (but failed) to hide her disgust. To this day the college application process creates a whole lot of frenemies among high school students, whose competitive drive cuts an invisible cord between once-friendly and helpful classmates—and parents! My high school was no exception.

Even in that environment, however, the underlying approval that came from being accepted felt so, so good, as if some higher college admissions power had given all my life efforts up until that day a stamp of approval—*you did good, kid.* And there was the undeniable sense of comfort; I knew where I would be headed next, and I had been accepted somewhere I could be proud of—a highly ranked university, a "good" school. It felt great in the moment, and I felt worthy of the overflowing pile of items the Duke Store sales associate efficiently rang up with care. She had seen all of this before.

So as I scroll through social media all these years later, I fully understand the joy and exhilaration on these students' and parents' faces. In fact, the first time I saw one of these college acceptance videos on social media, I teared up. Watching a student surrounded by classmates and teachers at a charter school serving mostly first-generation, low-income, historically excluded students, I couldn't help getting caught up in the anticipation and elation. In that moment, the video felt like a communal celebration of a long-awaited milestone. To some degree it was.

However, as I continue scrolling now, seeing what seems like the millionth highlight reel of college acceptance, my enthusiasm wears off. Instead of thinking about the students and families on the screen, I think about my own experience of getting rejected from my "dream school," which I applied to via Early Decision during the fall of my senior year. Yes, that elation and relief I felt in the spring at Duke was in part the result of the despair I'd felt a few months earlier when I'd received a thin envelope from that other institution encouraging me to "explore other options" and wishing me "all the best."

Seeing these videos online, I think about today's high school seniors who have not gotten their dream acceptance letter, about how they feel being endlessly bombarded by these images and videos. It's one thing to process disappointment and rejection, which is a normal part of life. It's entirely another to be reminded of it at every digital turn. By the time my alma mater posts a compilation of student acceptance videos on their social media accounts and I see a friend post her own daughter's acceptance reel, I feel like I am being trolled.

It's easy to fall for this romantic notion that acceptance into a "good" college or university guarantees a lifetime of success. While certain experiences during early adulthood can fundamentally change lives in glorious ways, most adults with at least a couple of decades of living under their belts will agree that life doesn't come with guarantees, especially around "success." Why, then, are we falling for this idea when it comes to young people?

To me these videos represent a greater conversation around how we—and by "we" I mean parents, caregivers, educators, and students—have made getting into certain colleges an end-all, be-all, make-or-break finish line. In doing so, we've inadvertently created an overvalued, excessively rigid, and downright false judgment around what constitutes a "good" or "bad" launching pad to a successful life. We become caught up in a cycle that dismisses the fundamental skills critical for long-term well-being in favor of short-term results. The consequences of doing so are dire.

It's no secret that many affluent families spend an inordinate amount of time and money focused on undergraduate college acceptances. With the Operation Varsity Blues scandal, a criminal conspiracy to influence undergraduate admissions decisions at a few highly selective universities that landed celebrities, financial executives, and others in prison, we saw how this pressure to gain parental bragging rights has led adults to make dubious, unethical, and illegal choices in the pursuit of college acceptance.[1]

One of the many "new normals" that students and families were forced to adjust to in the midst of a global pandemic is stunningly low college acceptance rates. In recent years, announcements of hyper-selectivity have become the norm for Ivy League schools and their peers. Yale admitted only 4.7 percent of applicants to the class of 2026, and Harvard a paltry 3.19 percent.[2] At the same time, overall applications rose by 10 percent in 2022.[3] Frank Bruni, author of the 2015 *New York Times* best seller *Where You Go Is Not Who You'll Be*, describes this staggering reality as driven by "economic pessimism" or "the sense among parents and their children that every last possible competitive advantage must be seized."[4] And even though the majority of US institutions actually accept the majority of college applicants,[5] this frenzy has created a sense of desperation that has led some parents to make unfortunate choices that ultimately don't support the well-being or the long-term success of their children.

This frenzy is not just experienced among the affluent and well connected. We often look at data around college graduation and lifetime earnings and mistakenly assume that college graduation is the sole missing link to economic mobility for children growing up in low- and middle-income households. As the cost of college and university soars, some students and parents have been saddled with enormous loans, all to receive a college diploma that provides no foolproof guarantee of long-term prosperity.

The laser focus that families and schools direct toward competitive college admissions is harming students' well-being and reinforcing the fundamental misconception that only a select few elite colleges are the appropriate launching pads to support students' long-term success. Recent data has revealed that college selectivity is not a reliable predictor of student learning, job satisfaction, or well-being.[6] Rather, students' levels of engagement in college—whether they participate in internships that apply classroom learning to real-life settings, have mentors who encourage them to pursue personal goals, or engage in multi-semester projects—correlated more strongly with positive outcomes after college.[7] These valuable experiences are often underemphasized in service of helping students craft the "perfect" application and résumé. As John Duffy writes in *Parenting the New Teen in the Age of Anxiety*, this slim definition of achievement "folds our kids into a very small box that allows precious little space for play, experimentation, and thriving."[8] The high levels of fear activated by the flurry of information and daunting statistics surrounding the college process often end up steering parents and children alike, quashing students' creativity and freedom to create their own blueprints for true fulfillment.

As we begin to question this outdated narrative equating college admissions and success, we are met with the opportunity to reimagine the kind of support we provide for young people as they embark on the next chapter of their lives. Instead of focusing on racking up accolades, recent data highlight the importance of social well-being and emotional development as key to building strong habits and refining skills that impact long-term success.[9] There exists no perfect equalizer, no singular magic bullet, but we do an incredible disservice to students in investing wholeheartedly in a competitive, demoralizing process that masquerades as a single-track pathway to a successful life.

College acceptance itself has also falsely become a symbol of parenting triumph as well as personal and intellectual/educational success—or failure. Students erroneously conflate college acceptance—or rejection—with their intelligence, ability, and long-term professional and financial potential. Parental anxiety permeates every conversation, as if eighteen years of child rearing and carpooling and science fairs and sports tournaments all culminate in this final evaluation. Within the halls of public, charter, private, and parochial middle schools and high schools across the country, "getting into a good school" has become a default marker of character and worth. I recently received an email from the parents of a fifth grader wanting to know what it takes to be admitted to a "top-tier college." This is hardly the first time.

Year after year, I've watched entire families—including family pets!—be overtaken by the roller-coaster ride toward college acceptance or failure. I remind them that getting into college, unto itself, does not make a life, and they all believe me, up to a point. Parents, caregivers, and educators regularly admit to lying awake at night, worried about children's academic gaps and learning lags, as well as their long-term social and emotional well-being. The three conditions affecting teens and young adults ages thirteen to twenty-two were anxiety, depression, and adjustment disorders—and rates of all exploded in the spring of 2020 as the COVID pandemic reached its first apex.[10] Female students in particular have been increasingly suffering; in 2021, almost 60 percent of teen girls experienced persistent feelings of sadness or hopelessness during the past year, and nearly 25 percent made a suicide plan. Across all young people, poor mental health outcomes have reached disturbing new heights, raising alarm bells for parents and educators alike.[11] And yet we've been so overly focused on the concerning data that we've given little focus to creating sensible, strategic solutions to help students move forward and learn to navigate their lives amid such turmoil. The false finish line created around college admissions is not just exhausting and misleading; it is fundamentally crushing the social well-being and emotional development of our kids.

In our quiet moments away from the immense pressure to be accepted, most of us are well aware of how damaging the college acceptance pressure has become.

It doesn't have to be this way.

The idea that college acceptance is some kind of magic carpet to lifelong success helps no one. In fact, it encourages us to overlook critical skills that young people today will need to develop in our ever-changing world. In the coming chapters, I will share fundamental skills that every student can benefit from developing throughout their schooling and beyond. Our over-emphasis on college acceptance as a finish line has meant we've collectively undervalued these critical skills in favor of predetermined markers like grades, test scores, and college acceptances.

For some students, including those who may not have sufficient access and exposure in their immediate worlds, a nurturing college experience can expand opportunities and perspectives around what's possible for them and their lives. Still, without many of the underlying skills I discuss in the upcoming chapters, long-term well-being may very well remain out of reach.

I've now spent more than two decades working with students from all socioeconomic backgrounds, from all over the country and around the world. From their stories, along with my own upbringing as the child of immigrants, I have a front-row seat to thinking about what needs to change.

My office is located in the heart of Silicon Valley, in a downtown area not far from where I moved as a middle school student, and a few miles from tech notables such as Apple, Google, and Meta. The whole area has been highlighted as a cradle for academic stress and anxiety.

In my work, as well as my own life, it has been abundantly clear that the incessant focus on grades, test scores, endless extracurricular activities, and awards is NOT what makes students happier, more "successful," or more driven and purposeful. True growth and engagement come from identifying the best system to address and complete everyday tasks and to-dos, as well as authentic exposure to different perspectives and a self-awareness of what is energizing and what is exhausting. So many students crave genuine connection and supportive friendships. By teaching students how to reframe or opt out of draining experiences and to navigate everyday disappointment in effective and meaningful ways, we allow them to create their own blueprints for success and fulfillment.

A few years ago, on a personal mission to look at the educational barriers to social and economic mobility that hold many kids back, I also began traveling around the country, interviewing educators, administrators, students, social workers, and community leaders to better understand the underlying issues so many students encounter on their way to adulthood.

What I learned didn't surprise me:

- Most students lack day-to-day executive functioning skills needed to succeed as adults.
- Many students who don't have family or friends who have achieved the success they desire aren't clear on how to move toward those dreams.
- Students with limited resources frequently lack exposure to people, organizations, and opportunities that could expand their worldview as well as direct and redirect them toward goals.
- Social and emotional coping skills critical to long-term well-being and success are underemphasized and viewed as secondary, or even tangential, by many parents, teachers, and administrators.

My work in understanding different barriers in kids' lives—and thinking about ways to address and even dismantle some of those barriers—has helped me recognize how those disparities shortchange all young people of the opportunity to flourish personally and professionally. Through my work, I have seen students develop meaningful career trajectories through using the skills highlighted in this book. I have helped students who were mistakenly told they weren't able to attend college, much less earn the master's degree they ultimately attained. I acted as a mentor and then a sponsor—terms I define in the section on connection—for a student who had spent several years in the foster-care system as she graduated from college and went on to earn a six-figure salary working for a technology firm before age thirty. A few students navigated mental health crises that required hospitalizations and long-term treatment. Student stories like these have shown me that the never-ending checklists, must-haves, and to-dos we place on students often work against them in the short and long term. The faulty finish lines we demarcate, however well intended, often have the opposite effect, preventing kids from gaining the critical-thinking and life skills that truly can and will change their lives for the better.

By the time college graduation rolls around, well-heeled students with high levels of social capital are accustomed to tapping connections from long before their college acceptance. Focusing on the skills highlighted in this book will not make up for the host of systemic challenges that can act as barriers to access and opportunity, but, with intentional efforts, they can start to make a notable difference.

What I've realized is that we critically underestimate the time, structure, and support we can offer all kids, and we repeatedly overlook the powerful impact of supporting students as they develop these foundational skills.

As we continue to address the impacts of a pandemic that magnified the limitations of the faulty finish lines we create for kids, we have an incredible opportunity to reconsider our educational structures and priorities. Now is the time to redefine what success looks like in the classroom and beyond. By moving beyond a shortsighted overemphasis on grades, test scores, and "résumé-builder" activities, we can give students the opportunity to better consider how they want to be of service to themselves, their families, and their greater communities. What's more, they can do all of that in ways that bring a sense of enthusiasm, joy, and calm in a world that constantly over-whelms with stimulation and uncertainty. In doing so, we can also support greater equality of opportunity among young people.

The bottom line is this: the current one-size-fits-all (but available to few) checklist of "résumé builders" is an old, staid model that isn't doing anyone any favors. Instead, we can show students how to be the architects of their own futures in a way that focuses on curiosity, com-munity engagement, and belonging. By placing greater focus on previ-ously undervalued skills—organization, planning, prioritization, flexible thinking, and authentic, non-transactional relationship building—we can nourish the creativity, innovation, connection, and leadership that are increasingly at the heart of true success in our fast-changing world. By placing greater emphasis on foundational life skills from an earlier age, we can give more students from all backgrounds and experiences the time, structure, and support to reflect on their own individual interests, values, and experiences in tangible ways.

HOW TO USE THIS BOOK

ERASING THE FINISH LINE HIGHLIGHTS HOW CERTAIN FOUNDATIONAL skills can utterly change life trajectories and promote overall well-being in remarkable ways. It shows how all of us—parents, caregivers, educators, basically anyone and everyone who cares about our future—can help our youngest generation navigate this ever-changing world in a way that promotes their social and emotional well-being as well as economic stability.

As part of my research for this book, I interviewed some of the students I worked with many moons ago. They are now young adults in their late twenties and early thirties who have now taken the various skills they learned and followed their own pathways—many different pathways, in many different places, toward uniquely fulfilling versions of success. A few were straight-A students; most were not. Some came from families who were far better connected and more financially secure than others. In most cases, they've pursued their own authentic paths and developed their own blueprints for success using the underlying principles I explain in this book. I also reflected on my own upbringing as someone who has experienced significant economic and social mobility and benefited from exposure to opportunities and proximity to resources that positively affected my life in extraordinary ways.

In the coming chapters, I'll share some of their stories as I introduce the foundational skills that empower kids to develop their own pathway to success and well-being. I'll discuss redefining success in terms of essential executive functioning skills rather than the grades, awards, achievements, and test scores we've misguidedly deemed to be markers of success. Time and time again, I've seen how focusing on underlying routines and skill building over résumé building has helped students develop their own blueprint far beyond any initial goals or expectations. I'll also show how exposure to an expanded worldview, along with shared experiences, helps kids develop a sense of curious engagement and an ability to build community: friendships and relationships filled with stronger ties as well as weaker connections.

Throughout this book, I've sprinkled tangible, practical, accessible ways we all can play a vital role in helping young people develop their own blueprint, which translates to a redefined path of lifelong success.

> It is my hope that kids will return to these foundational skills again and again, throughout their life—and that these skills will help them reflect, adapt, and redirect in a world increasingly different from the one their parents grew up in.

Erasing the Finish Line isn't about how we transform a kid. It is a model for how we can transform the world by focusing on the skills young people need to navigate a high-tech, pandemic-adjusted world. It doesn't mean we place less emphasis on the humanities or the sciences; it simply means we recognize that other long-ignored modes of developing oneself are at least as important in transforming a life as they are in transforming a society.

Our world is ever changing, often in ways that are socially, economically, and politically unpredictable. What feels like daily uncertainty and a lack of stability is the root of much of the anxiety and the sense of overwhelm that is shared by children and adults alike. Many jobs in demand today didn't exist two decades ago and therefore might be better suited to different kinds of education or training skills—and daily life itself seems to be constantly shifting, often as science and technology advance.

The most important aspect of my work is how it has helped young people feel about their journey and their role in the world. I regularly see students who once felt defeated and alone bounce out of my office with enthusiasm about learning these foundational skills. They've become more intrinsically motivated and excited about their options and possibilities. I've also seen the energy in audiences at schools around the world when young people have an "a-ha!" moment, realizing that they, too, can use these foundational skills to optimize their potential and change their daily lives—and then the future as well.

I am an optimistic realist who has worked with thousands of young people and their families around the world and seen, time and time again, the power of listening to kids and supporting them in developing a sense of control over their journey. When we do this, we enable them to thrive well beyond their wildest dreams and, in the process, erase the faulty finish line that college admissions has become.

CHAPTER 1

EXPANDING OUR VISION BEYOND
THE FAULTY FINISH LINE

AFTER SPENDING THE PAST DECADE VISITING DIFFERENT SCHOOLS and communities, I can confidently say two things: one, nearly every community has its own set of false finish lines, and two, none of this happens overnight. Nearly all parents and caregivers find themselves in the midst of hundreds of false little finish lines that start far earlier and become far more ingrained than we realize. Remember those pregnancy apps that say the baby should be the size of, say, a mango in utero, during this particular week? Or comparing a child to the height and weight percentiles for infants and toddlers at the pediatrician's office? Or the ways teachers and parents can become unnerved if kids don't hit certain milestones at certain times? These milestones can certainly be valuable indicators of whether extra support and intervention might be necessary at a given time. However, they can also cause unnecessary panic.

Somewhere down the line, the agony that can come from these false finish lines starts to make kids nervous, too. There starts to be this nagging belief that if they don't make the traveling soccer team or qualify for advanced fifth-grade math or AP classes as a high school junior or land first chair in the orchestra or win the 4-H rodeo, that something, anything, everything might fall apart. All our goals, plans, and dreams hinge quietly on these narrow and never-ending false finish lines. In time, some of the milestones that initially kept parents awake become sources of children's angst as well.

All students benefit from developing a certain set of skills throughout their elementary, middle, and high school years, and some classes and activities can be enormously helpful in developing those skills. For instance, participating in a school play can provide students with organizational, prioritization, and communication skills. Being on the debate team may help some students learn how to form a succinct argument quickly and flex their thinking in multiple ways in order to be convincing. (Notice that I **didn't** say "being *the star* debater" on the debate team.) Being a reporter for the school newspaper can help with critical-thinking skills, creativity, and meeting deadlines. (Notice again that I **didn't** say "being the *top reporter* or *editor in chief*" of the school newspaper.) Adaptable thinking, curiosity, and meeting deadlines are important skills in childhood *and* adulthood. Shifting our focus to place more value on core academic and personal development as well as life-management skills can be the foundation for lasting fulfillment in multiple areas of life.

One of the many points in the college admissions process where I've seen our detrimental faulty finish line mind-set is when high school seniors apply to a school and get deferred, which can feel like a derailment for students and families more than we imagine.

DEFERRAL

"I did everything right. I, I, I did everything they told me to . . .," Lauren says, her voice trailing off. Her brown hair tied in a loose bun, she is wearing an oversized sweatshirt emblazoned with COLUMBIA that casually envelops her petite frame.

After weeks of disrupted sleep, Lauren feels hopelessly on the verge of a breakdown. She's a teenager with nine college applications due within a week, but not a single one is ready to submit. Or at least that's what she thinks.

She'd spent weeks nervously awaiting an admissions decision from her "dream school." The email had finally arrived but not with the news she'd hoped for. Instead of being accepted, she'd been deferred. That moment when she learned this news has been replaying in her mind ever since, each time ending with questions like, *What else could I have done? What was wrong with my essay? Why did they take the other girl at my high school and defer me?*

Lauren had applied to her "dream school" Early Decision in November of her senior year. Being deferred in mid-December meant she wouldn't know whether she would be accepted until sometime in the spring, and the odds were not in her favor. At many schools, the number of students who are deferred from Early Decision and ultimately accepted is low; at Duke, only 110 initially deferred students joined the class of 2026, which is 5 percent of all accepted students.[1] Over the past few years, MIT reports having admitted between one hundred and three hundred students in Regular Admission who were deferred in Early Admission, and at Georgia Tech University, approximately 20 percent of deferred students were ultimately accepted for the first-year classes of 2025 and 2026.[2] Lauren's notification date had effectively been punted, which meant that in addition to processing the disappointment of not getting the news she wanted, she now had looming deadlines to finish the applications to other schools that she had been avoiding.

The deferral has left her school counselor concerned. He is now strongly encouraging her to apply Early Decision II to another school. Problem is, there's no other school that Lauren is excited to commit to attending if accepted. At this moment when everything seems in flux, she feels too overwhelmed to make a decision. According to her school counselor, Lauren's application might get lost in the shuffle if she applies to other schools during the regular decision application cycle. She is a strong student, but according to the school counselor, she's not "top of her class." As a result, he tells Lauren and her parents quite plainly that she is "running the risk of not getting in anywhere *good*."

Early Decision is a college enrollment strategy where a student applies to a school, and as part of their application signs a note saying that if accepted, they commit to enrolling in said university. In other words, if you let me in, I promise I will attend. The strategic machinations of whether to apply Early Decision have been around for years, since before I applied to college in the 1990s. Some colleges now fill more than half their first-year class using the Early Decision process. Over the past few years, colleges have offered more than one deadline to apply Early Decision, leading to Early Decision II and Early Decision III deadlines in January and beyond. The reasoning for asking for a seemingly binding commitment is not tied to student wellness, of course. It is tied to enrollment management and yield—making sure the applicants whose grades, personal statement, and achievements are pored over and who are ultimately accepted attend the university.

Now, as Lauren sits before me on the other side of a virtual Zoom room, we are on opposite coasts, but I can clearly see the emotional impact of uncertainty and overwhelm in real time. Trying to sound witty and charming and wise in a host of short essays while experiencing an underlying state of panic is difficult for any teenager, even a writer as talented as Lauren.

As we've talked, she's been fighting back tears, but now she snaps back with precision. "Okay, let's go," she says. She regains her determined composure and returns to editing, seemingly unaffected, as if her face has been splashed with a bucket of cold water. I see sentences forming on my screen as she writes in our shared Google document.

"Lauren, it is going to work out," I say gingerly, repeating words that someone told me many years ago that I didn't, at the time, believe any more than she believes them now. "We just don't know how it will turn out. Right now is hard, and I get it. Not knowing how it will work out can feel overwhelming."

"I know, I know, but can I complain for one minute?" she says with a sly smile and a tilt of her head, and when I nod, she shares a bit of gossip from her elite private high school on the Upper East Side of New York City.

To the outside world, Lauren is confident, decisive, and bold. Her career aspiration is to be a human rights lawyer, and she's earned As in many of the Advanced Placement courses at her high school. She's interned at a nonprofit organization fighting human trafficking, shadowed a criminal court judge, and is a highly ranked debater. She acts in plays and writes poetry and spent more than a year organizing an online writing group and exchange with a group of girls her age in Afghanistan. They met weekly until the country fell to the Taliban in August 2021.

For years, I've maintained a strict policy of not working during the last two weeks of December. I'll happily work more hours throughout the year to have those two weeks completely off—no meetings, no phone calls, nothing but unstructured time to read, write, watch movies, walk, and work out. I tell everyone and anyone that I will be unavailable. Over the past fifteen years, my focus on executive functioning skills and proactive planning created a system where high school students can manage their college application process and complete all their applications around Thanksgiving of their senior year, in part to avoid the sort of end-of-the-year overwhelm Lauren is now experiencing.

A few days before my self-imposed holiday bliss is set to begin, Lauren sends me a note telling me that she's been deferred. Even though I hadn't worked with Lauren on her application process, I've known her mom professionally for years and offered Lauren insight and perspective as a family friend. Not long thereafter, I catch up with Lauren's parents as I am walking my dogs in the morning, and I hear the heightened strain through the phone line. Lauren's mother admits she herself hasn't been sleeping. *Should they have advised her differently? What could they, and she, have done differently? Should she have applied Early Decision somewhere else?* The school counselor's mere suggestion that Lauren might not get in anywhere "good" unless she applies Early Decision II to another school induces unbearable levels of stress for Lauren and everyone in her immediate orbit, including her parents, sister, and the family dog, a snowy white shih tzu named Lola.

Despite my upcoming break, I offer to act as a sounding board as Lauren comes to the realization that she is exhausted from a long semester, feels dejected, and has a mountain of work to complete. Lauren is not one of my students, I reason, and I am doing this because I want to—in large part because I have empathy for her situation and can relate. I am confident she will have options she will be happy with in the end, but she's in the messy middle phase of her journey. And personally, I've been there. In some ways, Lauren reminds me of my teenage self, and if I could go back in time, I would sit my teenage self down and tell her to chill out. And take more studio art classes.

Lauren thought she did everything she was supposed to do: she took the rigorous classes, earned top grades, studied and received top test scores, and participated in interesting, unique activities that were meaningful to her. She has the street smarts of a teen who seamlessly figures out the fastest way to get cross-town using public transportation and the wit of someone who has continuously been coming up with a counterargument. She is interesting, engaging, thoughtful, and curious. She creates the most elaborate birthday cards and can get lost in reading a good book on the subway. I knew that no matter where Lauren was ultimately admitted to college, she would continue to take advantage of opportunities that came her way and develop her own blueprint for success. Her parents were supportive, driving her to debate tournaments and sitting around waiting to pick her up from play practice, but Lauren was always in the driver's seat. And yet perhaps the reason I agreed to give up some of my holiday break to wade through the depths of her college application mess was because I saw how clearly the college application process—and the faulty finish line it creates—was eroding her sense of self and her sense of worth.

"I have a question for you," Lauren starts, trailing off into an inquiry around whether I thought she would get in anywhere and how this would all turn out. Gently, calmly, and firmly, I patiently move in circles reminding her of her agency in the process, reassuring her of her different options, and encouraging her to move forward and focus on what she can control and to let go of the rest. Patience can be tough for a teen told to wait in a world where so much feels instantaneous.

Lauren has undeniable levels of privilege—her parents are well-connected professionals, and she attends a prestigious private school with notable alumni. She's lived in New York City all her life, with access to cultural and educational opportunities that she and her other classmates take for granted. Still, what I've found for students like Lauren is that this level of access and opportunity creates a hollow and narrow definition of what success looks like—throughout school (*These classes! Those scores! This activity! That honor!*), throughout the college application process, and in life (*This car! That job! That spouse! This house! That summer community! New, bigger, better job!*). In time, the artificial markers of achievement undervalue the foundational skills highlighted in upcoming chapters. It becomes of secondary importance that students take time for thoughtful exploration and become actively engaged in their school and greater communities in ways that are meaningful for them. The need for rest and purposeful reflection becomes devalued, and the benefits of exploration and shared experiences are underemphasized. In short, we focus on short-term achievements and markers of success at the expense of skill building that can be essential for long-term social and economic stability as well as for social and emotional well-being.

"Let's look at your list of what you want to finish over the next few days," I say to Lauren, knowing that breaking down all of her to-dos into manageable chunks will help restore her sense of confidence. As we scroll through various sections of a seemingly endless Google document, she suggests a few to-dos, and then she figures out how to prioritize them.

Over the course of ten days, Lauren slowly begins to recognize that the college application process, which is filled with flaws we cannot quickly change, can be reframed as an opportunity to reflect upon and actively convey who she is and how she sees the world. She loves writing, and once she moves beyond her fear of not having any "good" college options, she begins to feel emboldened enough to trust that she will ultimately have options where she will thrive.

Part of helping Lauren regain her sense of autonomy and agency—essentially, helping her feel that she can choose how to spend her time and, eventually, her life—is rooted in encouraging her to break her day down into three buckets: work (when she works on applications), movement (when she goes for a walk, stretches, or does something fun that gets her moving), and rest (when she relaxes on the couch, takes a bath, listens to music, or goes to sleep). Instead of spending every waking minute focused on her college applications, she can set a timer, work for a concentrated amount of time, and then put on a jacket, hat, and gloves and walk around the block for a fresh air break.

As she begins to follow these guidelines, she comes to see the diminishing returns of sitting in front of a computer all day and that looming deadlines don't mean the work needs to overtake every moment of every day. This new way to organize her time means her work gets completed sooner and with less stress.

"Hey, this is actually pretty good," Lauren offers with a hint of surprise, finally allowing herself to kindly evaluate one of the essays that she's been staring down for hours from a wider lens. "I like how this is turning out." In the time we'd been working together over Zoom, this is the first bit of self-compassion I've witnessed from her.

More words appear on my screen; she's starting to nitpick and overedit her already-great work. Her perfectionist tendencies are finding problems where she and I both know there are none.

"Stttttttooooooppppp the madness," I say in a joking voice but with underlying seriousness. "It is done. It is wonderful. Step away from the document." She laughs.

Thinking about the college admissions process as a faulty finish line wasn't just about helping Lauren organize her time and to-do list, though that was important since she felt that often paralyzing combination of overwhelm and exhaustion. It was also about encouraging her own self-awareness and helping her recognize her unique perspective. In doing so, we could reframe this as an opportunity for self-exploration and discovery of who she is, what she is interested in, and what are the many different places—there is *never* just one—where she could continue her educational journey. It was also about her accepting where she was in the moment and recognizing she had choices in how she moved forward.

When it came to deciding where to apply, I encouraged Lauren to look beyond the rankings and so-called prestige factor to the qualities that were important to her outside of the college experience. For starters, there are ways we underestimate how location matters.

"If access to voting rights is important to you, it might be interesting to look at where you could volunteer or get hired to work on a local or state election of interest," I suggest, encouraging her to expand her vision beyond a somewhat myopic list that was similar to so many highly achieving students at high schools across the country.

At first, she balked at my reframing and wondered whether I didn't think she was "good enough" for the schools already on her list. But once she started looking at different schools and spoke with students, she learned more about experiential programs that could help her build skills and expose her to experiences that would be helpful for life after college. She came to realize my point wasn't that she would choose where she would attend college based on the presidential or midterm election cycle but rather that she could move beyond thinking there was only one type of school, one type of place, in one type of location where she would and could thrive.

Lauren ultimately met her application deadlines, and in the process, she regained her sense of agency and worth. She expanded her initial vision of success, and even though her stress initially prevented her from thinking clearly, we came up with manageable to-dos and found ways for her to organize, prioritize, plan, start, and complete tasks. We often take for granted the benefits of receiving outside guidance to come up with a system and the time, structure, and support that make tasks more manageable, especially when students are feeling the situational overwhelm Lauren was experiencing during that time. And, when we assume students are doing well by using their grades, test scores, and achievements as markers of overall well-being, we can miss the bigger picture.

CHAPTER 2

NAVIGATING THE WORLD WITH NEW FOUNDATIONAL SKILLS

Eleven miles separate Charlotte Country Day School, an independent school in one of the wealthier enclaves in America, and Thomasboro Academy, a public K–8 school where nearly 100 percent of students are eligible for free and reduced lunch.

Charlotte Country Day School is, in many ways, a genteel country-club version of a K–12 education, a private school with a pedigree where connections and internships and job offers could be a phone call or casual cocktail conversation away. The facilities mirror those of a well-endowed small liberal arts college, and the school completed a $90 million capital campaign in the 2020–2021 school year to fund a wide range of facility upgrades.[1] When the upper school dean initially invited me to speak to students and parents, he soon asked me, "How comfortable are you around very wealthy people?"

Not long before that speaking invitation, Charlotte, North Carolina, was ranked last in an analysis of economic mobility in America's fifty metropolitan cities by the Harvard and University of California, Berkeley, Equality of Opportunity Project. The landmark study found that *where* children are born has a significant impact on their opportunities for economic mobility.

Using analyzed data from the parents of children born in 1980–1982, the study measured income of the children thirty years later to see the impact on upward mobility.[2] In 2015, Harvard professor and lead researcher Raj Chetty went one step further to analyze the same data and look at what happened when kids moved from what he deemed lower-opportunity areas to higher-opportunity areas. The results were notable: moving from low-opportunity spaces to high-opportunity spaces earlier meant better life outcomes for kids, including a higher likelihood that they would attend college and then earn more money over their lifetime.[3]

Charlotte philanthropists and city leaders set out to determine why children born into the bottom 20 percent of the income distribution in Charlotte had just a 4.4 percent chance of making it to the top 20 percent of the income distribution. In other words, if a child was born poor in Charlotte, North Carolina, the chances of escaping poverty were really low—and, according to the data, lower than in any other metropolitan city in America. It wasn't long before Charlotte allocated resources, formed committees and a task force, and pledged millions of dollars to address the issue. Public discussions and focus groups with experts from research institutions including Harvard University and the Brookings Institution soon followed.

It seemed interesting, and at the time also clear to me, that a key missing element was helping students with certain foundational skills needed to learn and thrive beyond getting through high school and accepted into college. After spending years helping middle school, high school, and college students organize their binders, manage their digital folders, clean out their backpacks, and get excited thinking about different routines and systems along with ways to develop connections and gain perspective, I saw how these often undervalued skills changed life trajectories. In my mind, any focus on test scores and graduation rates was shortsighted if the work wasn't rooted in giving students the ability to navigate their own worlds by focusing on these skills.

So I was intrigued on a sweltering, humid Sunday afternoon in the Queen City when one of Charlotte's well-connected nonprofit executives agreed to meet me at a local coffee shop in South Charlotte. Eighteen months after my initial visit to Charlotte Country Day, and after nearly a year of email exchanges, we met a few doors down from the local independent bookstore, Park Road Books, shortly before I was supposed to have a launch event for my recently released book on social media and technology.

"I've visited with students," the nonprofit executive explained, discussing the past few months he'd spent on a listening tour around the city, trying to understand how his adopted hometown had such barriers to upward mobility. "They want to do well. They have these big dreams and hopes and aspirations. But they are frustrated because they have no idea how to get from here to there."

"What do you think it would take to improve education in schools?" the executive asked me philosophically. Being neither a resident of Charlotte nor an expert on economic mobility, I wasn't qualified to identify the city's specific barriers to upward mobility. However, even in my limited time there, I sensed two things: Charlotte was a big small town run on connections, and despite being home to transplants from all over the country, the city's roots ran deep. "That's the million-dollar question," I replied. "I would start by doing a needs assessment."

The opportunity to complete an initial needs assessment in Charlotte provided a fresh challenge. But at a deeper level, as I began to learn about the research behind the Equality of Opportunity Project, I realized there was another reason I was so curious and attracted to the work: my own personal experience with economic mobility. If the study had looked at kids born in 1979, my family might have been included. And if so, I might have been counted as a success story. By the time the opportunity to do an initial needs assessment in Charlotte came along, I was nearing a midcareer point and having a bit of an existential crisis. Because even with my own hard work in school, which included good grades and strong test scores, the most pivotal turning points in my own life had been the result of a conversation, a connection, or an unlikely invitation. And since I'd experienced significant social and economic mobility over the course of my life, I consequently spent time and energy navigating seemingly disparate worlds with no real sense of "home." At times, it felt empowering to be able to move with relative ease in different environments. And at other times, as for many of my peers in similar situations, it could also feel lonely and exhausting. I began to look back and ask myself, *When? Where? How? Why me?*

A few years earlier, I began to examine the ways I benefited from many experiences that seemed of little consequence at the time. In looking back, I could see how many of them had utterly changed my life trajectory. I thought about the skills I worked with students on and how many of those same skills benefited me at different points throughout my journey. Somehow they had each led from one opportunity to the next, all of which would have left eight-, ten-, or twelve-year-old me wide-eyed and in disbelief.

This is the main reason, in retrospect, the opportunity to spend time in Charlotte soon became all-encompassing. There's really no other way to explain why I would come to spend thousands of hours and fly thousands upon thousands of miles to learn the stories of students, parents, educators, and leaders in a city so far from where I lived, and later throughout the United States, ultimately saying yes to opportunities that consistently sapped me of mental, emotional, and financial resources. The deeper I dug, the more I became entrenched in thinking through the skills and experiences that made all the difference in my life and the lives of others.

The Equality of Opportunity Project offered some answers that fit into the story of my life. Right before middle school, my family moved from rural Connecticut, where my parents had ultimately landed after immigrating to the United States and first settling in Bridgeport, to the San Francisco Bay Area, which the study identified as one of the metropolitan regions where a child was most likely to experience upward mobility.[4] I still say that moving across the country right before junior high was a cultural shock that proved to be one of the most challenging times in my life, and I also believe that the experience was unequivocally the best thing that ever happened to me. The move created more career opportunities for my parents and different educational opportunities and expectations for my younger sister and me. It also increased our access and exposure beyond the world we knew.

Several months after that initial trip to Charlotte, I began interviewing educators, administrators, students, social workers, community leaders, and well-connected public officials living in Charlotte and elsewhere throughout the United States, and I listened to their stories about what they thought had changed their life trajectory.

A common thread emerged: for those who had experienced economic and social mobility, something had happened, most often around the pre-teen middle school years but also in high school and college, that ultimately altered the course of their life.

During one of those interviews I met Jasmin, a recent college graduate who came back to Thomasboro Academy to squeeze on a couch between her former teachers and school support staff. Jasmin was in her early twenties, though she could have easily passed for a high school student. Her caramel-colored box braids reached past her waist, and she paired a fashion-forward flowery dress with knee-high boots in a way that conveyed an inherent sense of style. Her initial quiet, soft-spoken nature revealed an underlying sense of humor and determination once she became more comfortable. Jasmin attended Thomasboro through the fifth grade and felt a connection to the school and to the staff. She was a favorite reading buddy of a longtime volunteer at the school, who had known Jasmin for more than fifteen years. When she was in middle school, Jasmin was accepted to a well-regarded magnet middle school across town, where many of her class-mates were highly affluent, well-connected students from South Charlotte and elsewhere throughout the city whose families knew how to garner the best resources for their children.

For Jasmin, her middle school years provided a new perspective through exposure and shared experiences that could have impacted her life had they intentionally continued through high school and beyond. She became friends with classmates from different socioeconomic backgrounds and was a person who said hello to nearly everyone in the hallways. When district rules transferred her back to a high school in her neighborhood, resources were scarcer than across town. By the time she applied to college several years later, she didn't ask anyone for help and received just one acceptance letter, despite a transcript with mostly As and Bs.

Driving around the winding roads of Charlotte to my other interviews, I kept thinking about Jasmin. She had done many of the "right" things to achieve economic mobility: attended a magnet middle school, earned good grades, and graduated from college in just three and a half years, despite struggling with the sudden deaths of two family members along the way. All throughout her life, she had heard of the importance of getting into college and graduating—without much emphasis placed on life beyond that. When we first met, she was a few years out of college, juggling two eleven-dollar-per-hour jobs and living at home with her family.

I knew that much of the work we do in my office would have been helpful for a student like Jasmin—she wasn't at the bottom or top of her class but somewhere in the middle 60 percent, where students are routinely overlooked in a system with limited resources. To be frank, the kids down the road at Charlotte Country Day or at Lauren's school on the Upper East Side of Manhattan need these skills just as badly. But wealthier kids don't often require the same economic or social mobility to get a shot at their ambitions, and, in some cases, the need for these skills can be obscured by opportunity, access, and resources. In Jasmin's case, learning how to organize, plan, prioritize, and feel comfortable asking for help and following up on offers for support wouldn't have erased the host of systemic challenges she would continue to face, but they might have started to give her a more effective tool kit.

Like Jasmin, many lower-income public school students in Charlotte and elsewhere don't have family or friends who had achieved the level of success they aspired to. They lack the connections needed to access networks, resources, and social capital that were within a few miles of where they lived. One high school student I met aspired to attend a highly selective university but hadn't taken a sufficiently rigorous academic course load in high school—largely because no one had guided him to do so, and the information wasn't as readily available or easily digestible as one might imagine.

What Jasmin had succeeded at—those grades, getting that diploma—had never taught her how to think about life beyond the faulty finish line of college admissions. The message and mantra she received throughout her childhood was that college acceptance was key. She had successfully graduated from college, and yet, when it came to her postcollegiate ambitions, Jasmin seemed to be straddling the line between what Richard Reeves, a senior fellow at the Brookings Institution, terms as vague hopes and active aspirations.[5]

According to Reeves, "vague hopes" are loosely stated goals that are not currently backed up by daily habits or actions toward achieving the goal. "Active aspirations," on the other hand, are goals that a person is actively pursuing, and daily habits or actions are intentionally working toward a goal. When we first met, Jasmin wanted to be a speech therapist and was interning in a speech therapy office ("active aspiration") but hadn't done the work to put together a compelling written application to apply for her master's degree in speech pathology ("vague hopes").[6]

I admired Jasmin's tenacity and also noticed in our conversations that she took pride in doing things on her own. She had a small network and little awareness that she could benefit from a bigger one, and she was resistant to any efforts to expand beyond a well-insulated comfort zone she had created for herself. And yet she had so many of the characteristics we say we want to imbue in our kids: independence, grit, resilience. At the same time, her pride and instilled sense of independence were preventing her from accessing resources that could have benefited her in college and in her job search.

In the months after our first meeting, Jasmin and I talked about how middle school was a time when she was more open to encountering ideas, meeting people, visiting places, and having experiences that were unfamiliar to her family or neighborhood friends. There were available resources she hadn't accessed. As she got older, she'd become even less likely to reach out for help. She was also more prone to shying away from uncomfortable situations and new experiences that felt like a stretch. She admitted to completing all of her college applications on her own, turning down the limited resources available at her school. I could see how becoming comfortable with being uncomfortable and developing a larger, more diverse social network could help her achieve her goals and dreams.

It was the question that would continue to keep me up at night—how can *all* students develop skills I knew were critically important to navigate a life beyond the faulty finish line of college admissions? Not for the first time, I was struck by the fact that in different circumstances, my life story could have turned out very differently. It made me alternately uncomfortable and infuriated, thinking about the ways we hang on to a checklist vision of to-dos for success that focus on predetermined finish lines and in doing so can virtually ignore or overlook the underlying skills it takes to get there.

Simply put, Jasmin and countless students like her hadn't learned how to navigate a life beyond the one they knew at home. These foundational concepts—around systems, connection, perspective, and acceptance—were ones I turned to again and again with the students I worked with, and I knew they were vital to helping each student develop their own blueprint. These were the underemphasized skills I knew to be foundational and fundamental—and key to promoting long-term well-being.

PART ONE

DEVELOP A SYSTEM

Early in my career, I began noticing a pattern. When I would begin working with students, I would ask them to identify their most challenging classes. They would typically respond by sharing the class or classes where they were receiving the lowest grades. I would then ask to see their materials, and they would become sheepish. In most cases, their materials were in utter disarray, and there was no real system in place for organizing, planning, and tracking their workflow. That lack of structure created feelings of stress and anxiety and impacted their ability to learn, engage, and process information with confidence. Even so, most students overlooked the importance of focusing on the initial underlying system before addressing the content.

Students typically resisted that approach; they wanted to know how to ace their chemistry test or edit their English essay. Some parents and caregivers would also become frustrated with my focus on what they considered to be nonessential skills. They, too, were fixated on grades and test scores as short-term markers of improvement, in part because even the most well-meaning, child-centered schools are typically labeled as "good" or "bad" based in part on their student body's recent test scores.

Still, I gently insisted from one week to the next that we start by focusing on the underlying system. Little by little, students began to feel a greater sense of ease and calm. They began to expect and look forward to **regrouping**, a term I use to describe getting our system back into order. We would go through binders and later digital files and folders without judgment, with the goal of creating a system that worked well for the student. One simple goal we would often set: to organize themselves so that they could find any document or digital file in under a minute. Soon, our sessions became somewhat fun. When their materials were in order and they had a plan for completing their tasks, they were better able to focus, plan, and prioritize. For many who stuck with it over months and years, their results began to exceed any and all initial expectations. That newfound confidence in identifying what needed to be done and creating a plan for moving forward spilled over into all areas of their lives. They got more sleep. Many seemed, on the whole, happier and healthier. Their extracurricular and athletic endeavors reached new heights. All these years later, it's still a magical evolution to witness.

Even now, though, when I begin working with schools, I see some of the very same resistance I've seen in students and parents for decades. It's not surprising, given the metrics we use to evaluate school performance are often rooted in test scores. With a heavy load of academic content that needs to be delivered and absorbed, taking time out of their busy days to practice executive functioning skills that take months or years to develop can quickly be sidelined. In a world where fast results are prioritized, it can be easier to leave this kind of long-term skill building for some other time. Sadly, the ripple effect of *not* focusing on these skills is felt throughout the school day, elevating stress and dampening student learning and engagement.

In a pandemic-adjusted world, it is even clearer that helping students develop a system and focus on executive functions is more foundational to their learning, engagement, and overall well-being than any one grade, test score, or college acceptance letter will ever be. In fact, studies indicate that developing executive functioning skills including organization, time management, prioritization, working memory, and adaptability are a more reliable predictor of success in academics and in life than IQ, test scores, or socioeconomic status.[1]

Middle school and high school are especially critical times to focus on these skills because they're times when we ask more of students than their still-developing brains can manage. Suddenly in middle school, students are tasked with juggling multiple different classes, each with varying short- and long-term expectations. Then we layer on different technology requirements and ways of assigning and turning in work, along with extracurricular activities and family obligations, plus the demands of everyday living. These expectations are especially daunting for kids who experience trauma, abuse, neglect, or some combination of highly stressful issues at home. For many children, the effects of the COVID-19 pandemic—being unable to attend school, having basic routines disrupted, and dealing with heightened levels of uncertainty—amplified levels of stress and turmoil that we will continue to address in years to come. Research indicates a high number of adverse childhood experiences, or traumatic experiences in childhood defined within categories of abuse, neglect, and household dysfunction, correlates with delayed development of executive functioning skills.[2]

Unfortunately, technology can exacerbate the need for these undervalued skills. Since the 2010 publication of my first book, *That Crumpled Paper Was Due Last Week*, where I wrote about the need to help students navigate disorganization and distraction, tablets, online learning platforms, social media, and other online resources have staked their claims for our attention. This technological advancement has given kids more to manage, but we still fail to supply them with even the most basic support they needed decades ago.

Our educational system as a whole is unprepared to help students develop these necessary skills in any comprehensive, consistent way. In elementary school there is generally more time, structure, and support in place to help students get through the day and figure out what to do, where things go, and how to get things done. By middle school, we wrongly assume that students have the underlying skills in place. Quite frankly, this has proven to be a recipe for disaster. As feelings of overwhelm spiral, students often disengage, consciously or subconsciously believing that opting out is emotionally easier than constantly feeling frustrated and unworthy.

Having spent much of my adult life devoted to supporting the success of tweens and teens, I've seen how important it is to decode their complicated and nuanced world in a way that is empathetic, relevant, pragmatic, and solutions focused. After over two decades of working with students and consulting with schools on developing a system based on executive functioning skills, I begin with five core skills that we'll discuss more in depth: organizing, planning, prioritizing, starting and completing tasks, and adaptable thinking. Some of my first students, who are now in their late twenties and early thirties, a few with children of their own, have returned to tell me that the skills and systems honed in my office continue to support their professional and personal lives every day.

CHAPTER 3

START AT THE BEGINNING

"IS ANA HERE?!"

I could hear Nira's voice booming from three rooms away. Within seconds, she appeared at the door frame of my back office. I looked up from the computer. Her wide-eyed excitement and triumphant smile foreshadowed her news. "I just had to drive down to tell you in person," she gushed, rocking back and forth with frenzied anticipation as she stood in front of my desk. "I GOT IN!!!"

By the time Nira flew into my office that warm spring afternoon, I had known her for three years. Her genuine smile and earnest enthusiasm were infectious, and her cheerful disposition often radiated pure excitement. In that moment, I was thrilled for the happiness she felt, because she, like every other child in this world, deserved to feel joy and validation.

"I am going to get ice cream!" she blurted after a few moments. In several years of knowing her, I was used to sudden announcements of new information. It was as if she was finally experiencing a moment of reprieve from years of anxiety and anticipation. She was suddenly free to go get ice cream in the middle of an afternoon usually filled with activities, sports, and homework.

Her jubilation wasn't just about her acceptance to Notre Dame, which came after a slew of other acceptances—she'd received far more yeses than she anticipated, along with a few denials and a spot on a waitlist. It was about the progress she had made academically, socially, and emotionally—building her executive functioning skills, developing authentic friendships, and getting support for issues that concerned her.

Throughout high school, Nira was a busy kid whose frenetic schedule was buoyed by family, school requirements, and extracurricular activities. When she first came into my office, her binders were in disarray, and she kept most of the requirements for assignments, tests, and quizzes in her head. She struggled to prioritize and would get sidetracked by noncritical tasks. She also had a level of time blindness, which meant she would get lost in reading or working on a project and not realize that she needed to, in her case, get to sleep.

I often meet with students whose complicated organizational system isn't working. They've gone in circles around it, tried to make it work repeatedly, yet remain dedicated to it. Somewhere along the line, these students have gotten the (false) message that if they just try harder, the system they have created—or cobbled together—will somehow work. Sometimes, they even get upset if I suggest alterations to their existing system or to adapt a new system altogether. Their parents tell me before the first appointment that their child wants to continue doing everything a certain way, to which I reply, "Well, how well is the current system working?" Once students are introduced to a system that is streamlined and easier to follow, which increases the likelihood they will use it consistently, they realize their main obstacle to gaining the knowledge was their resistance to trying something new.

WHAT ARE EXECUTIVE FUNCTIONING SKILLS?

Resistance to prioritizing executive functioning skills, and to approaching these skills in new ways, is understandable, given how sorely undervalued these skills still are in our educational system. "Executive function" is an academic term that has recently, relatively speaking, made it into the parenting lexicon. It describes the abilities we need to focus, concentrate, and complete tasks effectively and efficiently—tasks that are not automatic and instead require focus. Adele Diamond, professor of developmental cognitive neuroscience at the University of British Columbia, focuses much of her research on children's development of executive functions. She breaks down executive functions into three core functions, plus three higher-order executive functions:

Core Functions[1]

1. **Inhibitory Control**—Students who are able to maintain attention on task, persist, and keep focus despite distractions can be seen as having strong attentional control, a subset of inhibitory control. Those with good self-control or response inhibition, another subset of inhibitory control, refrain from blurting things out, grabbing what another student has, or reflexively reacting when their feelings are hurt. The third aspect of inhibitory control is cognitive inhibition, such as resisting mind wandering or ruminating (going over and over a mistake you made). Inhibitory control plays an important and often undervalued role in socialization and character development. For instance, a student who blurts something out in a fit of anger may face reproach from peers and adults. A student who isn't able to manage and tune out distractions may have difficulty following directions or completing work.

2. **Working Memory**—Students with good working memory are able to hold information in their minds and use that information to create connections that might be logical or creative. They also may be able to relate this new information back to previous experiences. A person who has strong working memory skills might be good at mental math or might learn something today and then relate it directly to something from the past with a creative connection.

3. **Cognitive Flexibility**—Students who exhibit cognitive flexibility are able to adapt and think critically to come up with connections and solutions that might seem outside the box or not self-evident. They can adapt to change and to new information, even if it means that their previous conclusions are incorrect. With so much information coming at us, it can be especially important to be comfortable

with different ways of processing information to find solutions, or pivot when our initial plans might not be possible given unforeseen barriers or challenges outside our control.

Higher-Order Executive Functions[2]

1. **Planning**—A student who is able to plan can organize, prioritize, and break larger projects into smaller, more manageable tasks that they can then focus on completing, ideally in a way that they are able to follow through on and that reduces paralyzing stress, fear, and overwhelm.

2. **Reasoning**—At a time when there is so much information coming to us at once, students who use available details to efficiently process information acquired through different senses can determine the best path forward.

3. **Problem Solving**—Students who can take the available information, break it down into manageable tasks, identify opportunities for growth and problems, and determine next steps can continuously move forward with a solutions-oriented approach. Instead of being overwhelmed by potential roadblocks or challenges, they use adaptable thinking and reasoning skills to solve problems.

In my work with students and consulting with schools, I've adopted an approach that reflects Diamond's overall interpretation of executive functions with a hands-on, action-oriented curriculum that addresses the current combination of physical and digital materials that encompass the lives of many middle school, high school, and college students. When it comes to developing a system, I focus on these five initial focus points with students (overlap with Diamond's definitions of core and higher-order executive functions in parentheses):

1. Organizing (planning, problem solving)
2. Planning (planning, reasoning, cognitive flexibility)
3. Prioritizing (reasoning, problem solving)

4. Starting tasks and completing tasks (inhibitory control, working memory, planning)

5. Adaptable thinking (cognitive flexibility, reasoning, problem solving)

Within the scope of these initial five focus points, we work on other executive functions, including inhibitory control, working memory, and greater self-awareness. I begin with these five initial focus points in part because they provide a framework that feels useful and manageable to most students. From there, we expand our system building to include greater self-awareness around identifying and accessing resources, and recognizing what strategies work best.

WHY THESE FIVE FOCUS POINTS?

When students begin to focus on organizing, planning, prioritizing, and starting and completing tasks, they can build predictable routines that free up their time and energy. Once these routines begin to feel more second nature, students can find themselves expending less energy on getting started and more time and energy focused on completing the actual work. Then, slowly but surely, the repetition of their routine makes task completion feel easier, creating more time and space to encourage adaptable thinking and problem solving when challenges might take place. In time, students become more motivated to proactively manage and complete their work while also tending to their health and well-being.

Psychologists Edward Deci and Richard Ryan established the Self-Determination Theory, which suggests that autonomous motivation, often referred to as intrinsic motivation, develops from a sense of agency (the idea that students recognize that they have choices), a sense of competence (feeling that they can make good decisions), and a sense of belonging (a feeling of connectedness and relatedness to others).[3] Combined, these create the solid foundation for curious learning and enthusiastic engagement that we want for all school-aged children as they develop into young adults entering the workforce.

Providing the time, structure, and support to help students develop the skills needed to create a system enables a fundamental shift from what we learn to *how we learn*. This is especially important in the age of technology and digitalization when an overload of information and distractions fragments our focus and shortens our attention spans. As the pace of change quickens, we also need to support students and young adults in cultivating their ability to adapt beyond our fixed and rigid pathways. By pausing at moments of inflection, students develop "lateral thinking," a term coined by Edward de Bono in 1967 to describe a way of creatively solving problems using reasoning that goes beyond question-and-answer, step-by-step solutions to integrate experiences in newly imaginative ways.[4]

I have repeatedly seen how developing these skills, along with a focus on nutrition, sleep, and stress management, enables students to become more engaged and excited about their possibilities. Beyond the initial system-building skills of organization, planning, prioritization, task initiation and completion, and adaptable thinking, students benefit from intentional attention to their self-awareness skills, especially with knowing when and how to access needed resources, and inhibitory control, which we'll look at more in Part Two. Ultimately, building executive functioning skills can contribute to better self-acceptance, which we'll discuss in Part Four. I'm not exaggerating when I say that focusing on these skills ideally beginning in elementary and middle school (or as early as possible) changes the course of people's lives.

WHY MIDDLE SCHOOL AND HIGH SCHOOL ARE KEY TIMES FOR STUDENTS TO DEVELOP A SYSTEM

To be clear, we begin to develop our executive functioning skills pretty much from the moment we are born. Think about how babies make connections and communicate their needs or a preschooler's stories have a logical beginning, middle, and end. Arguably, at some stages of child development, these burgeoning skills might make us feel like we're negotiating with a leader of an autocratic regime. While kindergarten and elementary school allow for some structured support in building these skills, beginning in middle school, we wrongly assume students can figure out their own system, without the time, structure, and support they need to do so. Some students certainly can do so, but far more find the lack of guidance leads to feelings of overwhelm.

From a brain development perspective, the prefrontal cortex, which is key for the development of executive functioning skills, isn't fully developed until we are in our early twenties—and boys' full brain development generally completes a few years after girls'.[5] This may help to explain why so many boys struggle with organizational skills, though I see girls needing support with organizational skills as well, particularly as they are asked to juggle digital tools that create opportunities for both socialization and distraction. By not providing all students with the time, structure, and support they need, we are systematically setting them up for failure. Still, the distractions created through different channels of social media and technology mean that all students need additional support in developing a system.

Just as important: our executive functions are affected by our mood, stress, and sleep. We don't always fully appreciate the different stressors students face or how they impact their ability to develop and implement a system that works for them. Perhaps a grandparent is sick, or parents have separated, or there is drama in a friend group. Perhaps there is residual stress from trauma experienced several years ago that seems invisible now. We often underestimate how much stress and trauma impact executive functioning skills.[6] These days, we're all living in a pandemic-adjusted world that feels filled with uncertainty, and it is safe to say that nearly all children experienced some level of stress and trauma related to the pandemic.

What may surprise some is that students with diagnosed learning differences, who benefited from working with learning specialists from an early age, received the ongoing support needed to develop their own system. While some of these students put incredible effort to get basic assignments completed and may have struggled with reading comprehension or math understanding, they received support to learn to clearly organize, plan, prioritize, begin and complete tasks, and now had a system they could turn to time and again. As a result of creating a set of predictable routines, as well as advocating for themselves, many of these students with learning challenges were able to thrive academically.

I began to see how a student who might take longer to complete work and who needed to put in more time to process and learn new information but had the time, structure, and support to develop a system from an early age would see benefits. On the flip side, I would also see how students who relied on their memory and magnetic charisma would start to flounder in middle school or high school. Usually, that was when these students would find their way to my office.

In short? We've ignored the vital importance of helping all students develop executive function skills that provide a critical foundation for success from middle school through adulthood. That's even more true now that social media and technology have utterly transformed how students learn and process information, as well as how they socialize with one another and engage with the world. Today, there is an underlying expectation that students can navigate this digital world, but little to no teaching or coaching has been provided to them as to how to do that effectively. This issue has gotten worse over many years, and we need to give kids the skills to cope with a world that's increasingly full of distractions and conflicting priorities.

BACK TO BASICS: GETTING ORGANIZED

The need to get organized and manage distractions seems straightforward to anyone who has worked with middle school or high school students. Perhaps you've seen a backpack full of crumpled papers or a student so overwhelmed with short- and long-term assignments and expectations that they shut down. Maybe you know a student who is distracted by social media, video games, or "the entire internet," as more than a few students have shared with me over the past fifteen years. Or maybe a student's thinking becomes so rigid that even a slight deviation causes panic and overwhelm. Put simply, students who cannot organize, prioritize, start and complete work, or navigate changing expectations are often adversely affected academically, socially, and emotionally. And although the academic impact seems obvious—a student who doesn't turn in work receives a zero, which affects grades and long-term academic outcomes—the long-term social and societal consequences are far greater.

Nira's initial organizational style was overly complicated and somewhat haphazard, and her constant state of overwhelm tested her time-management skills equally. "I actually think [time management] is one of the things I am strongest at," she says, reflecting today on her younger years, "which is funny because do you remember me in high school? I was a mess." In Nira's mind, she was a procrastinator. I understand her self-analysis, though I saw her as someone who had perfectionist tendencies and needed more downtime to process and transition between work (school, activities) and rest (relaxation, sleep) than her high school schedule allowed. Her mind already worked in overdrive—something that can be powerful but can also lead to a detrimental spiral of overthinking and overanalyzing when trying to complete work while sleep deprived. When she left to go to college, the increased amount of unscheduled time required her to readjust—after stops and starts—and figure out how to put more time, structure, and support in place.

Because she did eventually get work done and did well in her classes, it was easy for her and her teachers to overlook her executive functioning deficits in organization, planning, prioritization, and time management. I've seen this many times with students who get good grades—maybe they are labeled as smart or gifted or whatever unhelpful labeling used at the time—and their poor organizational skills are overlooked or deemphasized. Some of them keep it all in their head, and given their academic performance up to that point, adults mistakenly believe they had it all handled. Honestly, the keep-it-all-in-your-head system can work for some kids—up to a point. Almost without exception, as workload and expectations increase, those same "on top of it" kids tend to accumulate missing assignments and careless errors, all of which impact their overall school experience.

During Nira's high school years, her parents worried about how much time and energy it took her to complete her work. Like many students whose anxious frenzy and consistent distraction are hidden behind consistently high grades and test scores, her disorganization and time blindness contributed to her anxiety. For example, she might not recognize how long a writing assignment or science lab project would take to complete to her level of satisfaction and then put it off until the last minute. Because she held herself to high standards, she wasn't satisfied turning in something less than what was, in her mind, "perfect." Putting work off to the last minute led to staying up late and skimping on sleep, followed by a host of other health challenges. It was a debilitating cycle.

Unlike students I see who don't end up completing assignments or complete them and then forget to turn them in, Nira always completed her work and turned it in on time. However, her initial work habits took an enormous toll on her well-being. The amount of time and effort she gave required propping up from family members, who might wake her up, drive her to school, or run errands for her. None of this would be available in the same way when she left home for college or beyond.

Outside of class and schoolwork, I watched Nira develop from a high school freshman who felt she had few friends to a high school junior who ran for class treasurer—and won! As her confidence blossomed, she became a thoughtful, empathetic leader in and out of school. One of her most meaningful volunteer experiences was at the Day Worker Center, a place a few miles from my office focused on creating a safe and reliable space for day laborers to find work and pursue job training.

During her junior year of high school, Nira started working with a therapist for her anxiety around travel, especially flying on planes. She wanted to apply to colleges that would necessitate air travel. Deep down, she knew she would be able to travel on planes and wanted some support to manage the stress and the feeling of being out of control.

"I remember one of the prompts colleges asked for was talking about working through a challenge or struggle," she recalls. "Now that I've worked in admissions for graduate programs, I get why colleges ask that. In a college or a graduate program, it is not going to be just highs. There are going to be lows, and it is important to have some sense for how people respond when things are challenging."

Today, Nira laughs at the questions she faced as she applied to college. "It was perplexing for a lot of people because it was so hard for me to fly. So it was kind of like, 'Well, why would you go somewhere far?' But I applied to many places that were far. I ultimately went to a place that was far away." This irony continued in her career choice, where for many years Nira was the associate director of a program that recruits and trains new teachers, a job requiring frequent travel around the country.

Looking back, one of the reasons she was so excited about her acceptance to Notre Dame was that she had submitted her essay on anxiety and considered her acceptance a validation of her mental health journey and, ultimately, of what she saw as her authentic self. And yet it was also this moment of acceptance that brought her a sense of false completion and relief. College life and the years beyond would bring Nira a new set of challenges around organization, time management, planning, and prioritization, ones that were hidden in the busyness of high school.

"College is such a growing-up experience," Nira reflects. "Up until college, you're just so focused on going to class and trying to get a good grade in that class that you don't understand everything that it entails to grow up.

"The hardest part of college was learning to manage time and keep track of what I was responsible for and holding myself accountable when my mom wasn't there to drive me to soccer, and there was no one there to wake me up in the morning," she muses, admitting she can't fully understand why she put things off as a teenager and young adult, and reveals she no longer does so. "One of the biggest things I started to learn in high school, continued to learn in college, and continue to work on now is how I use my time and if I am using my time productively and efficiently." Today, she has the self-awareness to understand what resources are available to her and what she needs to do and use to best support herself.

When Nira was in high school, she would sometimes feel overwhelmed by her many to-dos. Before pulling out her written planner, I would hand her a piece of plain white printer paper and give her five minutes to write down everything and anything that was on her mind—assignments, to-dos, errands, upcoming activities, and random due dates. Five minutes was usually more than ample time for her to complete this brain dump. Once she was done, I would have her put a star next to the ones that required urgent attention within the next twenty-four hours and then those that needed to be addressed within the next two or three days. She would identify things she couldn't control and those that she could. Within fifteen minutes, she had a semblance of a plan where there was once steam coming out of her ears.

During her freshman year in college, Nira was again in a situation where she didn't know many classmates and was trying to figure out where she fit in socially. "I kept trying to be cooler than I was and trying to hang out with people that I perceived to be more popular or a little edgier or whatever," she reflects. She would stay up late talking and socializing with people and not get any work done.

"My daily sleep routine was off," she concludes. "It would be 1:00 or 2:00 a.m. and I'd be trying to read a journal article or chapters in a book. My mind was not in a great place at that point, and I would have class at 8:30 or 9:00 a.m., so it wasn't like I was getting enough sleep. And then after class, I would be tired and take a nap or be lazy. And the cycle continued and was a real challenge for me."

I often see this cycle with middle school, high school, and college students. Students who are overscheduled, without the time they need to transition from work to rest, or who struggle to manage distractions end up staying up later and feeling exhausted during the day. The impact of sleep deprivation means work takes longer, focus is harder, and emotions can be more difficult to regulate. It is one way that social anxiety can directly impact academic performance; staying up late affects students' ability to organize, plan, prioritize, focus, and think clearly. Put simply, sleep deprivation affects our executive functioning skills and makes us feel as though we're in survival mode. It can be hard to break the cycle of going to bed later and trying to play catch-up, especially when a student gets caught up trying to manage outside expectations instead of stepping back to understand what works best for them, regardless of what others are doing. There are so many times when parents are frustrated with their children's ability to manage distractions and get work done, and yet the student regularly has twelve to fourteen hours of school, activities, and commute time before even getting home at night.

Once Nira became more comfortable with accepting who she was and knowing that there was always room for growth, she started to feel better, and she settled into friendships that felt authentic, rather than striving and posturing. She also became comfortable with her ability to move between groups of friends, realizing, "I was always kind of a floater and felt close with a variety of people. And that has worked well for me," Nira shares today with confidence.

Throughout college and then during her first years teaching, she used what she'd learned working with me to manage her time better and to prioritize her work and life load. Becoming more comfortable in who she is, finding a sense of community in her work and personal life, and recognizing how she works best means she feels okay to take a break or shift nonurgent or important to-dos to another day. Nira began to recognize how much time it took her to complete things and to allocate time accordingly. She learned she functions and feels best when she goes to bed between 9:30 and 10:00 p.m. and wakes up between 6:00 and 6:30 a.m. She's found a continued sense of connection in her spiritual practice and at her church. Lately, she has tried to get up a bit earlier so she can create a morning routine of stretching, yoga, and mindfulness. It is one way she's learned to support her mental well-being.

"We live in a world where you're probably always going to have a lot on your plate, and you're never going to have time to get everything done to the ability or level that you want," she contemplates. "Learning how to manage my anxiety and stress in therapy was probably one of the best things I ever did in my life, because it put me in such a good place to work well and also feel fulfilled and happy and not put all my stock or worth into my work product."

Ultimately, Nira's intentional implementation of a system that works well for her led to her own greater self-awareness and a comfort in knowing what time, structure, and support she needed to be successful. It has been an ongoing journey, and it didn't start or end the day she received that college acceptance. Today, she's developed her organization, planning, and prioritization skills to a point where no one task ever feels overwhelming in the way it once did in high school, and she is comfortable and confident to adjust and adapt as needed.

"The irony," she muses, "is that your work product actually gets better when you're okay with who you are and you relax a bit."

CHAPTER 4
DELIVERABLES

"EVERY SUNDAY NIGHT, I AM ON THE PHONE WITH THE TEAM AND we're talking through the week," Andrew explains, comparing his Sunday-night work ritual as a strategy consultant to the ways he learned to plan and organize his work in middle school and high school. "It's like, here's where we need to land, by a Thursday client deliverable, and here are the steps I think we need to get there. What does everyone else think? What is doable, what's messy, what is the quality of the data?"

It's been more than fifteen years since Andrew first walked into my office. He has since graduated from high school and college and worked for several years before going back to school for his MBA. He graduated from business school in May 2020, at the height of the pandemic, and took a job as a strategy consultant because it was the only one offered at a time when much of the world had shut down. When we first reconnect, he reveals a specificity in his near-future goal, explaining that he turned down three job offers in recent months, as he's quietly in search of his next opportunity ("cone of silence," he implores). He has been using his networking skills to talk to friends of friends at different companies in hopes of returning to the sector he sees as his life's work: affordable housing.

"I think I still have one of your weekend schedulers for finals up in my room at home," Andrew admits, referring to the study schedule that students create to prepare for their final weeks of a grading period, when they may juggle a number of different exams and projects. "The schedule gave me structure and accountability. It was like, you're going to plan your Saturday out, focus on this subject, take a break, make some lunch, walk around the house, and then start on this subject. I really loved that. And it was nice because when I got to college, I thought the same way."

Years ago, I created a study schedule for the week before and week of finals—a spreadsheet to empower students to feel autonomy and set aspirational intentions for how they would spend their time over those two weeks. I found that students felt more in control of their schedule and choices when they wrote out a plan, broke down tasks into manageable time blocks, and identified how and where they could spend their time. My focus has never been for students to follow the schedule 100 percent—and I tell them that. Even if they follow 80 percent of a proposed schedule, they will likely get far more done than if they went into that block of time without any semblance of a plan. On crunch weekends right before final exams, students like Andrew felt empowered when they saw that despite an increased workload, they still had time to exercise, take breaks, and sleep. And setting up that accountability with someone other than the parent or caregiver was helpful as they tried to ingrain new learned behaviors to a point where they would see motivating results. Over time, the structure of the study schedule was one of many routines that became predictable and second nature, something many students like Andrew later used in college and work experiences.

"I will say that the structure was set at a young age, at least the aspirational structure that I knew was the right structure to follow," he recalls. "And it became subconscious to stick to that, like, *Oh, I know I should be doing this, this way.*"

It strikes me, in our conversations, that Andrew is now in his early thirties and nearly the same age as Luis, a current client I work with who is employed as a mid-level financial analyst at a major global organization. I started working with Luis after his supervisor was in the audience when I gave a talk at her children's school. She sent me a note through my website, briefly explaining that much of what I had described in my work with students didn't apply to her children as much as it did to one of her staff members. She wondered whether I might consider working with Luis or even having an initial conversation. She clearly wanted Luis to succeed and was worried that his struggle to meet deadlines and follow through on deliverables would derail his long-term promotion prospects. I initially declined, citing time constraints, and then later agreed to take Luis on as a corporate client—in part to see in real-time the ways that the same work I was doing with middle school and high school students directly related to work-force development. Like Andrew, Luis had high expectations for himself, with personal goals around career development advancement. But it was clear that if Luis wasn't able to get a system in place, it would soon prevent him from reaching his potential.

Both Andrew and Luis are intrinsically motivated, personable, and determined, with a strong work ethic—but Andrew had the added bonus of building these skills in high school, a key time in his developmental growth. During middle school and high school, students face increased expectations—and technology requirements—while navigating puberty and societal expectations. Research shows ninth-grade grades to be a predictor of college access, graduation, and success.[1] In other words, when students fail to develop a system before high school, they can falter through their teen years and into adulthood.

In the first year I worked with Luis, I knew that he needed consistency to build predictable routines and create systems where there once were none. He made monumental strides, catching the attention of leaders at his firm with the turnaround in his performance evaluations ("a complete 180"). It might have turned out differently if Luis's boss hadn't taken the initiative to provide him with coaching, something I keep thinking of as I see the ways Andrew implements those same skills as second nature.

***

"Structure is still super important, especially as a way of building account-ability," Andrew explains, making a connection between the work we did together and his role managing projects today. "In management it becomes about seeing that every person feels empowered and also feels supported, and also persuaded to get their work done in the way you know it needs to be done." He goes on to share how he takes notes and creates a to-do list, using a piece of printer paper to map out projects and create a list of deliverables. For him, each week brings a new piece of printer paper. His work style today mirrors freedom from distractions, finding the right space, and being present—strategies learned years earlier. Today, he has a preference for quick check-ins throughout the week with different staff members, looking at the overall agenda, reviewing the timeline and expectations, and finding ways to anticipate and respond to different incoming issues.

"Maybe I am literally parroting what you taught me?" Andrew wonders aloud.

Throughout Andrew's high school years, when he and I worked together, he was well intentioned and conscientious. He was also well connected, engaged, and active, participating in sports, student government, and community service opportunities. He had high expectations of himself, determined to take a tougher course load of AP and honors classes, knowing he would have to work hard and might not get an A. He loved the coaching and community that playing a sport provided, even though late-night practices, games, and tournaments took up most evenings and weekends.

Despite his motivation and high expectations, Andrew could *also* be an overscheduled procrastinator.

Like many students, he would end up trying to pack in one more thing, balancing that fine line between getting it all completed seconds before a deadline or watching everything fall apart. He experienced a paradox of enjoying being busy, while also needing time for rest. Wide swaths of free time seemed to make him nervous, and he admitted to procrastinating most when he wasn't participating in a sport and had more free time after school. And yet he also needed more time than was possible to transition between his school day, his after-school activities, and evening homework time. He was often left trying to complete work when he was exhausted and was less able to focus and concentrate. The work then took longer to complete, and he would sometimes put off assignments or projects that weren't due the next day, until finally a pileup of work could lead to feelings of overwhelm and exhaustion. He would then get frustrated with himself when he fell behind or didn't perform as well as he expected.

And, of course, Andrew required a certain amount of sleep for his mood, focus, and overall well-being—in other words, so he was not grumpy. Recent research has unequivocally shown that sleep decreases anxiety and supports the consolidation of memories, thus aiding with executive function skills. A study done at the Center for Health Sciences examined associations between sleep and concurrent and later mental health symptoms among the national US sample of 11,670 early adolescents aged nine to ten years to find that parent-reported sleep disturbances were associated with internalizing, externalizing, and depressive symptoms.[2] For students like Andrew, learning how to prioritize sleep can make a world of difference. His mom, attuned to the needs of each of her three children, once told me that as a younger child, Andrew preferred having a few afternoons free of activities and commitments. While his older siblings were happily shuttled from one activity to the next with little transition time, Andrew was the youngest child who craved extra downtime to process, rest, and recharge.

In working with students, I find ways to use work, movement, and rest as the three overarching buckets to help students classify their time and energy. Using these simple overarching buckets, as I did with Lauren when she was working on her college applications, is especially important when supporting students with system development and implementation. Some students see that work takes less time when they get more rest or that they benefit from having more movement even if they aren't participating in an organized sport. Work often requires the most executive functioning skills—for Andrew, that entailed anything involving concentrated focus and study, which could include class time, homework, and study time. Movement means being active in a way that provides the ideal release of serotonin and dopamine, a combination shown to improve mood and overall well-being. Andrew was able to focus better and be in a better mood when he had time to be active, which as a student meant playing organized sports and now as an adult means swimming, playing tennis, and biking around New York City.

I was not surprised to learn that Andrew keeps in close touch with friends from elementary school and middle school. Despite now living across the country from his childhood home, he still watches soccer on the weekends with his friend from elementary school, who was also his college roommate. His current roommate is a friend from when he was six years old, and he rattles off the happenings of childhood friends with remarkable familiarity, in part because he and his family have recently been guests at many of the weddings of his childhood friends. Unlike Nira, who knew few classmates coming into high school, Andrew started high school knowing many of his classmates and kept in close touch with those who attended other area schools. It likely helped that both of Andrew's parents were well liked and well connected. He grew up understanding the ingrained importance of authentic, genuine friendships, and for the years her children were in middle school and high school, a referral by Andrew's mom seemed like the number one reason people called my office—she was a trusted resource.

After high school, Andrew headed to University of California, Davis, where he started off studying plant sciences before deciding to major in environmental policy and city planning, with a minor in economics. His personal light bulb moment came during his junior year in a seminar class focused on city housing. "This professor was like, 'Oh, all you environmental science kids want to save the world from global warming,'" he recalls. "'What if you allow people to live closer to where they work so they don't have to drive a '92 Ford Explorer to work every day across the Central Valley?'"

The real-life example clicked for Andrew, who spent his formative years in Silicon Valley, which had experienced explosive changes to housing costs since his parents grew up there. Andrew was familiar with the fact that many people lived in the Central Valley and endured long commutes so they could afford the cost of housing and, ideally, purchase their own home. When the professor focused on all the quality-of-life improvements—health, education, overall well-being—that happen when a person doesn't have to commute two to four hours to work each day, Andrew discovered his North Star: affordable housing development. "It's probably one of the only light bulb moments in my whole life," Andrew reflects, "and it really set a course."

Andrew landed his first job working at a local housing authority in the Central Valley by sending out emails and meeting everyone who agreed to meet with him. Soon thereafter, he started researching every single affordable housing nonprofit in Northern California and learned about a national nonprofit working to eliminate homelessness and housing insecurity for low-income families and seniors.

"I knew that was where I wanted to work and networked as hard as I could to get that job at age twenty-three," he recalls. Through watching the way his parents cultivated relationships over the years, Andrew intrinsically understood the power of making connections and maintaining relationships. It felt natural for him to ask his father whether he knew anyone working for companies and nonprofits focused on affordable housing and impact investing. Just as important as those initial introductions, though, Andrew had the confidence to follow up on leads and build the strength we all eventually need to churn through the meetings that often come after making an initial lead. "My dad asked a few people, and one of his friends was like, 'Oh, I know someone at three of these places,'" he explained. "So I talked to junior people at three of those places, and asked them for three more people to talk to. It's a friend of a friend, then you meet someone else, who then introduces you to someone else."

Andrew's perseverance paid off after eight months of phone calls and in-person meetings. He got a real-estate development assistant position at that leading affordable housing organization, working in a cross-functional role as a project manager for nearly five years. The system building that had been set at an early age in middle school and high school and reinforced in college was second nature to him. He brought those skills into his job search and then later to running projects that could be tricky and require pivoting. "I think back a lot to high school, or middle school too, and cutting yourself off from distractions—find the right space and get it done while you're there and be present with the work."

After several years, Andrew decided to apply to business school, in part because attending graduate school felt like a natural next step that he saw as an unspoken requirement to succeed long term in his industry. Many of his colleagues in similar roles went on to get a master's in public policy or city planning, and the vast majority went to UC Berkeley. Andrew decided to do something different, applying to and ultimately attending a business school on the East Coast. He thought that earning an MBA was going to help him because he wasn't an undergraduate business major, and he wanted to explore what else might be out there. Even so, his business school internships were at real-estate companies that worked adjacent to the affordable housing space. When his final months of business school were upended because of the pandemic, he realized his plans required a short-term adjustment. "The goal was always to be back in affordable housing. I felt like I'd already invested so much of my life in it, that it was those types of problems and people who were interested in working on those problems that I wanted to be surrounded with," he says in retrospect.

Not long after joining a strategy consulting firm, he realized that he needed to quietly and actively keep looking. He looked up old classmates to catch up and ask whether they might know anyone doing affordable housing or related impact work. One of his friends went to high school with a woman who is a vice president at the investment bank where he now works in the urban investment group. "We chatted in August of last year, and then she just kept me in mind, basically. They ended up having an opening in December, and I interviewed through the winter and got the job and started in March," Andrew explains, using his connection skills to land his new opportunity.

"It's fun to be back in the impact space," he says. "I am in a different position with a different view, but I am enjoying the work." Unlike his role at the affordable housing organization, where he was using funding to manage affordable housing projects, his new role has him evaluating a wide range of community and economic development opportunities through real estate projects, social enterprises, and lending to small businesses, in particular businesses owned by individuals who have been historically excluded.

How are the executive functioning skills and overall system coming into play today? "The short answer is that it's like constant triage, but also having to complete tasks and close loops on things," Andrew reflects, admitting that his new team is the smartest and hardest-working group of individuals he's ever been around. In many ways, it feels like a never-ending evaluation of what needs to be done immediately and what needs to be checked on in the near term to make sure no details are missed.

"For me, visually, it's still a grid," he says, referring back to that initial finals study schedule. "It's literally a piece of printer paper that has deals written on it and then all the things that need to get done to cross that thing off. That piece of paper basically gets ripped up at the end of the week, and a fresh one gets started."

Throughout the early stages of his career, Andrew has been able to use the system he started to develop in high school to create his own structure to pursue the career focus and aspirations realized in college. Being open, flexible, and patient has allowed him to approach each conversation, experience, and opportunity with a level of humility and self-awareness. And, at every stage of his school and career, his ability to maintain stronger friendships and weaker ties has enabled him to pursue opportunities that might not otherwise have been available, ultimately creating his own blueprint.

This is one of the surprising realities of developing executive functioning skills. The process is often more enjoyable than students, and adults like Luis, initially imagine. Over and over again, I've watched relief register on the faces of thousands of individuals who, with ongoing support, have developed a system that works for them. Almost invariably, people discover the joy of mastering skills that help them identify who, what, and how they want to be in the world. Equipped with executive functioning skills, they gain agency over their daily happenings and the longer-term trajectory of their life.

It feels good to be connected. It feels good to bounce back from disappointment and thrive. It feels good to set lofty goals, identify and understand the smaller steps required, and work toward that objective. In short, it feels good to feel as though we are on top of things. As Andrew and Luis and others have experienced, the confidence that stems from mastering executive functioning skills becomes foundational to creating an individual blueprint for success that integrates our sense of purpose with our interests and skills.

Given how quickly our world—including our working world—continues to shift and change with ongoing technology innovations that affect how we work and live, it is ever more important for students and young adults to develop these core skills at an early age and gain the confidence that comes from creating systems that are flexible and adaptable. Staying organized, managing and filtering out distractions, and prioritizing urgent and important tasks to come up with a workable plan are critically important as we prepare students for a future—and an economy—that we can't yet clearly define. If we can make sure we support kids in developing these skills, we're supporting their current academic, social, and emotional well-being and preparing them for an evolving future of possibilities.

CHAPTER 5
LEARNING TAKES LONGER

Within seconds of first sitting down at one of the dining room–sized tables in my office, Henry began tapping his fingers along the edge of the table. Before long, he was in the middle of a full-on drum set. "Henry was recently diagnosed with ADHD," his mother said patiently, "and we're still sorting out what that all means." Henry's mom was supportive, and I appreciated that she was direct and solutions oriented. She knew her son was talented and capable, and like many parents who walk into my office, she wanted to find ways to help him feel more in control of school and his life.

"So, your summer reading is *Pride and Prejudice*?" I offered cheerfully to Henry, silently wondering why the high school required students to read the same summer reading books for the past thirty years. I enjoyed both Jane Austen's book and the movie adaptation, and I also think there are more options for students to read. "Yeah." Henry stopped drumming for a moment and turned to look over with a smile before returning to his impromptu set.

During the summer after his sophomore year in high school, Henry had been referred to my office by the neuropsychologist who diagnosed him with ADHD. At the time, Henry had a 2.8 GPA, which his high school counselor said would limit his choices for college. In Henry's mind at the time, everything was about where he was going to go to college and how that determined his future, which would later determine his career and livelihood. Beneath his easygoing, fun-loving exterior, Henry was nervous and overwhelmed, trying to figure out how to do better in school when it felt so difficult to concentrate.

Without the time, structure, and support to develop a system, students eventually tend to spiral, feeling overwhelmed and underprepared. For example, students like Henry who consistently forget assignments or don't have a system to prepare for assessments or break down larger projects into smaller tasks often find their grades suffering. Beyond the grades, though, this feeling of overwhelm erodes their personal and academic confidence. Although they may want to take a more rigorous course load that might be intellectually appropriate, they may not qualify for classes where acceptance is in part based on grades in previous courses. This can all lead to lower motivation and decreased engagement, often persisting well into adulthood. Today, middle-aged men are increasingly on the sidelines of the job market; about 89.7 percent of men ages thirty-five to forty-four were working or looking for work as of November 2022, down from 90.9 percent before the pandemic.[1] Male friendships have also been on the decline; 15 percent of men report having no close friendships at all, up from 3 percent in 1990.[2]

As we each sat in my office with our copies of Jane Austen's masterpiece, I asked Henry to read a page and let me know what he thought was happening. That approach failed almost instantly, and I sensed he was losing interest by the second. I knew that the back-to-school reading exam (*welcome back!*) and future class assignments comparing and contrasting different themes from the book would require a deeper understanding. Reading online summaries or watching the movie could act as supplements, but I wanted him to also gain confidence from figuring out the best way to read and understand the book.

Starting to work with a new student involves a bit of trial and error, to see how they respond to different approaches and tying personal interests into the work at hand. I quickly realized I needed to redirect our efforts.

"It is a truth universally acknowledged, that a single man in possession of a good fortune, must be in want of a wife . . . " I began reading the first few pages aloud, offering appropriate quips and commentary and asking Henry for his own thoughts. Before long, the once-hesitant amateur drummer sitting in my office started laughing softly at the sardonic humor in the classic novel. "Hey . . .," Henry quipped, "this is actually funny, once you understand what is happening."

In between our next few sessions together, Henry began listening to an audio version of *Pride and Prejudice*, using different online resources and scaffolding techniques to improve his reading comprehension and overall understanding. We related the book's themes to his own teenage world and used the summer reading assignment as a gateway to develop different study strategies. He began working in fifteen-minute blocks of uninterrupted time, followed by a five-minute break, which felt manageable to him. Over the next two years, he would work his way up to fifty minutes of focused effort reading and annotating his book to help with overall comprehension, but in the beginning, fifteen minutes of focused work was a major victory. The active studying tips helped him stay motivated, and by the end of the summer, he believed he had a system in place to help him read, process, and learn new information.

By the time his junior year rolled around, Henry was more confident organizing his binders and paper planner and began to create a work rhythm. It didn't happen instantaneously, and he loved to question me and try to find loopholes. Still, most days he would come home after school from swim practice, spend an hour playing the drums (which at the time was a hobby he liked doing for fun), and then start on homework. The movement and creative outlets helped him focus when he sat down to complete assignments in the evening, and over the next two years, he felt more confident in his academic abilities and, ultimately, in being a more active member of his school and greater community.

"I want you to focus on the habits, not the grades and scores," I would repeat, somewhat mantra-like. I sometimes use the term "habits" to describe the predictable routines that can ultimately reduce the time and energy needed to organize, plan, prioritize, and start and complete tasks. "If you focus on the habits, the rest will come."

The shifted focus from grades to habits offered Henry a powerful reset. Each time I would ask whether he was doing his personal best within his current circumstances, Henry would reflect and come up with something else he wanted to improve upon. His underlying competitiveness was honed from years of playing sports, and his enthusiasm, along with his engrossing intonations, make him an engaging storyteller.

There would still be weeks when he would walk into the office with an overstuffed, unorganized backpack, complete with papers shoved haphazardly into the front pockets of binders. I have very few personal pet peeves, but if I did, having loose papers stuffed in the front pocket of a binder rather than organized in sections by dividers would rank high on the list.

Though easily distracted, Henry was motivated to do well. Like many kids who have seen few academic wins in the classroom, Henry was initially hesitant to share any big or bold school-related goals. I understood and instead helped him focus on habits, including organizing his binders regularly, writing down all assignments in his planner, and coming up with an organized plan before he started his list of to-dos. Those seemed doable and also helped him gain a sense of control. Whenever I sensed a bit of spiraling and overwhelm, I would calmly repeat the refrain to focus on the habits and the rest would come.

Years later, Henry recalls that initial summer reading *Pride and Prejudice* and how focusing on habits rather than grades has since proven fundamental to his approach to work today. "You showed me it is okay to slow it down and take pauses, to write notes down so you can remember what you just read. At the time, it was hard for me to stay focused and remember what I had read on the last page, and I'd get stuck reading the same thing over and over again."

"If you had asked me what GPA I wanted when I first came to see you, I would have been happy with a 3.0," he revealed, "and if you had me focus on my GPA, I probably would have stopped trying when I got that." Instead, as we focused on habits and incremental improvement, his GPA actually ended up improving from 2.8 to 3.4 to 3.8 by his senior year. A school administrator's recommendation helped to move him off the waiting list at his college of choice, a school where he wouldn't have met basic entrance requirements when he initially walked into my office a few years earlier.

Far more meaningful than his grades, scores, and ultimate college acceptance was Henry's newfound perspective and confidence. "I didn't realize you worked with Henry," his principal once exclaimed when I visited his school during the final months of his senior year. "He's become such a leader in his class." Henry's metamorphosis from the easily distracted, self-labeled class clown as a sophomore in high school to a class leader less than two years later was the result of several underlying elements to creating his own blueprint: figuring out a system that worked for him, accepting that he needed to slow down, being okay with that need, and setting incremental goals for himself.

At the beginning of every semester, I ask students to identify their own short-term academic and personal goals and then tie those goals back to daily habits and choices. After coming up with an academic goal, students identify two or three daily or weekly habits, routines, or choices they can cultivate to support that goal. Examples include using a written planner daily to map out homework, setting up daily work blocks to complete homework without distractions, creating a study plan that breaks up learning into smaller chunks over an extended period of time, and creating written flashcards in advance to help study for tests.

Personal goals are my way of reminding students that life shouldn't be just about completing work and assignments. They are integrally important for all students, because having something they want to work on personally allows the opportunity for reflection and problem solving in a way that often ties into their academic progress.

The first time I asked Henry to identify some personal goals, he wrote one down without hesitation: play the drums in front of more than fifty people. "I started playing the drums, I think, when I was thirteen years old," Henry recalls years later, explaining that at the time he was playing the trumpet in the middle school band and found himself grooving to a song that had a back beat of drums. "I kind of realized at that moment, 'I like this song probably because the drums are in it.'"

Henry was fortunate that his dad played drums for fun. After school and on weekends—whenever it was appropriate to bang around a drum set, given neighbors and other constraints—he would go into his dad's designated drum space and try to play his favorite songs. For many of his high school years, he was self-taught, and it was the way he found himself letting go of the pressures he felt in school and sports.

One seasonably warm fall day Henry rushed into my office. He had played the drums in front of the entire school. Immediately I saw how transformational making this incremental goal was for Henry, so much so that I also described this moment in my first book, *That Crumpled Paper Was Due Last Week.* Up until that point, he had played recreationally in front of family and friends. By reaching personal and academic goals, Henry began to believe in himself and his potential.

Even so, he never thought that going to a music school would be in his realm of opportunities. When he was accepted from the waiting list to a college in Los Angeles, he felt a weight off his shoulders. "I was like, 'Oh, I got into a good school.'"

And yet that wouldn't prove to be his ultimate destination. In the back of his head, he thought about Berklee College of Music.

"I heard about Berklee because some of my favorite drummers had gone there. I never thought I would be good enough to get in there. I hadn't been trained in drumming," he surmised. "So I was like, 'Okay, I will go to LA. There's music around; I'll figure it out.'"

By the time Henry began the second semester of his freshman year, he felt as though he had it all figured out. He would minor in music and start playing the drums again. He started learning music theory, reading drum music, and looking at music sheets, figuring this was the way to have everything he wanted—to play the drums and have a college experience at a school he enjoyed. "About three-fourths of the way through the second semester of my freshman year, my instructor says, 'Look, if you want to do what you want to do with music, it's not going to be here.'"

"I had a real decision point at the time," he recalls. "Do I want to go all in and try to be admitted to Berklee and try to give this thing a shot or do I just stick it out?" He had already set up his housing plans for his sophomore year, had picked his classes, and had a community of friends at school.

In many ways, Henry had reached a crossroads. The confidence he gained through developing a system helped him reach goals, meaning he now faced an opportunity that once felt completely out of the realm of possibility. He came to see what takes others years to see—that sometimes, creating your own blueprint means overcoming judgments of others (and ourselves!) to accept a pathway that seems atypical, coming from a college-prep high school where he considered himself a jock more than a musician. And yet it was the confidence that came from developing a system that made him believe he should give it a shot, a dream that might be considered unconventional by others in his immediate orbit.

Henry returned home the summer after his freshman year and decided to take a gamble on himself, taking a leave of absence, living at home, and taking drum lessons from local instructors in preparation for his October audition at Berklee in Boston. It was a courageous decision to invest in his dream but also a risk that came with few assurances. He was fortunate to have parents who were supportive and also had high expectations: taking a leave of absence didn't mean he was going to sit around the house. From the end of his freshman year in June to his audition in October, Henry went all in and learned as much as he could about music. In December, he was invited to attend Berklee. By January, he moved to Boston and became a full-time student, at a school that just a year prior he never thought he would be qualified to attend.

As excited as he was, transferring was a complete shock to his system. He went from an LA lifestyle in a college environment where he was minutes from the beach to living in Boston midwinter, where he didn't know anyone. It was a huge change and a daunting challenge, and, like most people, he, as well as his friends and family, may have wondered more than once whether he'd made the "right" decision.

"It's a completely different culture," he says, thinking back to his early days as a new music student in Boston. "We joke a lot about the Berklee bubble because everyone there is just doing music, studying music, researching music, practicing and performing; 24/7, I am eating and digesting music."

Suddenly, being the self-taught music kid from his high school didn't mean much. He was in an environment where everyone else had been studying music theory longer and had been playing more intensely. A few had parents who had spent decades in the music industry. Everyone was advanced, and he felt as though he was back in his first few years of high school again, struggling to keep up at first and then stepping back to figure out how to slow down and learn what he needed to learn in the way he needed to.

"Learning how to learn is the most critical skill I think you can learn as a person in general," Henry concludes today. "I was coming from a place of being behind compared to a lot of kids, and I needed to figure out how to fast-track a lot of these concepts and use my innate skills to my advantage."

Music theory turned out to be his most difficult classes, especially when professors would play notes and ask the intervals and the distance between two notes. As a drummer, he knew rhythm, but getting the tonality was difficult. He bought a handheld recorder, recorded every class, and listened to them over and over to hone his auditory skills. He went to all office hours, developing relationships with his instructors, who often taught both the introductory and advanced classes.

The whole experience took him back to the summer he and I started working together, reading *Pride and Prejudice* out loud at the oversized table in my office. "In school they tell you to read a book and absorb everything, and now it's time to take a test. For me, learning to slow down, take notes, and record classes made all the difference. Recording the classes and listening back, reviewing my notes or even asking other people to compare notes were concepts I used once I accepted I can do more than what they are telling me to do." Knowing that he understood the *process* of learning helped him navigate challenges that otherwise might have felt impossibly overwhelming.

Learning how to learn, at his own pace, even when he felt behind or overwhelmed, has been a theme in Henry's life not just in college but in nearly all of his professional experiences. It has allowed him to self-teach concepts he needed to thrive, as he juggles new and different experiences that have been alternately overwhelming, crushing, and exhilarating.

In the years that followed school, Henry pursued his interest in music while also building a career working as a business analyst, which he continues to do today. "Going to a school like Berklee, I was imagining becoming a rock star touring the world, or whatever. But success for me got redefined when I hit the checkboxes for financial stability, which is a huge contributor to why I am not a full-time musician," Henry admits, even though music remains an important part of his life. Henry's love of music bumped up against aspects of the industry he didn't love as much, and his desire for financial stability and to eventually start a family led him to proactively evaluate trade-offs and build his own blueprint that combined the two and, as he says, "use both sides of his brain." He likes the problem-solving aspect of his job and values the ability to work in technology and balance multiple interests. "I don't think I could do just one thing—I would get bored," he surmises.

"I've found myself on a career path that utilizes my skills and pursued interests to fuel my career from a technology perspective, from a problem-solving perspective," he reflects. "The problems that I'm working with and resolving are interesting to me." He poured some of his savings into buying a condo, looks forward to using his paid time off on travel, and remains true to a daily schedule that allows him to maximize his strengths and focus given his ADHD, including working out in the mornings and creating predictable routines as touch points throughout the day.

With a winding journey, Henry found multiple ways to pursue personal and professional interests, and the underlying skills remain vital to his ability to move forward, set goals, and focus on pursuing evolving and meaningful life goals. There's no one set timeline, and the structure and systems that help him learn, process, and solve problems carry through regardless.

Toward the end of one of our most recent conversations, he turned and exclaimed, "It's funny—all these years later, and it is still like we're sitting in that front room in your office just chit-chatting." And so it is.

PART TWO

DEVELOP CONNECTION

Not too long ago, I was in an academic advising appointment with a high school junior and her mom. The previous school year had been difficult, thanks to a serious concussion that sapped her mental energy and required a great deal of rehabilitation. With the school year fast approaching, I asked what she was looking forward to or hoping for in the form of a fresh start. After a brief pause, she said, "I'd like to find some real, supportive friendships. I have friends, but they're a lot of drama. I don't want to deal with that anymore."

We don't often realize the mixed messages that we, as adults, send around friendship, connection, and belonging. From early ages, we can unintentionally encourage what I call **transactional socializing**—forming connections with the underlying focus that now, or at some point in the future, we will need something from a person or group. That ask may be a recommendation, an introduction, or even a follow or subscribe on social media. Transactional socializing, coupled with a never-ending pursuit of popularity—acquiring a greater number of connections rather than developing meaningful connections—is increasingly influencing how, when, where, and with whom we connect. When you add in the high-drama, high-intensity influence of relationships that are alternately catty and mean, as they often are in middle and high school, including among parents, it is no wonder students are confused about what constitutes authentic, nurturing connections. In my book *Social Media Wellness*, I discussed how likes, loves, comments, and followers have become a new barometer for popularity. When we pursue and form connections with ulterior motives, we're overlooking opportunities to develop genuine, mutually supportive connections.

One of the more worrisome results of these trends is a growing epidemic of loneliness that's severely impacting kids from middle school onward, as well as countless adults who may be "connected" to many people yet have few, if any, enduring and meaningful friendships. This widespread loneliness is one of several major factors in the growing mental health crises among young people.

How we connect, why, and with whom is an increasingly urgent issue, impacting health and well-being at the most fundamental level. It is key for social and emotional wellness, and sometimes for safety as well. Lacking meaningful connections has also been shown to increase the likelihood of high-risk behaviors, from bullying to violence[1] to self-harm.[2]

Steering away from transactional socializing is critical in other ways, including in advancing career and other life goals over time. In an age of so many online exchanges and engagement, we underestimate the value of connecting with others on a human level and maintaining genuine connections without expectation or preconceived notions. In reality, moving away from transactional socialization to build a core network of supporters can ultimately result in opportunities that are far less accessible through other means.

In my life, the ripple effects of supportive connections have proven endless. I feel fortunate to develop a remarkable network of personal and professional supporters. More often than not, the unexpected gift of a connection forged without any presumption or presupposition has led to some of the most lasting impacts on my life. In fact, bringing together my second- and third-degree connections has at times been extraordinarily beneficial for others. One quick example: When I was working on finishing the first draft of this book, a friend I had known for more than a decade phoned to share the birth of his son and his recent appointment as interim head of the school where he began as a teacher. He was excited but also nervous about stepping into this new role with an infant at home and expressed his desire for some additional guidance and support. I thought for a moment and offered to reach out to a highly regarded, recently retired head of school whom I kept in touch with over the years. Months after I'd put them in touch with each other, my friend reached out to say how enormously helpful this new connection was to his transition into the new role.

A key part of connection is, of course, the ways we learn to communicate, including how we introduce ourselves, how we make and maintain friendships and relationships, and how we navigate different social situations and potential stressors. These skills may come far more easily to some than to others. As with academic skills, we must meet students where they are, focus on helping them cultivate effective interpersonal skills, and create opportunities for students to grow and thrive in this area.

As students move beyond the initial stages of building a system discussed in Part One, inhibitory control—or the ability for a student to suppress an urge to respond in a "knee-jerk" way and instead choose a behavioral response more consistent with long-term goals—is one key starting point for developing connection. In an academic context, students with strong inhibitory control can stay on task, remain disciplined, and be persistent and focused despite distractions. In a social context, inhibitory control means having self-awareness and self-control, understanding what is appropriate in a given context. It is also about developing a tool kit to seek necessary support before, as one elementary school principal explained, everything breaks loose. (She had just come from a parent meeting after a fourth grader was sent home for getting frustrated and punching a classmate.) At a certain point, students with low inhibitory control—those who constantly interrupt, are unable to regulate their emotions, and struggle to stay focused—can suffer from social stigmatization, isolation, and other dynamics that can and do impact their self-esteem and health.

On a basic level, skills like holding a conversation, engaging in small talk, knowing how to write and respond to written messages (including text messages and emails), and being able to identify and appropriately ask for support are far more crucial to students' success in school and life than we've acknowledged. Online socialization has made this issue even more urgent, since it has the potential to further degrade our communication skills. Simultaneously, students must keep track of a longer list of spoken and unspoken rules, many of which are invisible to adults. In real life and online, tone, greetings, gratitude, and appreciation all matter. Nearly any Gen Zer will tell you the difference between "K!" "OK!!!" and "Ok." The last one can be interpreted as hostile.[3] I don't make the rules.

In my experience, connection and communication skills are too often overlooked in students who are seen to have high cognitive intelligence—that is, when students get strong grades and test scores in academically rigorous classes, adults often make the mistake of underemphasizing their ability (or inability) to authentically communicate and connect with others. I regularly advise students whose emails begin without a proper greeting or who are unable to properly introduce themselves when calling someone on the phone. Some of these skills may be highlighted in elementary school, but by middle school they are often deemphasized. That strikes me as odd because when I ask adults what stands out most about their middle school and high school years, their memories are often centered on socialization, communication, and connection.

How can we better support kids in creating meaningful connections that boost their well-being and improve their lives? Our focus here is on identifying basic social needs, including supporters and clarifiers, who can be mentors or sponsors. It is about finding multiple nonoverlapping circles of connection and understanding that we are each born with inherent social capital, some more than others, and often of different value depending on environment and context. And that openness and curiosity—alongside core communication skills—can create opportunities for **levers**, or moments that can change our life trajectory.

CHAPTER 6
FLOATING

LIKE MANY CHILDREN OF IMMIGRANTS, I STRADDLED TWO CULTURES, feeling limited pride in my heritage as I focused on learning an individual handbook of norms my classmates took for granted. Looking back, I realize how spending the first twelve years of my life in rural Connecticut allowed me some of the trappings of an all-American childhood despite limited financial means. Our town's recreation league subsidized a host of kids' activities, which meant my parents could afford to sign me up for a host of activities to keep me engaged and busy—soccer, basketball, softball, swimming, and even one tennis camp. Our proximity to the University of Connecticut main campus meant we had access to free and low-cost cultural and sporting events that might have otherwise been out of reach.

When I was in the sixth grade, my mom received a job offer from a computer company in Silicon Valley. I wholeheartedly begged my parents to move, seeing it as an exciting and fresh new start.

Major transitions like long-distance moves can significantly impact kids' well-being and performance, and I was no exception. Moving to the Bay Area was one of the most significant opportunities of my young life—one of the levers that had an all-encompassing impact on my life trajectory, in ways I wouldn't recognize until many years later. Starting in junior high school, I was navigating an overwhelming combination of being new to the area; feeling out of place in a sea of Silicon Valley wealth, status, and connections.

In what felt like a land of unknowns, I became an observer, trying to comprehend what seemed like an entirely new culture. For the first time in my life, I found myself navigating a new workload that was considerably heavier than any I'd had previously. As challenging as my new academic work seemed, the social scene felt impossible. I tried befriending a tight-knit group of girls who were in my classes and had attended elementary school with one another. At best, they were unwelcoming. It didn't help that one of the girls decided that I was her archnemesis. She proceeded to do all the typical mean-girl things—tell her friends to exclude me, switch tables when I tried to join them for lunch, and make sure I wasn't invited to after-school and weekend activities. Fifteen years later, I would run into her at a yoga class in San Francisco and was dumbfounded when she offered me a heartfelt apology for how poorly she treated me.

From a research perspective, the cross-country move propelled me from what could be seen as a lower-opportunity space to a higher-opportunity space, complete with new classmates from higher socioeconomic backgrounds with far more resources than I previously imagined possible. Even though my home in rural northeastern Connecticut wasn't devoid of resources, this new place felt like an entirely different stratosphere. I also found myself in an environment dominated by much higher expectations—academic and otherwise—and this exposure led me to greater expectations of *myself.*

Quite by accident, my solution to navigating all this newness was to become what I now refer to as a **floater**, a role I've continued throughout high school, college, and in some ways, my adult life. Like Nira, whose story I shared in Chapter 3, I developed singular friendships and connections with different classmates and peers who might have considered themselves to be part of a specific group or clique. To be clear, this was not the accepted norm in junior high and high school and even college; being "popular" and being defined by belonging to a certain friend group still dominates the norm in many communities. As an adult now working with parents, students, and faculty members in school, I see how this need to find positioning within a group dynamic still creates scenarios where adults behave like middle schoolers. At the time, one of the benefits of being new to the community was my fresh perspective—I might have placed more weight on my initial rebuke by that friend group if I had grown up there. I adjusted and figured out other ways to make friendships and connections that felt supportive and authentic and gave me enough of a sense of belonging. Several of these connections were from my world-language class, which required a good deal of partner and small-group work, and other connections formed from being involved with the school newspaper and yearbook.

Today, I still see how shifting group dynamics and lack of connection to a defined group impacts kids, many of whom can feel "less than" owing to social connections or lack thereof. This dispiritingly persistent social insecurity isn't just prevalent among students who think they don't have any/ enough friends. It's also about students who would otherwise be perfectly happy with two or three close friendships or who have close friends without belonging to any one defined "group."

In the rise of social media friendships, popularity extends beyond school hallways, venturing deep into cyberspace and its many technology platforms. In some ways, online communities that are prosocial and supportive can encourage connection and belonging. At the same time, these online communities also have the potential to narrow our definition of social acceptance. With likes, loves, comments, and followers adding new hurdles to popularity, social media can create additional ways to encroach upon students' sense of self. My own junior high experiences were limited to the school day—now, for kids who engage online, reminders around perceived popularity can bombard them day and night and on weekends, often in silent and unspoken ways parents and trusted adults may not always fully grasp.

Given that socializing—and so many other parts of our lives—are increasingly turning into a transactional competition, we can get unintentionally caught up on "winning" the social game, which boils down to being well known and well liked. This "race" to become and remain popular ultimately narrows our focus to the people who can help us accomplish certain agendas and, in the process, undervalues the importance of openness, which can be seen having a "lower friending bias."[1] In other words, when we socialize in a goal-oriented, here's-what-I-need-from-you or here's-what-I-can-get-from-you sort of way, we overlook people who could add depth, meaning, and value to our lives, and we also tend to become less curious about other people who may have different backgrounds or perspectives. Together, this decline in **openness** and **curiosity** contributes to a more polarized and less fulfilling social life. Over time, that approach works against our goals by weakening our social ties and limiting our connections to an excessively curated, insufficiently diverse group of people. In addition to becoming dangerously lonely, we also end up having fewer opportunities to create genuine connections with others and then may struggle to get whatever support we may need—personal, professional, academic, and so on—from the people we do know. In short? The more we feel comfortable connecting with people and finding similarities across differences, the more expansive our world becomes. Being out in the world with people from different backgrounds and with different perspectives, and learning to be comfortable with being uncomfortable, has never been more important.

It's helpful to step back and realize, too, how much our entire conceptual understanding around friends and friendships has shifted so quickly, and how those shifts change the language of connection that our kids internalize. Social media terms like "friending" or "following" or "being connected" have also distorted our understanding of what connections mean. You may not have met your online friends/connections/followers in real life, and you may not communicate regularly, which is in many ways essentially the online equivalent of an acquaintance. Though there are exceptions, of course, these online connections are less likely to offer the kind of support we seek from meaningful, nourishing friendships. You might say that they're "friends" but not friends.

Of course, most adults realize it's entirely normal to have a hodgepodge of online and in-real-life (IRL) friends and acquaintances—close relatives, neighbors, a favorite barista, old friends, rooted friends (those we may not see for weeks or years and pick up as if no time has passed), acquaintances we haven't seen since middle school, as well as professional colleagues, professors, and so on. Some of these ties are weaker, and others are stronger. They can all be important, even if they all have distinctly different levels of connection and support.

Based on what I hear from students, what's often lacking are meaningful connections. It's a reality that's reflected in adults, too; nearly half of Americans report having three or fewer close friends.[2]

To change this, it helps to take a long look at how we frame socializing from a young age and examine ways we can encourage more openness and curiosity in friendship development. Early in elementary school, we start sending messages around friendships—so that boy/girl friendships are dissuaded by "Wouldn't they be a cute couple?" delineations. In adolescence, cross-sex friendships can be accompanied by a harmful stigma; girls run an increased risk of being described as "promiscuous" and boys as "gay."[3] For young boys in particular, forming relationships with members of the opposite sex can be regarded as a violation of prevailing norms, increasing their risk of experiencing meanness or bullying.[4] The loss of relationships with girls, therefore, has a particularly negative impact on boys' sense of peer integration, as it narrows the pool of attachment figures available to meet social and emotional needs.[5] By middle school or earlier, kids become aware of their popularity. Perceived popularity—popularity derived from social visibility and reputation—is relatively stable during late childhood and early adolescence, even across school transitions.[6] After the middle school transition, aggressive behavior becomes increasingly associated with perceived popularity.[7] Parents', teachers', and other adults' concerns around popularity may not be helpful, and adults, too, fall prey to feeling pressured to know more people or the "right" people.

Before and during those years when popularity becomes a priority, young children are often encouraged by parents and caregivers to hold on to a few close friends or a designated group of friends. Often, those friendships are forged by proximity or convenience. They might be the children of their parents' friends or kids they see at regular activities. The messaging, however subtle or overt, quickly gets confusing and potentially overwhelming. Kids are supposed to be popular—invited to every party, well liked, friended, and followed—yet they also need to nurture "close friendships," some of which were chosen for them, rather than by them.

To be sure, the social power brokering that occurs among elementary, middle school, and high school parents—however well intended it may be—trickles down to kids, who slowly but surely gain a distorted view of what meaningful social connection even is. Because we're ultimately focused on social goals, we fail to notice all the ways this approach to socializing is degrading kids' self-esteem and ultimately robbing them of meaningful connections.

Interestingly, popularity may not be nearly as important as we've been told it is. Psychologist Mitch Prinstein analyzes two different kinds of popularity: high status and high likability. More often than not, the two do not correlate; many people who are likable have little status, and only about 30 percent of those who have high status are also likable. In fact, most people with high status—a type of popularity that doesn't exist until adolescence and is driven by a conviction that one person is better or more important than others—are largely hated by others. Indeed, it has been found that the most popular kids in high school or those who hold high status as adults can be at much greater risk for substance use, loneliness, anxiety, and problems with relationships.[8]

Prinstein argues for the importance of likability for long-term social and emotional well-being. That's understandable because likability is rooted in authentic connection rather than transactional socializing. At the same time, there are noteworthy limitations to a focus on likability. Our own biases—we all have them—can exert excessive influence over whom we find likable or attractive at first glance. Recent research from Professor Raj Chetty and his colleagues at Opportunity Insights suggests that friendships among people from different backgrounds are still stratified along class lines, especially among people with the highest socioeconomic status.[9] In other words, people tend to be friends with those from similar class backgrounds, regardless of other differences.[10] In future chapters, I'll discuss how this narrowed friending bias impacts students' ability to connect, but for now, it can be seen as another impact of trans-actional socialization.

Once we do acknowledge the very real impact of transactional social-ization and perceived popularity on social and emotional well-being, the question becomes, what do we do about it?

IDENTIFYING BASIC SOCIAL NEEDS

We know that feeling a sense of connection and belonging is fundamen-tal to our well-being and our ability to build a meaningful and purpose-ful life. Instead of focusing on popularity, I suggest reframing our whole notion of connection, beginning by making sure each child has supporters and clarifiers in their lives. **Supporters** are people, generally peers or those around the same place in life, who are available, interested, and willing to provide positive, prosocial support. They could include siblings, cousins, classmates, or friends in and outside of school. Everyone benefits from hav-ing multiple supporters—ideally in spaces where they spend a good deal of time each day. A key is helping students understand that if they have peers who *aren't* supportive, well, perhaps they are being misclassified if they are seen as friends. For instance, frenemies, those who are or pretend to be a friend but are also in some ways an enemy or rival, aren't supporters. **Clar-ifiers**, on the contrary, are generally adults who offer clarity and wisdom. This could be a therapist or counselor, a coach, an aunt, uncle, grandparent, or trusted family friend. A parent or caregiver could also serve as a clarifier, though as students get older, it is helpful to have clarifiers outside their immediate family.

Two important types of clarifiers are mentors and sponsors. Mentorship, on the one hand, is characterized by a passing interest, perhaps a few hours here or there or even on a regular basis. Reading tutors or college applica-tion counselors are great examples of mentors. They provide support and advice as needed to help the student progress, though student effort tends to be the driver. Sponsorship, on the other hand, involves an active, tangible effort to provide support for the direct *economic* benefit of the person being sponsored. Sponsorship doesn't need to involve a long-term relationship, but it involves a well-connected person's active efforts to support another person's life trajectory. We all need mentors to help us stay the course, but to create opportunities for social mobility and economic stability, we also need sponsors. Sponsorship could mean recommending a student for a relevant program and then following through as the student navigates the application process to matriculation (including helping navigate financial hurdles), or connecting a student to others who can provide support and skills to have a successful experience in school, an internship, or an initial job. In her book *The Sponsor Effect: How to Be a Better Leader by Investing in Others*, Sylvia Ann Hewlett calls on sponsors to "endorse [their protégés] noisily": both in public and behind closed doors.[11] Loud endorsement could include introducing a student to people, places, or happenings relevant to their interests and then providing active support as they pursue opportunities. While we often think about sponsorship in the context of work and career, students are just as likely to need sponsorship as they move through school.

In my life, I've benefited from the support of many types of clarifiers—adults who aren't my parents—whom I can call on for advice or a listening ear or to work out a challenge. As the child of immigrants who experienced social and economic mobility, many of these clarifiers have been critical in helping me expand my possibilities and understand a seemingly invisible handbook of unspoken, unwritten social norms that weren't part of my childhood. Some I talk to more regularly than others, but through the years, I've actively stayed in touch with a host of individuals who are ten to thirty years older than I and who have come into my life during different experiences at different times. Those who have been sponsors in my life have helped me land my first internship, get my first book deal, and even navigate the purchase of my first home. The key to symbiosis in these relationships is that I have been open to receiving clarity, and they have been open to providing it. Some clarifiers stay for a season, and others I've known for decades. Some I speak to once or twice each year; others more frequently. Their intergenerational wisdom provides a life perspective I might not be able to get from a peer.

At the same time, and this is key, many of the people I might have reasoned would be great mentors or sponsors didn't pan out or play the role I assumed they would. But others, who ended up playing the most influential roles in my life as mentors and sponsors—the alumna from my university I sent a cold email to, or my high school dean of students to whom I speak regularly, or the education reporter whose efforts ultimately introduced me to my literary agent—all resulted from my own openness and curiosity.

CULTIVATE MULTIPLE CIRCLES OF CONNECTION

Trends around kids feeling more isolated and less connected are mirrored in adults, too; friendship has undergone a steep national decline. The number of Americans who said they did not have any close friends has quadrupled in recent years.[12] In many cases, we've turned inward, focusing on relationships in our family, which can be necessary, even constructive. At the same time, without ongoing access to a diverse community of supporters and clarifiers, the strain on our family or those in our immediate orbit to be all and do all can be too much and can also prevent us from developing perspective.

An important way to encourage openness and curiosity in connection is to promote **multiple circles of connection**, particularly nonoverlapping circles of connection, which are individuals or groups of people we know and feel genuinely connected to, whether through shared experience, interests, or other contexts, but who don't know each other. Much of kids' angst is rooted in overlapping friendships—friends from school who are also on their swim team and in their community youth group. Seeing the same kids all the time works great when everything is going well, but especially as they reach the teen years, when friendship drama strikes or the normal ebb and flow of relationships happen, they benefit from having multiple supportive people and spaces to turn to. Another reason: over the past few years, as families have moved to different cities, states, and countries, some students have found their "one close friend"—the one they counted on for an overwhelming amount of social and emotional support—moves away. Or their "six-pack" of friends—a term one parent used to describe the bewildering way a group of six boys always arrived and left birthday parties together—breaks up. "My car can't even fit six kids, so it's good my son isn't part of that group," she lamented.

Instead of focusing kids' attention on that one tight-knit group of friends, they can benefit when we encourage them to seek out multiple spaces where they feel a sense of belonging. For some students, this happens naturally—maybe one circle of connection is their cousins, another is friends from orchestra, and another is friends from summer camp. For others, this may take a bit of effort. Parents, too, may be well advised to intentionally introduce their younger children to places and groups where others they already know might not go, if only to get children used to approaching new social spaces with greater openness and curiosity. For one of my students who has had challenges with emotional regulation, his social-skills group with other students learning to navigate social settings has created a safe, supportive circle of connection. As parents, teachers, and mentors, this often also means urging kids to expand beyond their social comfort level, something they may resist initially but that can be an important growth opportunity. Figuring out how to develop multiple nonoverlapping circles of connection, even if challenging at first, is likely to help kids feel less excluded later and is a way to organically encourage a floating mind-set where no one friendship or group is all encompassing.

Some strategies for helping children develop multiple circles of connection and encouraging a more expansive view of friendship:

- Take a step back and evaluate your own friendships—this may involve taking a piece of paper and writing down people you see or interact with daily/weekly/monthly/yearly and analyzing the diversity of your own friendships in terms of background and perspective. Do you have circles of connection that aren't overlapping? What is your own friending bias?
- Parental modeling can be far more effective and eye opening. Take the time to assess and reflect on your own efforts to expand friendships and relationships through openness and curiosity. An example: If you go to events at your child's school, do you speak

to the same parents every time? Do you ever introduce yourself to or interact with different parents, faculty members, and staff? How inclusive and welcoming are you to those who are new in the community? How do you engage in everyday conversations and small talk with others? When planning an event, do you make sure to make other families all feel included and welcome?

- Identify ways to pursue interests that are not in your immediate community or with peers who aren't at school or regular activities with your child—for instance, sign up for a dance class two towns over, or participate in a youth group that pulls students from different communities.

- Find something to do together as a family in the immediate or nearby community that doesn't overlap with people you already know closely or encourages you to expand the people you encounter every day. For instance, one family whose children I work with began volunteering at a local food bank on Sunday mornings, engaging with volunteers and clients that they would not have otherwise met.

- Use summer break or school vacations as a way of visiting a new place, going to camp with different peers, planning a day-long excursion or an opportunity to explore somewhere different, and in the process, expand beyond normal routines.

- Think of a parent's place of employment as a potential opportunity for engagement or exposure to different people, places, and opportunities. For instance, Luis's father was the manager of a high-rise office building, and he landed a job with attorneys whose offices were located there. That job experience provided Luis with invaluable exposure and a new circle of connection that was critical to his long-term professional success.

The key to these circles of connection is feeling a sense of belonging and understanding that there can be both closer friendships and weaker ties. Having a floater mind-set is not meant to devalue close, authentic friendships—instead, it is meant to support expansive openness that leads to exposure, shared experiences, and multiple circles of connection. Floating creates the opportunity for kids to have multiple close friends who might not all know one another. As kids mature, they usually discover that no one friend can be all things at all times and placing too much focus on one friendship or friendship group can create problems in the long term. Middle school and high school are developmentally a time when kids can outgrow earlier friendships, and the transition time between friendships can feel lonely and dispiriting. There is often so much emotion wrapped up in feeling a sense of belonging that feeling ostracized and alone can deter the development of critical social and emotional growth, confidence, and worthiness. Having multiple places to turn to during times of social transition can combat this loneliness and support kids' self-esteem through hard times.

Having multiple circles of connection can have long-term social and economic benefits, especially for those from historically excluded communities. It can help students become comfortable with new and different opportunities that might come their way by increasing peer and adult networks. These increased circles of connection may provide access to power and relationships that may ultimately positively impact upward mobility for students and their families.[13] In short, all (supportive) socialization has the potential to offer positive benefits.[14]

When I unknowingly became a floater in middle school, I began to benefit from cultivating nonoverlapping circles of connection. Having friends with different backgrounds and perspectives meant I developed a more open and curious mindset around socializing, ultimately creating more opportunities for supporters, mentors, and sponsors to have a positive impact on my life. In the end, *all* our lives are enriched when we're more open-minded and curious about people around us.

If openness and curiosity are beneficial in all these ways, why do we seem so determined to steer away from this approach to socializing? There are many reasons. As adults, many of us have grown up seeing how acceptance in certain groups can be critically important for social standing. We may have our own insecurities that resurface as our kids move through school. And yet it is our focus on certain group dynamics that can contribute to increased feelings of loneliness. Social media and technology also have noticeable impacts on how we connect, communicate, and engage with one another. In some ways, having access to the curated photos and musings of others online, at all hours of the day, allows us to feel perpetually connected regardless of distance or differences. In theory, it should also allow us to connect with more people outside of our social sphere, but many of us see more of the same. Researchers at the New York University Stern Center for Business and Human Rights found platforms such as Facebook, YouTube, and Twitter can serve to exacerbate polarization, as they employ popularity-based algorithms that maximize user engagement through inciting contagious fears or feelings of indignation, bolstering pre-established boundaries between communities.[15]

In my work today, I see how encouraging students to find multiple circles of connection can be a key preventative, because additional social outlets are especially critical when social dynamics shift (and they inevitably will shift, a fact cited in research as a primary reason that middle school moms are the most stressed group of parents).[16] Between one-third and one-half of all middle school friendships do not survive from one academic year to the next.[17] Kids who have largely been exposed to the same group(s) of friends during those years are more likely to struggle than those who have learned how to float and have established multiple nonoverlapping circles of connection.

Throughout high school and college and into present-day adulthood, I have remained a floater, benefiting from multiple nonoverlapping circles of connection. In college, a classmate who had been an acquaintance in high school turned to me one day and said, "Everyone always assumed you had it all together and you didn't care what people thought."

She had a point—I just had never thought of it that way. Perhaps I already had the acceptance discussed later in this book and just didn't realize it at the time. I found connections and perspective in volunteering outside of school and in working different retail and food-service jobs during the summers and year round. The jobs gave me the opportunity to talk with people of all ages and backgrounds, building my comfort level moving between different spaces with increased ease. I regularly meet up with friends when I travel to their hometown for work, and we often pick up like no time has passed. Research has suggested that interactions with older and younger peers provide unique opportunities for emotional and social development during adolescence; adolescents who have friendships across grades report less loneliness than other adolescents.[18] Data also indicates that mixed-grade friendships may protect anxious, withdrawn boys from being victimized by their same-grade peers.[19]

Looking back, having weaker ties and being acquaintances with classmates from completely different backgrounds was critical. An astute observer, I could do just enough to work on gaining the invisible handbook of knowledge I would otherwise have been oblivious to. I've thought about this a lot over the years and about classmates who remained tightly coiled with friendships of others who came from similar backgrounds and who lacked a wider range of perspectives that comes from exposure and finding similarities among differences.

Even though my parents graduated from college, they didn't have an undergraduate experience in the United States and were oblivious to many of the cultural norms that other families might think of as commonplace. And even though I spent six years in Silicon Valley before going to college and attended a private parochial high school, I lacked any understanding of the different companies and career options my classmates and their families traded as fact. My parents didn't have the connections that come from living in a space for a long time, having an extended network of family or friends nearby, or being deeply rooted in a community.

I can point to so many of these experiences—most of which felt uncomfortable at the time—as being foundational to my feeling comfortable moving through different spaces with far more ease than I would have otherwise. Early exposure and shared experiences across so many different avenues encouraged me to develop my own system, cultivate connections, and, later, develop my perspective and acceptance of the possibilities I wanted to pursue, irrespective of what others around me were doing.

I didn't realize it when I was younger, but I now see that being a floater has given me the freedom to move into and out of a wider variety of social spaces and places. Drop me into nearly any social or business circle, and I can usually find a way to connect with one, if not several, people. Experiencing that level of social confidence boosted my success in work and life. By rethinking how we frame socialization and friendships to kids, we can give them the freedom to stop pursuing popularity and begin focusing on creating supportive connections through openness and curiosity.

CHAPTER 7
OPTIMISM AND OPENNESS

Subject: College News!!

To: "Ana Homayoun"

Date: Wednesday, March 30, 2011, 4:08 PM

Hi Ana,

I got waitlisted by Stanford, rejected by Princeton, but none of that matters because I got into Harvard!!!!!!!

Thanks for everything!!!

Philip

PHILIP AND I MET IN THE SPRING OF HIS JUNIOR YEAR IN HIGH school. He attended a public high school in San Jose, California, that was consistently lauded as one of the best in the nation. Philip's high school classmates were occasionally overzealous and often obsessed with who was applying where to college, which was considered the ultimate finish line. Philip's parents had immigrated from China, and both worked as engineers in Silicon Valley. Having been educated in China, they hadn't been exposed to the typical undergraduate experience at US universities and weren't yet familiar with the college application process here.

Looking at Philip's transcript, it would be easy to assume that he was caught up in the college frenzy. He'd gotten straight As, 5s on every AP exam, and nearly perfect SAT scores. I would soon learn that he was also perpetually sleep deprived, pulling at least one all-nighter every week.

I liked Philip right away. He was thoughtful, engaged, curious, and funny. He seemed reserved at first, but once he felt comfortable, he opened up and could be downright chatty. He enjoyed playing the clarinet and had a keen interest in plant biology. Much to his mother's dismay, he grew sunflowers that towered over the shrubs and flowers that filled her garden.

In our first meeting, Philip asked some of the questions a child of immigrants straddling two cultures might ask. His main concern at the time was his summer plans. His classmates spoke of the importance of attending COSMOS, the California State Summer School for Science and Mathematics. COSMOS is a popular intensive residential summer program focused on science, technology, engineering, and mathematics subjects. The program is described as having a "challenging curriculum" that is "both hands-on and lab intensive." Philip was interested in science but was unsure he wanted to attend. He worried that spending his summer doing something else might set him back, especially because his hypercompetitive classmates saw COSMOS as an unspoken prerequisite for getting into a highly competitive college. For his parents, it would be a stretch to pay the program fee, which was several thousand dollars.

"Philip, if you don't want to go to COSMOS, *don't go to COSMOS*," I emphasized. Almost immediately, I could see his shoulders relaxing, his jaw softening. "You have this intense love of plants; why don't you think about doing something this summer exploring that interest?" I didn't have any other students growing illicit sunflowers in their mother's garden. "Why don't you put a résumé together and see if someone at Stanford or somewhere else might be willing to have you work in their lab over the summer?" I continued, intuitively blurting out the first idea that came into my head and naming Stanford because it was a few miles from my office. "I am happy to help you put together a résumé. Everyone knows someone who knows someone. *If* you are interested in having that experience." He nodded.

UNDERSTANDING THE IMPACT OF SOCIAL CAPITAL

Inherent in the idea of developing the multiple circles of connection is a greater point: How does everyone, regardless of background, receive access and opportunity *and* develop social connections that give them a sense of belonging? Access and opportunity shouldn't be limited to exclusive, pre-determined networks. We need to support the development of social skills that enable kids to build social capital *while also fostering genuine connections and a sense of belonging.*

Social capital describes how friendships and relationships are bound together by a sense of shared understanding. For well-connected, well-resourced adults, social capital can be a bit like the air we breathe. When we see the inherent benefits in our own social capital, it's like having clean air and clear skies; we appreciate it, but we also take it somewhat for granted, even if we put effort into maintaining it. It's an intrinsic part of our lives. However, when we lack the social capital needed to move forward, it's like living with the high levels of pollution we've had in California during wildfire season. The air is stifling, even toxic, and the skies are clouded and at times daunting. Altogether, the picture is impossible to ignore and con-tinuously impacts every aspect of our lives.

When we help students cultivate openness and curiosity in their approach to socializing, they can also better understand their own social capital, including recognizing the powerful role that mentors and spon-sors can play in their lives. Although the term "social capital" may seem to promote transactional socialization, it's by connecting with others in an open, curious way that we build sustainable, impactful social capital. We can achieve both—create genuine connections with more people and, in the process, build social capital, too.

A few weeks after my conversation with Philip about finding a research lab that tapped into his love of plants, Philip walked into my office with a draft of his résumé, which we edited together. He composed a short introductory email to those who might be able to help. He sent out what seemed like an endless number of inquiries that got no response and a few others that received polite rejections. In desperation, he changed the subject line of his email to "Please read! High School Student looking for

Summer Research Opportunity in lab." A professor at Stanford wrote him back, asking him to fill out an application and send along two references. After some back-and-forth, Philip ended up getting a position in her lab, which at first was an unpaid internship. Midway through the summer, the professor landed additional funding. Instead of paying to attend a summer program, Philip ended up being a paid intern.

Two of the things that have always made Philip easy to work with are his optimism and adaptability. He wasn't mired in only one way to do something and was open to hearing perspectives and then evaluating and reflecting on what might make the most sense of the available options. If one thing didn't work out as planned, he would find another path that did work out, often better than he'd imagined. Sending out hundreds of thoughtful cold emails to professors he didn't know takes a certain level of determination and optimism. Even when facing rejection or disappointment, he had a sense that things would work out. That optimism, coupled with his willingness to listen and be flexible as needed, made it easy for others to step up and act as mentors and sponsors.

Much of his work in the lab that summer consisted of making sure all the lab rules and procedures were followed, including cleaning protocol. Midway through the summer, he asked the professor whether he could do some lab work of his own and got the green light to run an experiment. That opportunity changed the course of his summer, and before long he was spending time in the lab, then coming in early or staying late to work on his experiment. Through the fall of his senior year, he continued working in the lab part time. When the professor suggested he use his lab experiments to apply to the Intel International Science and Engineering Fair (which since 2019 has been known as the Regeneron International Science and Engineering Fair), he did just that and was named a semifinalist.

Philip's college essay focused on plants—his love of plants and his research around them, including a humorous nod to his mom's annoyance around how his garden experiments affected her own efforts. When I read his essay for the first time, I thought, "Wow, he really loves plants." I was proud of how much he'd pursued his interest in his own way, but throughout the fall semester of his senior year, I still had one significant concern:

his sleep schedule and the impact it was having on his well-being. He was juggling a full load of AP classes with college applications and commuting back and forth to the lab over an hour in Silicon Valley traffic. On more than one occasion, he fell asleep in the chair in the office lobby waiting to meet with me and was then so tired during our meeting that he'd forget what he was going to say or struggle to complete a thought. Hoping to convince him of the critical importance sleep would play in his success, I shared research on the connections between sleep, emotional well-being, and productivity.

When we meet again several years later, I am comforted to learn that post–high school Philip has always prioritized sleep. "I've never pulled an all-nighter after high school, which I did regularly back then. I sleep eight hours a night, consistently, no matter what," he added. "Even in college, I never ended up doing that again. And definitely not in medical school. Definitely not in business school. I am not sure how I . . ." he trails off.

Going into his freshman year of college, Philip was ready to explore. He was equally interested in health policy, global health, and business. "Sometimes I felt like the stuff I was doing in the lab was a bit detached from what was happening out in the real world. I wanted to be part of the process that applied science to our day-to-day lives."

He wasn't quite sure which direction to pursue until he received an invitation from someone who would quickly become another sponsor. "She was actually my Harvard interviewer for college," he recalls. "She was very deep in the biotech world. And she was like, 'Oh, you should come staff this conference.'" He agreed and volunteered at what turned out to be a major biotech conference in Boston, and that initial exposure piqued his interest in the combination of business and science.

"After that conference, I just went down this rabbit hole of thinking about the business side of science, mainly in the form of biopharma and drug development. My journey since then could be categorized as balancing those two aspects. I did a lot of research in college. I did internships in biotech companies and in consulting, and decided I wanted to go into medicine."

In his senior year of college, Philip thought he wanted to get a job in consulting, like some of his peers. He had interned the previous summer at a smaller consulting firm doing research on the life sciences, and he received a job offer. "But I wanted an offer from one of the larger consulting firms like McKinsey, Bain, or BCG, and I didn't get any of those."

"I had no idea what I was going to do. Am I going to get a PhD? Am I going to find a job at a start-up? That was the last time I felt like I really didn't get something I wanted."

Right around that same time Philip's mother was diagnosed with breast cancer. That news prompted him to start learning more about the world of medicine, specifically from the patient perspective. His first job after college ended up being at the Dana-Farber Cancer Institute in Boston, where he spent two years helping with the clinical trials of patients with head and neck cancer.

"I didn't design the trial but basically did everything else in terms of executing and operations," he recalls. "And that shaped how I viewed medicine and science afterward. When I look back, I think my life would look so different if I did end up doing consulting. I'm not sure if I would be in medicine."

After spending two years at Dana-Farber, Philip was accepted to Yale School of Medicine, where he met another sponsor, a professor who was a surgeon and whose support led to Philip being named on research publications and speaking at conferences. She would come hear him speak and offer feedback to help him improve. His interest in the business side of science spurred his application to Harvard Business School, where he was accepted between his third and fourth year of medical school. He took a leave from medical school and headed back to Boston.

One thing that strikes me in my conversations with Philip today is how relaxed he is despite different priorities and interests. Philip has a simple organizational system that consists of a running Microsoft Word document of to-dos and replies to any email that would take less than thirty seconds to address right away. He admits to maintaining a consistent inbox zero, replying and clearing out emails daily, and doesn't have issues with distraction, which he believes is at least in part because he spends nominal if any time on social media. In early iterations of social media, he had a Facebook account for a brief moment, but his only real online presence today is on LinkedIn. This lack of social media has likely also left him freer to contemplate and reflect on his own blueprint, irrespective of what his peers or classmates may be doing. In environments that can feel highly competitive, he feels a powerful element of freedom to continuously create his own path.

"Balancing medicine and investing has become a big part of my professional life," Philip explains, reflecting that none of his medical school classmates and only one business school classmate have interest in a similar path. For him, it takes the pressure off feeling he might be competing for certain accolades and allows him to focus on what he wants to do and how he wants to contribute to the world. Ultimately, Philip is working toward becoming an oncologist, and eventually he wants to work for a biotech company creating new cancer treatments.

For Philip, work is mission driven. It's a mission shaped by experience and with the help of mentors and sponsors, which altogether have enabled him to carve out a meaningful, authentic career path. In many ways it also feels less competitive than his high school. "I can totally see in high school, they just set up these guardrails that force everyone to basically go down one lane, and it makes it extremely competitive," Philip concludes.

Philip starts to list all the different mentors and sponsors he has had since high school and how they've helped guide him as he developed his own career path. Many he keeps in contact with to varying degrees, including the Harvard alumna who originally interviewed him for college at a Peet's coffee shop and whom he since credits with introducing him to biotech. In my mind, his willingness to actively participate, even when—especially when—an encounter or experience felt uncomfortable, like sending out emails to land a summer internship in high school, is a shining example of openness and curiosity. He persevered then, as he continues to do in his adult life. And after going back to read that original email, his authentic thoughtfulness was clear in his writing even back then.

Today, Philip laughs when describing that initial *Please read!* email as "cringy," but it was his willingness to prepare a résumé, send out random inquiries, get rejected/ignored, keep trying, work in a lab for the first time, and later volunteer to work at a biotech conference—all firsts for him—that allowed him to take advantage of opportunities his sponsors had provided, even when placed in new situations that might have at first felt uncomfortable. That willingness to take chances that appealed to him has enabled him to carve out a uniquely authentic and fulfilling career path. And he's developed social capital through taking advantage of opportunities presented, in large part, as a result of his own openness and curiosity.

Far more so than mentorship, it's important to keep in mind that sponsorship is a two-way street. For a sponsor to offer opportunities and potentially create levers, there needs to be a person interested in being sponsored. Some people who insist they want a sponsor are not yet willing or able to listen to, follow up on, and heed advice that might go against their preexisting beliefs. Others who think they want a sponsor may not be ready for the impact of the sponsorship and may then self-sabotage or create obstacles as a way of blocking opportunities that may feel uncomfortable at first. Philip's sponsors helped to change the trajectory of his life and enabled him the exposure and shared experiences to see what was possible beyond the world his parents knew and beyond what his classmates in high school might have viewed as success. Still, it was his willingness to engage, to follow up, to be adaptable and open to new opportunities or changed circumstances that continues to make the impact of sponsorship reverberate as he moves along his professional and personal life path. These are powerful skills we can teach all young people—and like Philip, many will find they open doors that help them create a blueprint that's authentic to them and their own personal mission-driven sense of purpose.

CHAPTER 8

LEVERS

"**D**ID YOU GET AN OFFER?!" I BELLOWED INTO MY CELL PHONE, FORgoing any initial pleasantries. I was back in my room at the Embassy Suites after a long day of giving presentations at schools during a ten-day trip to Tennessee and North Carolina. I was scheduled to fly home early the next morning, and this was a call I'd been waiting for.

"I did," Aaron replies, cool at first. "They . . . they offered me more money than I ever imagined," he said, so excited he seemed to be stumbling on his own words. He then described a six-figure compensation package from the major technology company where he had been interning for more than a year. It was the same company that had been dragging its feet on making him a formal job offer. He went through the mix of base salary, bonus, and stock options in the offer letter before shrieking with joy in a long-awaited emotional release. At that moment, receiving the offer letter felt like crossing the finish line of a long race of years and years of trying to survive. He was *in*. He had *made it*.

Four months earlier, on a Sunday in late November, Aaron and I caught up over a casual dinner in Palo Alto, California. We had been introduced over a year earlier by a friend who thought to connect us because Aaron had recently graduated from college and had just started a two-year graduate program at UCLA. At the time, he was in the area for the summer, interning for a company a few miles from my office. I invited him to visit my office and was pleasantly surprised when he followed up and met me for coffee on the bench outside Manresa, a popular coffee shop and bakery around the corner from my office. From there, we kept in touch and connected every few months or so.

Midway through dinner, Aaron shared his anxiety around postgraduation employment. In short, he needed a job before he graduated. Some of his classmates didn't fully understand his concern—some wanted the summer off to travel or rest—but Aaron felt the financial pressure to begin work immediately. Despite having a paid internship while in graduate school, he had taken out extensive loans and had a limited safety net. He feared he wouldn't be able to afford housing if he didn't have a job lined up when he graduated from his master's program the following June. The funds in his bank account were low, and there always seemed to be unexpected expenses.

What I didn't know at the time was how Aaron's wily, compact frame belied his determination within a state of inner turmoil. By the time he was a senior in high school, he had already attended ten schools and moved fourteen times.

"I lived a paycheck-to-paycheck childhood," he later recalls, "which means there was very little stability and also very little predictability." He had spent his childhood shuttling between Atlanta, Oakland, and East Palo Alto, and he knew there was no safety net from his family. Even his close friends had a difficult time fully understanding the urgency of his predicament.

Aaron felt as though he had nothing lined up, despite efforts with informational meetings, good conversations, and email follow-ups. The technology company where he was interning had been saying for months that they would eventually make him a formal offer, and he thought they might be stringing him along. Months passed and no official job offer had been made. The many connections he amassed through his various leadership positions and activities had yet to make any real efforts to connect him with potential opportunities, despite Aaron's thoughtful and consistent follow-up. He was fully aware of the thin line between thoughtful follow-up and being a pest, and his ongoing attempts to secure a position had become dispiriting.

I wasn't surprised by Aaron's challenge to land a job, despite his flawless résumé, tireless work ethic, emotional intelligence, and personable humor. Black men have the highest unemployment rates of any race/gender group, as well as the lowest labor-force participation and employment rates among men.[1] Missing from official statistics are thousands of Black men with low employment, even further reducing their measured earnings rates and employment.[2] Additionally, Black men experience less upward and more downward mobility over time, relative to their parents, than does any other race/gender group in the United States.[3]

His experience reminded me of a time a few years earlier, when I was invited to a meeting held at the impressive library of an elite private high school a few miles from where we were having dinner that evening. The meeting was organized by a well-regarded nonprofit, an organization with a strategy of helping students gain admission to the local independent and private middle and high schools. The underlying hope was that access to exclusive school settings would allow students to transcend their families' current living conditions. The meeting's purpose, as I understood in advance, was to find ways to help more low-income and historically excluded students find "success."

The library looked like it could be featured on the set of the movie for an East Coast boarding school, furnished with dark wood tables, floor-to-ceiling built-in bookshelves, and stained-glass windows. It looked at once welcoming and formal, expensive and cozy. When I arrived, I smiled at the older gentleman already seated and said a polite hello. He had a captain-of-industry look, with patrician features, a square jaw, and gray hair matching his dark sweater and pressed collared shirt.

"Are you the diversity and inclusion person?" he asked. "Um, no," I replied, taken aback as he pressed on, curious as to why I had been included in the gathering. I mentioned my work with students and my books on education topics. Uninterested, he returned to the pile of documents he had been engrossed in before I sat down.

The nonprofit was known for its annual gala, well attended by many prominent CEOs, venture capitalists, and technology executives. Its board was composed of well-connected, highly successful folks. The captain of industry who had spoken to me turned out to be a longtime donor and chair of the board and one of the valley's original venture capitalists. He had no idea that I had grown up a few miles from his expansive home and that one of his children was a friend of mine.

Toward the end of the meeting, the captain of industry became increasingly exasperated at what he perceived to be a lack of success among the program's graduates. He expressed that frustration in a bit of an outburst. "We get these kids through middle school and high school," he bemoaned, "and we even help them graduate from college. But then they graduate and they are unemployed or severely underemployed."

The rest of the room was silent. I have no idea why I decided to speak up. "The problem," I began slowly, as I felt all eyes in the room fall upon me, "is that the same people who buy tables at your annual gala don't give these students an internship opportunity or hire them at graduation. And none of these students have parents or aunts or uncles or cousins to pass along their résumés."

I was never invited to another one of the organization's gatherings again.

Knowing that Aaron faced barriers for reasons that have nothing to do with his potential or performance, I made him a deal at dinner that night. He would make a list of the top ten companies he might want to work for. I would then brainstorm who I might know at each of the companies to try to set up an informational interview, with hopes of getting his résumé flagged to a hiring manager and get him an interview.

"You are going to have a job lined up before graduation," I promised, with an *if you visualize, it will happen* optimism. He looked uncertain, exhaling a small bit of relief that someone else might help him shoulder the burden that was troubling him.

RECOGNIZING THE POTENTIAL OF LEVERS

Given my own experiences, I know the power of levers, the term I used earlier to describe an event or experience that unequivocally changes someone's life trajectory. For many students and their families, the faulty finish line around college admissions is rooted in a belief that a certain college acceptance will be the main lever in their lives. It is true that being accepted to a particular school may have a tangible and long-lasting impact. Still, the singular focus and faulty finish line created undermines the real potential that comes from exposure and shared experiences.

For me, my move to the Bay Area, a coveted internship in college, and an article about my work in a national publication turned out to be levers—once they happened, a whole host of opportunities and experiences followed that led to other happenings down the line. Levers can certainly be positive or negative, and sometimes both. A lever might be a chance conversation that leads to a job that requires travel or a move, or an opportunity that leads to far greater things than once imagined. The fact is, at various times in life, nearly all individuals have levers that changed their life trajectory in some way.

Most of us have multiple levers over the course of our lives, and sometimes we only realize the greater impact years later, when we look back. Often, it is hard to predict what will be the levers in our lives, though there are ways we unknowingly put the foundation in place to make us more likely to benefit, or to continue to benefit from the potential positive impacts. Sometimes, levers are about taking advantage of the opportunity presented, with little hesitation. The opportunity to benefit from a lever can be temporary and may not always be available in the same way if we circle back. It is rare to realize the long-term impact—and yet, looking back, it can sometimes be uncomfortable to think about the tentacles of experience that develop out of what feels like a singular happening.

In my life, there is one particular lever that continues to stand out and motivate me to act as a supporter and sponsor to others when it feels appropriate and I am able. During my junior year in college, I was trying to land a paid summer internship and hitting a whole lot of dead ends. Unlike many of my college classmates, my parents had few if any connections that could be helpful, and they also had little understanding of how the internship process worked.

Feeling dejected one Saturday afternoon, I was doubtful that submitting a résumé through normal channels would land me a summer internship—after all, hundreds of students typically applied for one or two openings. I decided to scan my university's alumni database, figuring sending a direct email might be more personal. Looking through alumni profiles, I came across Clara, who was then a vice president working in a technology group in the Palo Alto office of a major investment bank. I knew nothing about banking, but I remembered a classmate mentioning that those jobs were among the hardest to get, so I figured they were coveted. Most importantly, an internship in Palo Alto meant I could live at home for the summer. I crafted a thoughtful email inquiring about internships, and to my utter surprise, Clara replied and later called me, speaking with me for no more than twenty-five minutes while she was waiting for a flight at the Providence, Rhode Island, airport. I don't remember much of what I said in that initial conversation, other than a promise that I worked hard and was a quick learner. Clara decided—for reasons I still don't fully understand, because we would never become close—to sponsor me and make sure I got that coveted investment banking analyst internship the summer before my senior year in college. At the end of our initial conversation, she offhand-edly said something to the effect of, "You should come work here this summer. Give me a few weeks."

About a month later, a contract arrived at my dorm room via FedEx. We had never spoken about salary or any other details for the summer internship, and I was floored to read the fine print and realize the internship paid $10,000, plus a $1,500 housing allowance. It was more money than I ever thought possible for a summer job. My parents were equally dumbfounded. I got the internship offer—which later led to a full-time job offer for post-graduation work—by circumventing all the normal channels, including connections I didn't have, a career center process that hadn't been fruitful—and ended up with an internship and later a job offer beyond what I even knew was possible.

Clara's sponsorship created a lever in my life, and, even more importantly, her efforts still have ripple effects in the way I think about being of service to others. How could someone do what I saw as moving mountains for someone they barely met? I've thought about this so many times over the years and when opportunities have arisen where it is appropriate for me to act as a sponsor for someone else.

So when Aaron expressed his concerns around finding a job, I was determined to find a way to help. And as skeptical as he seemed to be around my unwavering optimism, he was true to his word and sent an email in the first week of January with the subject line "Top Ten Companies." His email noted how he reflected on our previous conversations over the winter break and had come up with ten companies he had shortlisted as places to explore opportunities. He noted his ideal start date of July, a few weeks after graduation, and his desire for a full-time role in policy, communications, or public affairs. He also noted his ideal locations: Washington, DC, or the San Francisco Bay Area, along with a well-edited list of six technology companies, three private foundations, and a nongovernmental organization. *No rush in response!* he implored.

I immediately thought of people at two of the technology companies on Aaron's list to reach out to, one a stronger tie and another a weaker connection. The stronger tie: a friend I knew for nearly a decade, whom I saw every few months, who was a longtime executive at one of the companies. The weaker tie: the wife of a friend from high school who worked at another company long before its successful IPO and was still in a management position there. I considered her an acquaintance at best, though I was willing to go out on a limb and ask for a favor on Aaron's behalf.

We often confuse mentorship and sponsorship. On the one hand, mentorship typically incorporates advice and guidance but stops short of actively creating connections. Sponsorship, on the other hand, involves far more engagement and an active use of social capital (friends, network, connections) to proactively move the needle on behalf of the person being sponsored. Sponsors commit to either providing the lever(s) in someone's life or helping the people they sponsor to be in a better position to access those levers. So even though I didn't have a job to offer Aaron, I saw my role as using my network to find others who might.

To my complete surprise, my weaker tie—my friend's wife—again, at the very best an acquaintance—became personally invested. I later learned she had also experienced significant social and economic mobility. She met with Aaron before passing along his résumé and then met with him several times to prepare him for different interviews as he moved through the hiring process. She introduced him to colleagues as a way of building his support network within the company. My stronger tie also pulled through, flagging Aaron's résumé and helping him through the maze of the recruiting and hiring process at his company. Within three months, Aaron had two solid job offers at two different technology companies from his emailed list, complete with formal offer letters and expiration dates. Either position would have served the purpose of getting him in the door at a well-known technology company and would enable him to pay his bills.

With those two offers in hand, Aaron met with his supervisor at the company he had interned at for over eighteen months. Suddenly, the same supervisor who had been making vague offers of potential full-time employment for more than six months was faced with losing him. After learning that Aaron's job offers came with expiration dates, his internship supervisor begged Aaron to give her a few days. Within a week, Aaron had a third job offer in hand. This final offer from the company he had been interning at was by far his best option with regard to the position, salary, and benefits package.

"My grandma has been working for forty years. She's never made over $60,000," he said slowly, his voice cracking, a potent combination of exhilaration and overwhelm. It had been a long few months, few years, lifetime. At twenty-four years old, he now had a job offer—two months before graduation, where his total compensation package would be more than double his grandmother's highest salary.

When we hung up the phone, I should have been excited—and I was, to a point. I knew how much work went into Aaron getting his job offer and how many people acted as sponsors in big and small ways to create that lever. Despite all his own efforts to build social capital, his work ethic, his remarkable résumé, his superior emotional intelligence, and extraordinary communication and leadership skills, despite burning the candle at both ends for much of high school and especially in college and graduate school and doing everything he possibly could and then more, Aaron still needed multiple sponsors to ultimately land him a job he was well qualified for—one where he would go on to earn multiple promotions over the next few years, and be included in frequent meetings with senior company leaders and C-suite executives at a company with more than 150,000 employees worldwide.

I thought back to the captain of industry venture capitalist in Silicon Valley who had stood up at that meeting and bemoaned the students' lack of suitable full-time employment at college graduation. He was frustrated that his organization's early efforts—their "investments," as he called them—weren't leading to the desired long-term impact and life outcomes. Yet, at the time, his organization was full of well-meaning mentors, most of whom weren't realizing the need to step up to sponsor those who didn't share the same level of access. I also recalled Clara, the investment banker who had helped me land my summer internship nearly two decades earlier, which gave me exposure at a level I could never otherwise understand. In many ways, the solutions to systemic inequality and fundamental access and opportunity can be seen as complex and layered. In other ways, the solutions aren't nearly as complicated as we want to believe. The more we become personally invested in supporting authentic connection with others, the more we can start to find solutions.

PART THREE

DEVELOP PERSPECTIVE

Perspective is about expanding notions of what success looks like, what opportunities exist, and what is possible. It is about becoming engaged and exploring our immediate communities in different ways—and about looking beyond our immediate communities and listening to learn from the stories of others. It is also about realizing there is no one "perfect" or "right" pathway, and that there are many avenues to pursuing personal interests, including career options, housing, relationships, and more.

Some of our traditional notions of perspective building—for example, studying abroad, voluntourism—may not offer as much perspective as we've long believed. Traveling to an area recovering from a natural disaster or spending a summer or semester studying abroad might help kids become more independent. However, when these experiences translate into more time spent mostly with kids from similar backgrounds, they may not offer the expanded perspective that true immersion in a different environment—local, regional, national, or international—would.

Two inherent ways to gain perspective are through **exposure**—to people, places, and experiences with others whose backgrounds might be different from ours—and through **shared experiences** that help us find similarities across differences. We know that a lack of perspective promotes a narrowed, stringent, and often myopic definition of success. Our goal is to expand possibilities, move beyond the immediate, and promote curiosity and critical thinking as ways of seeing possibilities that might be available beyond an immediate community, some of which may take longer to see to fruition.

One idea I use to help students develop perspective is encouraging them to become **savvy consumers.** I initially started using that phrase while helping students identify where and how they wanted to spend their time online and in real life. We know that social media and technology can act as a double-edged sword—potentially expanding our perspective by exposing us to new possibilities, ideas, and opportunities, while at the same time creating underlying anxiety and worry about missing out or not doing enough. Savvy consumers, however, identify what is important to them, the qualities they want to highlight, and the experiences they would prefer to avoid. The idea of reframing social media and technology use as something they could actively choose to opt into and out of resonated with students, who began researching founders' stories, data/privacy policies, and related issues of different social media platforms before downloading them to use. I explain more about this in Chapter 11.

These days, I also encourage students to become savvy consumers as a way of reframing their overall school experience, including the college admissions process. It's a way for them to move beyond the anxiety-provoking, *Will I get in? Will they take me? Am I good/smart/brilliant/hard-working/unique enough to be accepted?* mind-set to a more balanced one: *Where are the multiple places where I can thrive? What are the other options for me? What am I looking for in a college/university? What does this opportunity offer that could be important for my personal and intellectual growth and overall well-being?*

Gaining a broader perspective allows us to be more adaptable, flexible, and capable of bouncing back from setbacks and disappointment. It can also counteract the effects of meanness and social exclusion. By looking at a situation from multiple perspectives, students can experience greater self-acceptance and a deeper sense of worth that can help them move beyond preconceived expectations and toward developing their own blueprint of how they want to explore and engage in the world.

CHAPTER 9
OPPORTUNITY AND ACCESS

B<small>Y THE TIME OLIVER—OLLIE TO ANYONE OTHER THAN HIS GRANDPAR-</small>ents—was thirteen years old, he had attended five different schools on three continents. His family's frequent moves gave him practice at meeting new people and being the "new kid," but each new location required an adjustment that involved a unique set of complications.

An avid reader, Ollie alternated between Marvel comic books and David McCullough biographies, sometimes using Audible to listen to prize-winning tomes about history. Earnest, quiet, and kind, Ollie didn't participate in organized team sports, though a weekend afternoon at home might be spent playing in the park with his younger brother, drawing in his sketchbook, or rooting for his favorite soccer team, Manchester United. Friday evenings were often spent playing video games with friends from around the world.

Ollie's advanced interest in geopolitical issues likely resulted from his parents' background and lifestyle. His accomplished father grew up in Hong Kong, Zurich, and London, and his mother had spent her formative years outside of Washington, DC. Ollie was curious and engaged, in a way that wasn't captured by grades and test scores. As a student, he struggled to keep track of assignments and turn work in on time, which created tension at home. Transferring between US and international schools on different continents also left gaps in Ollie's foundational knowledge of math, science, and the English language. Working with a math tutor addressed some of the foundational gaps in real time, but surprise quizzes and exams still unnerved him. He also struggled with organization, prioritization, and managing distractions, completing schoolwork at the last minute when he was stressed and rushed and less able to perform at his best.

When Ollie and I first met, I had spent a decade working with American families living abroad. (I still mess up time zones with embarrassing frequency.) Ollie would sometimes start our meetings by repeating conversations from around his family dinner table, add his own commentary, and then ask for my opinion. I would respond with open-ended questions, preferring to encourage him to probe more deeply into his own viewpoints and conclusions. World news events were an engaging distraction and also an area where he needed to set boundaries, including removing news notifications from his phone.

Ollie lived in an expansive, privileged, multicultural world that was also very sheltered. He was polite and generous, and he had the perspective of someone who has interacted with many different people from many different backgrounds since an early age. He was outwardly friendly and upbeat and felt more comfortable talking to adults than to peers his age. In spite of his resources, he loved earning his own spending money and was accustomed to traveling around the world with his family—skiing in Switzerland, sailing off the coast of Sardinia, and spending summer breaks in Bar Harbor, Maine. He would crowd into a beach home with his three siblings and mom as they spent extended time during the summer with his maternal grandparents, who now lived outside of Raleigh, North Carolina. When he was younger, Ollie attended a summer camp with kids from all over the world and at the conclusion of every camp session would spend hours trading messages across multiple time zones. As he got older, he spent part of his summers in New England beach towns working in retail.

During his last two years of high school, Ollie's worries around college acceptance started to spiral into overwhelming concerns about his future. He understood that his overall profile made acceptance at some of the more selective schools (which boast an acceptance rate of less than 10 percent) less likely. He would frequently become stuck correlating his college admissions process to worries about creating a life that mirrored the one he grew up in.

Ollie was experiencing what I see as a paradox of opportunity and access. Born into a family that offered him extraordinary exposure, social capital, access, and resources, it appeared that the world was his proverbial oyster. Certainly, that idea holds true; so little seemed out of his reach. Yet his perspective was walled off; confined to the ways he'd always known, he was unable to imagine any other way of living. And, without an understanding and confidence to explore beyond the world he'd grown up in and the basic underlying skills to develop a system that would help him navigate life, he might fall short of his personal potential.

The seeming paradox of opportunity and access suggests that students in highly competitive, well-educated, and affluent areas feel empty, exhausted, and overwhelmed in part because of their limited perspective and narrowed definition of success. When well-resourced young people have a limited perspective, it doesn't just impact their ability to develop their own blueprint and discover their own abilities, talents, and gifts to the world. It also undermines their self-awareness and self-acceptance. For many of them, it is as if nothing they will do is ever good enough, and their sense of self and well-being suffers as a result. This isn't a *poor little well-connected rich kid* argument or a plea to feel bad for the student with extraordinary access and opportunity. At a time when there are real structural issues preventing millions of young people from reaching their potential, it might seem counterintuitive to spend time and energy addressing the concerns of students who have been afforded so many options. And yet, in many of the communities I've visited, and including Bay Area schools right by my office, this narrow definition of success and its impact on student mental health and well-being are extraordinary. Ollie, like so many students from similar *and* very different backgrounds, needed to expand his perspective. He needed exposure to different ways of living, earning, relating, and achieving, if only to break out of the wide yet confining world he'd grown up in.

This seeming paradox explains why students in some of the most affluent, educated areas of the country are ridden with angst, anxiety, and overwhelm and why many of our current strategies aren't working. These students feel restricted, unable to consider a life blueprint that doesn't exactly mirror what they know. Ollie hadn't been exposed to the notion that there were many ways to create a meaningful life. He wasn't sure where he would want to live or what he would want to do for a living, and that uncertainty made him anxious, convinced that he was behind, that he should feel ready to define a concrete path by seventeen years old, like he thought many of his classmates were doing.

I've heard countless students voice similar concerns. So much of the anxiety students (and the adults in their lives!) feel around their future is rooted in a narrow definition of success, which results in part from a lack of perspective. For some students, *not* having a tunnel-visioned goal is equally stress inducing. Yet in a world where many of the jobs in demand today didn't exist twenty or thirty years ago, students' increasingly narrow definitions of success hold them back academically, socially, emotionally, and potentially professionally as well.

One of my college classmates was a highly motivated, perfectionist straight-A student. Her goal was to graduate from Stanford Law School and work for a top firm as a corporate litigator. I remember thinking that her goals seemed incongruent with her personality and interests, and I wondered more than once whether she'd watched too many law-firm dramas on television. Nonetheless, it was her version of what success looked like, and it acted as her North Star throughout high school and college.

A few years after she'd started her first job as an associate at a big law firm in corporate litigation, I ran into her. She was devastated by the realization that working for a big law firm didn't actually end up to be what she wanted and was worried that leaving a career she'd worked toward so hard and for so many years would equate to failure. It's a scenario I've seen play out in countless students who feel pressured to realize a singular, often excessively narrow version of "success." Fortunately, in time she expanded her perspective and realized that there were different opportunities where she could use her skills in ways that felt more purposeful to her. That redefinition showed her that success could be defined in many different ways.

What would have occurred if she'd been exposed to other options at an earlier age? There's nothing wrong with changing course, and sometimes doing so can prove enormously beneficial, as it did for her. Still, though, gaining broader perspective at younger ages can potentially help kids identify personal values earlier with less confusion and fewer lengthy and costly detours. Developing perspective allows kids to see that multiple possibilities could be feasible to move forward. When it comes to college admissions, students and families can become convinced that only one school or one type of school or one school pathway is "right" for them. In fact, more often than we realize, other pathways forward—from widening the scope of colleges they consider to attending community college or attending college part time—might better set a student up for long-term well-being and financial stability. In a world where technology and so much else are transforming how we live, learn, and work much faster than ever before, these options are not "less than." In fact, in many cases they can avert costly—in terms of money, time, and energy—missteps.

Given that the average adult born in the later years of the baby boom held an average of 12.4 jobs from ages eighteen to fifty-four,[1] teenagers' limited perspective can be viewed as developmentally appropriate. However, our collective faulty finish line mentality around college admissions often leaves students, parents, caregivers, and teachers with the illusion that being unsure is some kind of curse—or at least a detriment to a student's future prospects.

Of course, limited perspective doesn't just hold back students who have lots of resources, opportunities, and access. Students of all socioeconomic backgrounds can feel the negative effects of having a limited perspective, and no one volunteer trip or summer internship or outdoor adventure "does the trick." Developing perspective outside the confines of whatever world a student has grown up in typically happens through exploration and self-examination. It is a process that takes time but is too often cut short by the faulty finish line of college admissions, which suggests that certain types of experiences should be completed before fall of their senior year in high school, if only to inspire a standout college admissions essay.

Nicole's childhood was utterly unlike Ollie's, yet she, too, ultimately benefited from developing perspective. A first-generation college student from a low-income family, she admits that she hadn't been "shown the ropes," so to speak, around how to prepare for the college admissions process or college itself. She and I met more than a decade ago, when we were part of the same cohort of thirteen graduate students in our master's program specializing in school counseling and pupil personnel services.

Now a school counselor at a rural high school in the Placer County School District in Northern California, where she once was a student, she's cognizant of the irony that she works here all these years later. "When I graduated from high school, I wanted nothing to do with this place," Nicole admitted to me on a Friday afternoon at the end of a long week. "So in that way, it's weird to be back."

In her new role, Nicole now finds herself in a small town located along Interstate 80 in Northern California, with a population of around 2,500 in 2020. The school's attendance area covers an expansive fifty-mile radius, with students coming from as far north as Truckee, near Lake Tahoe, to Auburn, about thirty miles outside Sacramento, the state capital. The school is socioeconomically diverse, with some students living in homes deep in the mountains that barely have electricity and no Wi-Fi access, and other students living in multimillion-dollar homes in country-club–like settings. When Nicole looked up the school's profile for me, she realized that fewer than half of students at the school (43 percent) attended a four-year college after graduation, with 40 percent attending community college, 7 percent going to full-time work, and the rest a mix of military enlistment, vocational or trade school, and other opportunities.

In many ways, a socioeconomically diverse environment has the most potential for increased perspective, or the opportunity to see experiences and opportunities beyond our immediate world. One of five girls in a family that she describes as "super low-income," Nicole's own perspective of possibilities was limited as a student. Neither of her parents, who divorced when she was twelve years old, attended college. Her two oldest sisters did attend college, and her third sister did not. In high school, Nicole would do the bare minimum to get by. "If my grade dropped too low, I would bring it up. If it was too high, I would relax and let it drop. I would procrastinate and cry the night before a paper was due. I would get it done, and would end up with a C."

"I signed up for the SAT because I was with a friend who was like, 'I am signing up for the SAT.' And I was like, 'Oh, okay, is that something we do? I'll sign up for it too.'" Nicole describes her parents as uninvolved and unaware of what needed to be done. Much of her academic advising happened informally through friends.

After high school, she headed to San Francisco State, seeing college as an opportunity to get out of a home she desperately wanted to leave. She soon learned she didn't have the skills or resources to sustain herself on her own. It proved to be a perfect storm of too much. Trying to juggle a full-time job working at the Olive Garden in the Stonestown Galleria mall with a full academic course load was not something she was prepared for, academically or otherwise. When the financial aid office called her in, having found a mistake on her financial aid forms, the forms had to be resubmitted. Her financial aid application was moved to the bottom of the pile, and she ended up qualifying for just $500 of aid that semester, leaving a monstrous gap her low-income parents were unable to help close. "I cried and packed and left two months in," Nicole reveals, feeling defeated. "I had to write a letter to petition not to be charged, to excuse my fees."

For the next several years, Nicole bounced around, enrolling and dropping out of community college several times. She lived alternately with her mom and then her dad, and then got a job as a nanny. She moved to Los Angeles and then back to Sacramento, determined to go back to college and graduate. She went to American River College in Sacramento and met teachers who changed her life trajectory. "I had a couple of amazing teachers who basically showed me that I was capable. They connected with me. They had these conversations with me like, 'Wow, I like the way you framed this, and this was written really well, and here are a couple places you can do some edits.'"

"And I was like, 'What do you mean this was written really well?' I had never heard positive affirmations about my educational ability." That encouraging validation helped her plow through the awkwardness and discomfort of making a new start, and her expanded perspective helped her keep moving forward and finding solutions even when things turned difficult. "I took a math placement test and scored really low," she goes on to explain. "I thought, well, that's weird. I better just start from the beginning. I decided to enroll in the lowest math class and start over."

She eventually transferred to Cal Poly Humbolt, where she got her undergraduate degree at twenty-four years old. Knowing that she ultimately wanted to work in education, she didn't yet feel ready to pursue her teaching credential. She moved to Japan for a few years, then worked for an advertising firm in San Francisco. All of these experiences were part of an exploration process that solidified her interests and helped her expand her perspective.

"I knew I wasn't driven by money, and I wanted to be in education," she explains. "I started interviewing people who worked in schools and talked to someone I grew up with who was a school psychologist. She said, 'Nicole, you need to be a school counselor. That's the job for you.' And I was like, 'What does a school counselor do?'" Fast-forward to a decade later, and she in fact does love her job as a school counselor, but it's an opportunity that never would have been available to her if she hadn't broadened her perspective beyond the world she'd known growing up.

To be clear, I am not suggesting that we force young people to be exposed to experiences that are not personally or developmentally appropriate. What I know is that helping students thoughtfully and intentionally develop and expand their perspective can both act as a buffer to some of the angst young people are feeling and also give them a wider lens through which to define and redefine their interests, pursuits, and sense of purpose.

One of the most powerful ways to develop perspective is through **immersive exposure**. I define this as encouraging students to get out of their normal environment and, in many cases, beyond the reach of peers they already know, as well as parents or caregivers and perhaps current teachers as well, to stretch their understanding of life and possibilities beyond their own.

This type of immersion might be uncomfortable at times, which makes sense; the most significant, life-affirming experiences aren't always easy. Still, immersive exposure isn't as complicated as it seems. Young people can often find opportunities for immersive exposure within five to fifty miles of home.

For one student, working as a bagger at the grocery store provided him with immersive exposure and expanded his perspective. Until then, all of his activities were with childhood friends; he had never earned his own money or felt comfortable talking with adults, which prompted his parents to act as a buffer in certain social situations. In this new role as a grocery bagger, he was in a new environment, accountable for specific tasks, forced to interact with the general public, and solved problems on his own for twenty to twenty-five hours each week.

Another student of mine spent three years playing music at an elderly care facility near her school. She developed friendships with many of the residents who came to hear her play the piano on Tuesday and Thursday afternoons. They asked her questions about her day, and she learned about their lives and their likes, dislikes, and personal preferences. The experience allowed her a consistent opportunity to interact with people whose life circumstances were different from her own, to have regular conversations and develop intergenerational friendships, and to have a community separate from the one she grew up in.

Another one of my students years ago volunteered weekly—as part of his high school's required community service program—as an after-school tutor at a parochial elementary school. The school was located less than four miles from his private school but in a traditionally excluded and historically underresourced area that was a world away from his own in terms of access and opportunity. One day after tutoring, he came into my office and was offhandedly sharing about the experience: he loved working with the young kids and naively wondered why they didn't have more after-school activities where they could just run around and play. I explained there was likely a shortage of staff members and the focus was on making sure students reached grade-level milestones around reading and math. That led to his realization that the students didn't have access to the type of sports day camp he and his friends took for granted when he was in elementary school. This notion gnawed at him for weeks, until he decided he wanted to put together a sports camp for three weeks that summer for students—not for college applications or a résumé, or anything related, truly—and he became laser focused. When he first approached the elementary school, he was rebuffed. He did multiple presentations to convince the elementary school to allow him to create his sports camp, raised money, created an agenda, recruited volunteers, and for weeks drove around with a trunk full of donated supplies. His parents were absolutely baffled in the best possible way: their good-natured son who was usually easygoing and a master of free time (his mother once wondered whether it was healthy that her son spent more than half the weekend lounging on the couch) was suddenly giving up evenings and weekends, making sure logistics were in order, and organizing and emailing and recruiting his classmates to participate in this camp. His conscious effort to think beyond his own experience to what summer vacation for the students at this school looked like, and why they don't have a sports camp experience, was the way he developed perspective.

Immersive exposure isn't as obvious as it seems. We've long assumed that a lack of exposure is a socioeconomic issue—and it absolutely can be, but not always. Even well-meaning parents and caregivers who try to expose their children to a wide variety of experiences reach a limit to what is possible, especially given realities like limited vacation time and budgets. Also it's important to understand that developing perspective is often somewhat personal; an experience that expands perspective for one child might not do so for another. Similar experiences can impact different people in different ways.

But in a world where students get so many messages coming at them online and in real life on how they should act, look, and be, developing perspective through immersive experiences offline and in person expands their in-person understanding of the many different ways to live meaning-ful, purposeful, and engaging lives. When we help students broaden their perspective through immersive exposure in experiences that have them interacting and engaging with those who have a different background and life perspective from them, they can become happier, more intrinsi-cally motivated and resourceful, and better able to develop a healthy sense of self.

CHAPTER 10
EXPANDING POSSIBILITIES

"I LOOK BACK AT MY BROTHER AND WONDER WHAT HIS LIFE WOULD have been like if he did what I did," Christopher reflects wistfully. "He had multiple opportunities to get out of New Orleans, and he didn't take advantage of them."

For the first sixteen years of his life, Christopher grew up in the shadow of his larger-than-life older brother in a family beset by tragedy. As the youngest of three children growing up in Metairie, Louisiana, an unincorporated part of the New Orleans metropolitan area, Christopher lived with his parents in a well-worn home built on a swamp. Looking back, he describes his childhood as exemplified by experiences that might be typical for a child living in close proximity to extreme poverty, alcoholism, substance abuse, and domestic violence. He grew up accustomed to seeing red and blue sirens outside his bedroom window while falling asleep and hearing violent fights in his own and neighbors' homes. His early years were mostly unsupervised, his days often spent roaming the streets on bikes with his motley crew of eight friends, shooting BB guns, building tree houses, and getting into neighborhood fights. His older sister died at eighteen from a drug overdose, leaving behind her one-year-old daughter, whom his parents adopted and raised as their own child. His mother stopped working when he was around eleven years old, and his father cycled through extended periods of unemployment.

Christopher was eight years younger than his brother and always felt pressure to live up to his legendary reputation. His grandparents covered the tuition so Christopher could follow in his brother's footsteps at Holy Cross School, an all-boys Catholic school in New Orleans. His brother was the quarterback of the football team who dated the head cheerleader from a rival high school and was elected class president. Christopher played the same sports as his brother and participated in the same activities. Years earlier, Christopher's brother attended the Holy Cross Leadership Conference in Austin, Texas, meeting other student leaders from Holy Cross schools around the country. Christopher was determined to do the same, and by the end of his sophomore year of high school, he was elected junior class president and attended that same conference.

Christopher is friendly and outgoing, with sandy brown hair, a quick smile, and a self-effacing laugh, and it is no surprise that he formed fast friendships with students from around the country, including Ryanne from the San Francisco Bay Area, whom he kept in touch with after the conference.

About a week into his junior year of high school, Hurricane Katrina hit New Orleans. After several failed evacuation attempts, his family, accompanied by another family they'd been friends with for a long time, drove along the Panhandle through Mississippi and Alabama to Florida. By the time they reached Florida, water was coming up on the road. They eventually ended up at a resort in Palm City that opened up rooms to shelter those who had been displaced, and Christopher began spending time on the beach every day, watching news coverage of the devastation back in his hometown.

Within days, it was clear that there would be no school to return to. His high school, then located in the lower Ninth Ward along the failed Industrial Canal levee, was destroyed as water flooded the historic building complex. Then one day Christopher received the surprise phone call that would change the course of his life: an offer to come to California and live in the guesthouse. Ryanne's mother, Cindy, threw her energy into solving all the logistics, including getting him a scholarship to her daughter's high school and securing his plane ticket to California. The next day, Christopher packed two bags and flew to the San Francisco Bay Area.

"I had a very wondrous, adventurous, dangerous childhood," Christopher says, thinking about growing up in New Orleans. "But it gave me a lot of freedom. All of that freedom was stripped away when I moved to California, in a good way. When I moved, I could no longer do things that were going to damage my future."

Moving to California and living in the guesthouse of Ryanne's family meant a completely different lifestyle, in a neighborhood where the most noise at night came from the family pets. The transition wasn't without its challenges. Suddenly, he needed to surrender the task of raising himself, which he had done for years, and start getting up at 5 a.m. to go to school to finish homework, and then staying after school for wrestling practice and a second workout, which helped him stay out of trouble. He found himself living in a home full of boundaries and structure, with a "second mom" he'd just met, a woman who was adamant that he get the support he needed to go to college. It was an entirely new world for Christopher, and the idea of attending college, equally far flung. He'd always assumed he'd enlist in the military, like nearly all of his friends, or go to a local two-year college while working, like his brother. Up until then, those seemed like the main options on his table.

"It wasn't so much taking away as it was, 'this is what you get,'" he continues, reframing the experience of moving to a household that was the opposite of his home life in New Orleans. "When I got home after school in New Orleans, nobody cared if I did homework or not. Now, I get to have a family dinner every night with a colorful assortment of foods. I don't have to eat cereal by myself or hot dogs and hamburgers while I'm on the couch and no one is around."

To Christopher, the nightly family dinners stand out as a fundamental difference between his life before and after moving to California. While eating a balanced meal, the family would communicate, discussing ideas and sharing knowledge. He never had that level of consistent time, structure, and support for what he now calls "cohesive relationship building."

Transitioning to his new school was overwhelming socially, emotionally, and academically. "It felt like *Saved by the Bell*," he says, referencing the popular early 1990s television sitcom immortalized in reruns and a recent reboot. "I came from an all-boys school with uniforms. Here it was coed and everyone was in collared shirts." His learning gaps soon became clear. During his first Algebra II class, the instructor, who was also one of the wrestling coaches, handed him a copy of a test the rest of the class was scheduled to take that day. After assuring Christopher the exam wouldn't be graded, the instructor encouraged Christopher to take a look at the test and give it a shot to see what he already understood.

"I take a look at the test, and I break down in tears," he recalls with emotion in his voice years later. "I didn't know any of it, and this was Algebra II. It was stuff I should have been learning."

He would soon learn that his math understanding was at a sixth-grade level, and his reading comprehension and writing skills were not much more advanced. Two of the math teachers—both involved with the wrestling program and wanting Christopher to raise his grades and qualify for the team—started tutoring Christopher for nine hours a week, after school and on weekends, to get his math understanding up to grade level. Cindy, whom he still calls his second mom, was adamant that he rise to the challenge, providing structure, support, and high expectations that he had never before experienced. Over the two years that Christopher lived with her family, Cindy made sure he received writing tutoring, standardized test preparation support, and assistance with his college applications. That's how he found his way to my office.

During our first meeting, Christopher pulled a stack of papers out of his backpack. Despite all the tutoring and different levels of support, he had no clear system for organizing and managing his work, and he constantly felt pulled in several directions at once. I had intended to spend our first hour together helping him figure out how to prepare for upcoming exams, but instead we took a binder and five-tab dividers from my office supply closet and went through all his materials. We devised a system for getting his work in order and then reviewed strategies for planning his week and prioritizing his academic work, sports, and other activities. Over the next year and a half, we continued our work together, focusing primarily on managing schoolwork, preparing for exams, and completing his college applications.

"It was an opportune place for me to focus and learn and not be distracted by my childhood friends," Christopher surmises, thinking about the evenings in the guesthouse after dinner where he would do homework and watch DVDs. "I was distraction-free. Even today, I don't like distractions."

Being part of the wrestling team provided connection, familiarity, and solace. In New Orleans, he had won two tournaments but never saw himself as putting in any grand effort in the way he did when he arrived in California. In a new space detached from everything he knew, he focused on wrestling, buoyed by the support of the coaches who also acted as mentors and tutors. For Christopher, continuing with wrestling and putting considerable time and energy into getting his math knowledge up to grade level gave him the confidence to learn whatever is put in front of him. The connections he developed through being on the wrestling team—with teammates but also with coaches, one of whom ended up being a constant lifeline and support to this day—provided an anchor as he navigated the new living experience of being a houseguest adapting to new rhythms, expectations, and cultural norms.

When thinking back on his forced transition to a completely new environment, Christopher also remembers the feeling of overwhelm when meeting new people who lived in what he describes as magnificent homes. "When I was around these people of massive wealth, I was so overwhelmed and out of my depth," he remembers. "It was so foreign to me." Now, he looks back on that immersive experience as helping him become comfortable with being uncomfortable in new environments and expanding his perspective. Now, as an adult, he feels much more at ease talking with people from a variety of backgrounds, skills he's used throughout his career, first in sales and now as a recruiter working for technology companies.

Christopher also realizes how his parents and brother were never exposed to the experiences he has been. "My brother has always stayed in the confines of his immediate peer group, what they do and think and believe. And, unfortunately, that peer group is not diverse. They think the same way their parents think."

Much of Christopher's success in transition is a result of the time, structure, and support Cindy provided at a critical junction. Cindy was a forceful combination of warmth and positive energy, determined and organized. She was the ultimate sponsor, and her energetic enthusiasm made me think she was always in motion, juggling multiple projects and lighting up a room with her bright smile. When Cindy came in to speak with me about Christopher's college application process, she opened a color-coded binder filled with every document and resource needed to help him be accepted to college and also find a way to pay for it.

"Out of the fifteen colleges I ended up applying to, I got into fourteen—every school but Tulane," Christopher recalls, "which was a good thing, because I probably would have moved back to New Orleans."

In some ways, Christopher's story of accidental migration exemplifies the results touted in the landmark analysis of economic mobility in America's fifty metropolitan cities by the Harvard and UC Berkeley Equality of Opportunity Project mentioned earlier in this book, which led me to do those initial interviews in Charlotte, North Carolina. In the study, New Orleans was identified as one of the metropolitan areas with the lowest intergenerational economic mobility. Two of the most likely places for upward mobility are San Jose and San Francisco, the metropolitan areas directly to the north and south of where Christopher ended up moving.[1]

Looking back, he still has clear memories of feeling "out of his depth" when he first arrived at that private high school in California. One of his sharpest memories is from homeroom on his first day, when he watched his fellow classmates pass a cardboard box around to collect donations for Hurricane Katrina. All of his classmates contributed their spare change or a few dollars. When the box got to him, he froze. "I took the little cardboard box and passed it on, and somebody made a remark like, 'Oh, you're not going to donate.' At the time, I almost got angry. What do I do with this thing? Everybody is looking at me. Do I take it? Do I put the lunch money the family just gave me in that? I don't know what to do." To this day that memory surprises him and evokes a visceral reaction. At just sixteen years old, he'd been torn so suddenly from his home and his family by a traumatic event that his classmates had only read about and watched from afar.

Christopher's story wasn't just that he moved from a low-opportunity space to a high-opportunity space. Not only did he move; he also left his birth family and the place he grew up in because of Hurricane Katrina, a traumatic event that left permanent scars on the lives of millions of people, including Christopher, his family, and his friends. No one would wish for the circumstances that led to Christopher's exposure and shared experiences in an environment utterly different from what he had been accustomed to. In many ways, it tells like a Hollywood fairy tale, the teenager who cashed out on that one exceptionally lucky hand. His story is real, however, and the sponsors and mentors who came forward to support him—Cindy and her family, the wrestling coaches, and the way he was forced into an environment where he was constantly exposed to new worlds expanded his perspective and understanding of what was possible. The heightened expectations Cindy and others placed upon him to build his skills, to keep pushing forward, and to close his learning gaps helped him realize that he loved to learn. He also saw what he could do if he really gave something his all—both in school and in wrestling, and later as an adult with weightlifting.

There's always a price for navigating such traumatic experiences early, and Christopher has spent his adulthood dealing with the aftershocks of multiple levels of trauma, even if the immersive exposure and expanding perspective created social and economic opportunities he might never otherwise have known existed. Still, he sees the challenges he's overcome throughout his life in situations where he again feels out of his depth as a source of strength. There's a sense of peace knowing that although we can't always control the circumstances of our lives, when we can learn the skills and have experiences to help us tackle the challenges we face, we are able to find ways to thrive. In Christopher's case, developing perspective and understanding what could be possible as he was continuously encouraged to become comfortable with being uncomfortable changed his life trajectory. In the end, it allowed him to discover his innate curiosity and love for learning in an environment where he felt knowledge and education were celebrated.

CHAPTER 11

ONLINE AND IRL (IN REAL LIFE)

FOR MUCH OF ELLIE'S FIRST SEMESTER IN HIGH SCHOOL, HER DAILY lunch period was a recurring reminder of loneliness and social exclusion. She had come to her private high school after attending public elementary school and junior high, and few of her previous classmates attended her new school. In addition to adjusting to the academic rigors of her new school, she struggled to make new friends in a place where her out-of-the-box thinking, wholesome kindness, and quirky humor could be misjudged by peers who often traded in teen angst and dark, sometimes biting, sarcasm.

For those first few months of high school, she spent much of the first half of lunch hiding in a bathroom stall, scarfing down a peanut butter and banana sandwich, then headed to the library to pretend to do homework. A hard-working honors student and strong athlete, Ellie didn't feel like she belonged. Even her teammates on the elite-level varsity volleyball team she'd been invited to join were older and more socially advanced. Above all, Ellie yearned for a sense of belonging and a place where she could feel *at home.*

Worried about Ellie's social and emotional well-being, her parents suggested she join a local youth group that was made up of teens from neighboring high schools. Ellie resisted at first, but her parents insisted she try it out for three weeks. She liked it and soon became an active member throughout her next three years of high school. The youth group gave her a fresh start and perspective; she met peers from other schools and participated in nonacademic activities in a warm and welcoming environment. Over time, the social confidence she developed from her youth group friendships translated into increased confidence in reaching out to classmates she didn't know, and pretty soon, she had a group of friends at school to eat lunch with.

This is one of the many ways that perspective-building experiences can counteract the effects of meanness and exclusion. At the beginning of her junior year in high school, Molly felt similarly excluded virtually overnight when her friends began ignoring her. To an adult observer, it seemed like a bout of teenage meanness and exclusion, but for Molly, it felt devastating. Just like that, each school day became a slog where she felt alone and overwhelmed. She considered transferring to her school's online program and worked with her school counselor and therapist to weigh all her options. Ultimately, she decided to keep going to school in person. At the same time, she started working at a local bubble tea shop, several miles away from her high school in a completely different neighborhood so there was no overlap, and also started volunteering at a local animal-rescue organization, taking small dogs for walks and providing general care. Being immersed in new situations with new people allowed her to realize that the world is bigger than the myopic meanness she might be experiencing in her immediate environment.

I thought a lot about Ellie and Molly and feelings of exclusion a few years ago, when I began traveling to schools around the country to talk about social media and technology. When Ellie was a high school student, many of the social media apps that are now used by students as gateways for both connection and exclusion didn't exist. Molly, however, was living in a world immersed in social media and technology, and they weren't that different in age—at least in my mind. So much has changed so dramatically in such a short time that it can be easy to forget what life was like before smartphones.

My original motivation for learning the language of social media socialization—long before it had the all-encompassing role it does now in the lives of people today—was to understand the creeping distraction that was increasingly influencing how and with whom students were spending their time and energy. After all, when I first started working with students on these fundamental skills, there was no Facebook, Twitter, Instagram, YouTube, WhatsApp, TikTok, or Snapchat—and arguably a lot less information overload impacting our ability to organize, plan, prioritize, manage distractions, and make decisions that support our overall well-being.

In many ways, I've had a front-row seat to the whole experience. Having spent my formative years and my career working with students from an office in Silicon Valley, I had a unique vantage point to the impacts of social media and technology early on. All in all, social media acts as a double-edged sword. While it can help kids and adults alike to see possibilities and communicate with people beyond our immediate community, it also creates a culture of comparison that can narrow our social circles, as well as how we define success. Too often social media places the focus on perfectionism rather than progress and acts as a constant reminder that others may seem to be doing more, better, sooner, and faster than we are. That might feel motivating or overwhelming depending on our circumstances. Given the potential for the sharing of highlight reels and curated content, it can at best act as a window to new ideas and experiences and, in most cases, will never be anywhere as powerful as actual in-person experiences with regard to developing perspective.

In my work, my focus has always been to encourage students to make better decisions around developing a system that honors their time and energy management, seeing how their choices impact their connection to others, while also developing perspective around how and where they want to focus their efforts. Throughout the evolution, I aim to remain objective, student centered, and solutions focused. Above all, I come from a place of empathy and compassion for students' longing for support and connection, rather than from fear, anger, and frustration for the many ways technology and social media can upend our lives. Time and time again, I see students respond favorably to this approach, becoming proactive in changing their daily habits and adopting behaviors that support their well-being. It usually helps that I am not their parent or caregiver and act as an outside source. The goal has always been to encourage students to pause and make better decisions online and in real life, regardless of who is watching and how they are being monitored, and regardless of the popular apps of the moment in their community or among their age group.

That work was the focus of *Social Media Wellness*, my guidebook for parents and educators who need support in helping the tweens and teens in their lives navigate this ever-changing set of online and IRL experiences. In the fall of 2017, I began traveling to schools around the country, speaking to parents and students about my Three Ss framework: Healthy Socialization, Effective Self-regulation, and Overall Safety. Used together, the Three Ss help students, educators, parents, and caregivers to assess, reflect, and evaluate social media and technology use. Being around the work for so long made me realize how quickly what is hot and popular today can be obsolete tomorrow, so developing an evergreen framework that can be adjusted and applied was important in order to remain relevant.

Whenever I was invited to a school to speak about social media and technology, I wanted to learn the language of social media socialization within that particular school community. I knew that having a clearer sense of how each community was using social media was key to being seen as relevant by students, parents and caregivers, and faculty members. I designed a survey for each school to have students take a few weeks before my visit and used the results to personalize my presentations to the school community. Nearly all schools were receptive and asked for the resulting data to be shared with them. (One school that refused to have students take the survey was having serious troubles with students' online misuse, I later learned, and the administrators weren't keen on having survey results immortalize these issues.)

My research indicated that the ways students spend their time online can vary—by age, demographic, and location. Sometimes the variations are geographic, even school specific, while at other times the differences may be age based. While sixth graders at a school might be mostly using group texts and messaging applications, the eighth graders were more likely to be on a platform like Instagram. At one high school, first-year students might be spending their time on TikTok, while juniors and seniors were mostly using Instagram or a short-lived anonymous messaging app, for instance. At some schools, posts on anonymous message board apps would circle through the student population and wreak havoc, while at other schools students remained relatively unscathed.[1] And information about where students kept their phones at night was similar to the Pew Research survey finding that 72 percent of teens check for notifications as soon as they wake up, and 57 percent believe that they often or sometimes have to respond to messages immediately.[2] The impact of the digital world on students' lives has only increased in recent years; Common Sense Media found that teens use screens on average for seven hours and twenty-two minutes daily, not including screen use at school or for completing homework.[3]

The survey I designed asked students about their online use, as well as their behaviors and feelings around online use. It asked about the ways they spent their time online outside of completing their schoolwork, including the top ways they socialized online and in real life. It asked about their sleep habits and where their phone was when they went to sleep. At one high school, a school administrator noted that the junior class had a distressing amount of class drama, and the survey results suggested that the class was far more likely to stay up late to spend time online, and their phone was often right next to them when they did try to fall asleep. There's no way to prove those habits were directly related, but the survey results did suggest that the junior class was likely experiencing the most sleep deprivation in addition to the most drama. At a middle school grappling with the aftermath of meanness online, a high percentage of students self-reported that their parents didn't set any restrictions on time spent online.

The survey was meant to be an informal way to gather information, but the answer to one question caused me to pause at every public, private, independent, and charter school I visited. The question asked whether the student had adults or peers they could approach if they witnessed or experienced something that was inappropriate or made them feel uncomfortable. No matter the location of the school or the type of school—rural, urban, suburban, or somewhere in between—2 to 10 percent of students consistently self-reported that they did not believe they had an adult or peer they could turn to if something inappropriate or even harmful happened online. At one parochial high school in the Midwest, 17 out of the 591 students reported they didn't have a peer or an adult to turn to, and 149 out of 591 students reported that they didn't have any adult to turn to if something inappropriate happened online. That's a lot of kids—especially in an age where meanness and cruelty have exceeded some of our worst expectations. And though having supportive friends is important, having trusted adults is critical. At this school, *149 out of 591 students couldn't identify a trusted adult!* During the question-and-answer period after my student talk, one high school junior was vulnerable and became slightly emotional in sharing why she kept her online use hidden and didn't feel like she had an adult to turn to: her father adamantly railed against social media. She didn't stop socializing online, because it was where her friends were and how they made plans, but his judgment drove her use underground. This meant if something happened online that made her feel uncomfortable or was inappropriate, he was not on the short list of people she felt comfortable contacting.

It is fair to say that the allure of online "connecting" is real and scary. The research around the dopamine hit that comes with likes and loves is alarming, even more so when we think about the many ways in which the transactional method of socialization and connection is evident in our online lives and seeps into the messaging patterns that we inadvertently teach kids. Given the monetization of an online presence—whether it is having a video go viral or millions of subscribers to a newsletter list or online channel—there's been a commercialization and commodification of connection that can warp the way we see ourselves in the world and how we measure our own self-worth. It can also alter the ways our kids see themselves and their connections in real life.

How do we help students develop perspective in ways that feel safe and developmentally appropriate? Especially in a world that feels so uncertain, ever changing, and always online, it can be tough to step back and make the time and space for students to develop their own perspective. In a world where an online search can turn up so many results, and where students can be navigating online and IRL experiences that may be unfamiliar to the adults in their lives, it is not surprising that so many parents, caregivers, and other well-meaning adults can easily and unintentionally sabotage or undermine a young person's ability to develop their own perspective.

What are the ways we can support students in developing perspective in a world where so much socialization and schoolwork takes place using technology and apps we might not be familiar with?

Acknowledge and validate that the world is changing. We've spent a lot of time chastising helicopter parenting, parents' suffocating involvement in children's academic and personal lives in a way that doesn't allow a child to process, reflect, and make decisions on their own. At the same time, we need to acknowledge how parents in our immediate and extended communities may be experiencing a heightened level of fear and anxiety around very real concerns about students' daily news feeds, mental health and well-being, gun violence, bullying, and more. In our pandemic-adjusted world, we've had so many once-unimaginable experiences that have changed our lives in so many ways and changed the way we parent in so many ways. We're not in a moment to be judging parents, and their parenting styles in general, given that so many of us are still processing the impact of the past few years. This is, however, a moment to be engaged with kids, especially as it relates to their online activity. So many of us have overrelied on technology and social media use in recent years, and stepping back to reflect and address what is working and what isn't should be done in a way that is child centered and focused on social, emotional, and physical safety and well-being.

In an age of rampant online oversharing of commentary, photos, and videos, identifying safe spaces online for ourselves and for children can feel like a daunting task. Given how much of today's schooling and everyday communication happens through online channels, we need to prioritize healthy ways for tweens and teens to engage online and in real life, especially because so much of the world has become more tech focused.

Act like a breezy, curious television interviewer. I've always found that the best way to gather information about new and different trends among students is to ask open-ended questions from a place of curiosity rather than criticism. "Oh really? How so? That's so interesting. Tell me more." Watch a great television interviewer, and you'll see the key to getting an individual to share is gently asking follow-up questions with an inquisitive, nonjudgmental tone. The same is true here. And if students start using a new social media app, I encourage parents and caregivers to download the app and figure out how to use it as a way of gathering information while also learning their child's language of social media socialization. Teens want to talk, and as they share their observations out loud, it allows an opportunity for parents, caregivers, and trusted adults to gather information and for kids to process the information they have been seeing and hearing. Tone and facial expression can be dead giveaways—so it may mean that you need to practice a few times in the mirror or record yourself and play back your voice for tone (it works!).

Parents and caregivers often ask me about new social media apps or websites, since even the most engaged parent can feel as though they are playing a never-ending game of Whac-A-Mole around which new social media apps, video games, and websites their children are allowed to play/visit/download. This is where my focus shifts toward helping students become savvy consumers, willing and able to actively identify how and where they want to spend their time online and in real life. Here's one exercise I suggest trying: create a family policy where tweens and teens who want to download a new app have to research and write a one-page summary on the app, including the app's founder; origin story; early history; and privacy and data policies, including how data is used and whether there have been significant data breaches. Encourage them to highlight any safety issues using current events, and have them reflect on why they think using this app is important to their growth, development, and positive socialization. Finally, ask them to identify any potential risks or restrictions to using the app that they would recommend.

The one-page research summary serves a few purposes: One, it provides a window of time for students to reflect. Two, it encourages them to gather their own information and draw conclusions, which allows them to think about how and where they want to share their data, energy, and time. Three, it encourages them to discover past safety issues and decide whether it makes sense for them to download. I've had students complete this exercise and come out of it surprised how their interest shifts after having time to research, reflect, and develop their own perspective. In some cases, they decided not to use an app, even though they had parental permission.

Sweeping the ice can backfire. Curling is a winter sport where a forty-two-pound stone is moved down a sheet of ice. If you've ever seen a competition in the Olympics, it is a game of skill, strategy, and quick motion that can get intense. One team member launches the stone, while two other players work down the sheet of ice, feverishly sweeping in front of the stone. Sweeping reduces friction by warming up the ice, which allows the rock to move straighter and get farther than it would on its own. In life, there are times where figurative "sweeping," or moving slightly in front of a child and smoothing out the surface and reducing friction, may be necessary to help students navigate a new experience or to offer support at a specific time. At the same time, sweeping just ahead of the rock (yes, in this analogy, kids are the rock) can make things easier and help them go slightly farther, but it can also backfire and miss the mark.

As individuals and in groups, we often develop perspective when things don't go as planned or we face some sort of friction. Looking back, friction in the form of challenges, delays, and disappointments helps us learn how to adapt, redirect, and navigate under different conditions. If we're constantly sweeping the ice for kids, we're not allowing them to stumble, fall, get back up, and regroup. Nor are we allowing them to develop perspective around their own buoyancy, which is a term I use to describe a child's ability to process and bounce back. As students become more buoyant, they still process experiences but typically can move through disappointments more quickly and then focus on alternatives and solutions. Moving inches ahead to reduce friction means that we make things seem easier in the short term, but longer term, we don't want to prevent kids from having the experience to process, reflect, analyze, and move forward in a way that ultimately will take less time and energy with practice. In truth, this can feel like a difficult line to draw.

That being said, every family is different, and every child within a family is different. Sometimes, a little sweeping is critical for getting things moving forward. One might need more support or a different kind of support in different areas. Perhaps a child with a diagnosed learning difference needs some extra assistance to get the support they need on their way to advocating for their own needs. Perhaps a student navigating grief or mental health challenges may benefit from some temporary sweeping. Focusing on supporting students where they are, given their current situation and needs, allows them to develop perspective in a way that is appropriate for them. The goal here is not to make sweeping a long-term solution, since it ultimately has the potential to decrease confidence.

Deescalate, disengage, deactivate. A few years ago, I was doing an interactive workshop with seventh-grade students at a New York City all-girls middle school. The girls quickly admitted that they spent most of their time on Instagram, YouTube, and TikTok, as well as online shopping, and that a mean comment or message could derail their day. I knew telling them to "stop going online" or "deactivate their accounts" would be ineffective and render my entire messaging useless. Instead, I mentioned the Three Ss—Healthy Socialization, Effective Self-regulation, and Overall Safety—as a way to help them frame their own choices online and in real life. I wanted them to know they had choices about how they spent their time and they could curate their feed and choose what they wanted to filter in and filter out.

Suddenly, a girl in the front row raised her hand in the midst of an "a-ha!" moment.

"I follow all these other kids I am not really friends with," she began slowly, explaining how at the beginning of school, most classmates followed one another even if they didn't really know one another. "I feel bad when I see photos of parties I am not invited to, but I am not really friends with them so I wouldn't be invited. But I don't have to follow them." She seemed excited in her declarative statement, as if she had just realized her power in choice. I had successfully framed her options to be about her choices and her time, and she stepped into her power. Six months later, I came back to the school as a follow-up to our initial round of activities, and she came up to me to share how much of a difference curating her feed had made.

Social media and technology have proliferated in all areas of our lives in ways we don't fully realize. For kids, social media use permeates every aspect of their academic and social lives so quickly they often don't realize that they have choices in how and where they spend their time, online and in real life. I am always surprised at the level to which students using social media and other technology haven't been given tools to think through their experiences. When I work with students, I help them think about the ways they can de-escalate experiences and even opt out. We talk about ways to disengage online, especially when online conversations feel mean or aggressive. After being interviewed as part of the book video I created for *Social Media Wellness*, one student decided to deactivate several of the social media apps she didn't think were serving her and to focus on just using one app to keep in touch with friends and family.

Encourage energizing relationships—including supportive intergenerational friendships. An important element of developing perspective is being able to evaluate whether the ways we spend our time are energizing, draining, or neutral. When we're adults, we may have a little more geographic choice in the matter—if we don't want to spend time with someone, for the most part, unless they are part of our daily rhythms and routine, we don't have to. For kids who attend a traditional school experience, they may end a friendship or romantic relationship and still have to see the person every day. Time and time again, we see how social experiences affect academic engagement—think about a student who does better in a class when they like the teacher or a student whose academic performance drops off when they are stressed by social exclusion or drama happening among classmates who were once friends.

The more we can encourage students to focus on energizing relationships and to reprioritize and reframe draining relationships, the more students can feel as though they are in the driver's seat of their own social experience—much like the seventh-grader who curated her Instagram feed. When students can identify multiple different places where they feel a sense of belonging and connectedness—it could be with school friends, members of their jazz band, cousins who go to different schools, summer camp friends—the less concentric the circles and the less overlap among the different places, the stronger the network of connection. This means if one relationship goes awry, there are other places to turn for support, and the more likely students are to have a bit of bubble wrap around the socialization challenges that have felt amplified in our pandemic-adjusted world.

Intergenerational friendships with trusted, supportive, listening adults are often an undervalued source of support, and they are key to encouraging students to process experiences and develop perspective. In many ways, perspective sprouts from connection to different ideas, opportunities, and ways to see the world. That is one reason the survey data around not having a trusted adult to turn to was so troubling. Even though parents and caregivers can absolutely be one of the trusted adults, it is helpful for there to be other adults as well—perhaps an aunt, school counselor, therapist, or coach—because issues may come up where talking to someone outside an immediate family member can be helpful. I always tell parents and caregivers that it doesn't matter whether you are the trusted adult your child turns to—it is your role to make sure they have an adult you trust to turn to in a time of need. Absent that support, students might turn to their same-aged peers to try to navigate tricky, nuanced topics that may benefit from input and wisdom of an adult who can hopefully provide more perspective and clarity.

Focus back on supporters and clarifiers. At the school where Nicole is a counselor, the principal has a specific focus of creating a school culture that ensures every student feels connected to an adult at the school. "When a student is not doing well, one of my jobs is to figure out who they are connected to," she explains. "And if they are not connected, who can be their connecting person, whether it is the IT person or the English teacher or the art teacher? And then we have an advisor, and the goal is that they have the same advisor for all four years."

In the midst of all the turnover and change happening in education and schooling, amid technological changes and innovation, my call to action seems at once both simple and challenging: Does every child have two to three peers or classmates they can identify as supporters who are caring and encouraging? They don't all have to be at school, but it is helpful to have at least one supporter at school. For kids who are well known and well liked, this may not seem like a big deal, but I know from years of experience that for some kids, having one supporter is a great place to start. Parents and caregivers often mistake a supporter as someone students have to hang out with and plan activities with after school or on weekends. That could happen, but a supporter can be a classmate they interact with at school regularly who offers encouragement, even if they don't spend time together outside of school.

Do they also have two or three adults who can act as clarifiers, who provide clarity and wisdom and help process issues that may arise? They need not have answers or solutions. Simply asking open-ended questions without judgment and offering a listening, empathetic ear provide the opportunity for children to reflect on possible challenges and ideas.

Get support as needed. In our focus on grit, self-reliance, and resilience, we sometimes overlook the importance of recognizing when we need help, identifying the help needed, and feeling comfortable reaching out for that support. Some students may feel out of their depth, like Christopher did when moving from New Orleans to California, and not know even what kind of help they might need. In his case, trusted adults stepped in. Others might feel ashamed or overwhelmed at their inability to handle a problem on their own or will turn to friends for advice (or the internet!) when the reality is that they may benefit from specialized, individualized support.

We underestimate the importance of knowing when, how, and where to ask for help as a key step in developing perspective. As adults, creating an environment where kids know that we feel comfortable not knowing all the answers and that we are willing to get help can be effective modeling that reduces the stigma people mis-associate with asking for support.

What I've learned in my own life and in my work with students is that some kids grow up in environments where asking for help is commonplace, and others do not. In some families, there might be lots of helpers around—extended family communities of a grandmother, aunt, and cousins living down the street, or a nanny who acted as a primary caregiver. And there are some places where students feel comfortable asking for help—coaching for basketball, or music lessons, for instance—and other areas where they would hesitate, like addressing social issues or getting mental health support. Messages of rugged self-reliance have created an environment where it is frowned upon to seek help, and yet encouraging students to know when to ask for assistance and to be open to receiving support as needed can be critical for developing a system, a sense of connection, and perspective.

Here, too, is where modeling can be important. Do they see trusted adults seeking support and getting help when a need arises? Or do the adults in their lives send the message that it is always better to try to figure issues out on their own? Are the adults in their lives on a pathway of always learning, always growing, always curious? Do they value their physical, mental, and emotional well-being and work with a therapist, counselor, or coach as needed?

Every person's journey to develop perspective is personal and never ending. Over the past few years, so many adults have seen the confluence of events in their lives—including concerns around health and well-being; navigating family challenges, regardless of children's ages; and restructuring of careers in our tech-intensive, pandemic-adjusted world—provide unintended opportunities for developing perspective around what feels important. Building perspective is part of growth and development, and students need time, space, and exposure to process ideas and thoughts. One of the most effective approaches is finding comfort knowing that we don't have all the answers and don't have to. Instead, we can model how we are exploring, learning, processing, understanding, and reframing in a world that is constantly evolving.

PART FOUR

DEVELOP ACCEPTANCE

Several years ago, I was invited to speak at an all-girls school about overcoming the culture of perfectionism. It was a hot and humid afternoon, and I assumed the students would be restless, but eight hundred girls in sixth through twelfth grade showed up fully focused and engaged. Midway through the Q&A, a seventh-grader posed a question:

When did you stop worrying about being perfect?

I paused, smiling, wishing I could give her a neat and simple answer. "The moment I was accepted to college" or "the day I started my first job." Neither would have been true, though I did stop sweating a whole lot of small stuff after my emergency appendectomy when I was twenty-one years old. Her question was far more complex than she realized. Despite my very best efforts, I have never completely stopped worrying about who, what, and how I am. The intensity of that worry, of course, ebbs and flows, as it does for most of us.

For so long, we've looked at the pursuit of accomplishments— *Grades, check! Scores, check! Athletics, check! Friends, check! Social media following, check!*—expecting that happiness and success will spring from those achievements. When I've asked students how they are doing, some answer by summarizing their recent grades or mentioning an external achievement, sometimes as a deflection. Adults often do the same ("Libby's doing so well in her classes!" or "She just made the varsity field hockey team!"). As so many adults eventually discover when a crisis hits, however, that's not how we, or our lives, work. Having the "right" work/career, finances/house, and lifestyle/family doesn't "make" us feel whole or happy. We rarely, if ever, look around and decide that we no longer need to "measure up" anymore or be "perfect," and if this does happen, it's often quite late in life. The reality is, the externals can add fun, even joy, at times, but they can't ultimately "make" us happy. To feel better about ourselves and our lives, we have to figure out how to intentionally nurture our whole selves—a lesson we ideally learn *before* a crisis strikes and *before* our most active adult years are over.

To be clear, this achievement-focused orientation isn't a personal failure but a broader cultural one. Most adults weren't taught to value themselves or each other on a "whole human" basis or to evaluate their well-being outside of external achievements. Yet as we teach and guide kids today, this mind-set needs to be addressed and altered. Kids are growing up in a technology-adjusted world that values creativity, innovation, and collaboration. These skills all necessitate a higher level of mental, emotional, and social nourishment and maturity. In other words, to prepare kids for the world they're growing up into, we need to better encourage them to accept and appreciate themselves. By broadening our outlook beyond the faulty finish lines of past generations—college acceptance being just one of many—we can better prepare them for the world they will need to thrive in. At the core of this preparation is acceptance.

Acceptance encapsulates self-acceptance, self-compassion, and self-awareness, as well as an acceptance of others. It's about helping each person honor their gifts, talents, and interests while encouraging them to identify areas of growth. It's about proactively stepping back and giving ourselves permission to pause and assessing when to rest, recharge, regroup, and redirect, without guilt or shame. It's about encouraging kids to literally and figuratively curate their feeds, which is especially important when so much information comes at them at once. It is about identifying and choosing where and how we want to spend our time and energy, It's also about purposefully ditching checklists in favor of developing personalized blueprints and figuring out how and when to opt out or reduce impact.

Just like developing systems, connection, and perspective, modeling acceptance is a continuous and often lifelong process. There's no moment where we can go *ding!* and scratch that off the list. One of the biggest challenges to acceptance is our fear, as adults, that kids aren't "enough" in some way, whether academically, athletically, socially, or otherwise. This fear stems from the intensely competitive undercurrent that's increasingly dominating the ways we evaluate ourselves and each other. Which kids made the travel team, qualified for AP courses, have the "best" friends, got into an Ivy League school, and more—this list of Supposed To-Dos that we, as parents, teachers, and guides feel pressured to make kids conform to is only growing longer and starting at ever-younger ages. The fear that our kids aren't doing or achieving "enough" often drives participation in multiple after-school activities, even though getting home after 9 p.m. every night means students don't have adequate time to recharge.

This fear also contributes to well-intentioned but misguided efforts to push students even harder when they may need time to rest, recharge, reflect, and redirect. This same fear trickles down to kids, who then neglect their own needs. Whereas little kids will accept who they are with confidence—and will tell you who they are, what they like, and what they want to be when they grow up—somewhere around the early days of puberty this authentic and free-flowing sharing is replaced by a more restrained, socially acceptable version that slowly but surely constrains our sense of acceptance. We suddenly become very unsure of ourselves and our place in the world and judge ourselves based on the external validation we receive for various preapproved accomplishments and accolades. For some of us, those feelings resurface once our own kids begin school and remain into our forties or beyond. This creeping self-recrimination can, and often does, prevent kids and adults alike from pursuing important goals and dreams across multiple parts of their lives.

Ultimately, acceptance allows us to plan and prioritize more effectively. Self-compassion can ease any shame around feeling incapable of a task we're new at or think we're not "good enough" at and allows us to identify what is most important to each of us, at each moment. At a time when we seem to be juggling so many different and sometimes conflicting priorities, helping students step back and fundamentally accept who they are in the world is a critical piece of encouraging them to develop their own blueprint.

CHAPTER 12

DIFFERENT PATHWAYS

"You SEE, WHAT HAPPENED WAS . . . ," JOSEPH WOULD SAY TO begin his latest story as soon as he entered my office. His stories were typically detailed, entertaining, and involved a level of creativity and humor that would enliven any afternoon. Sometimes it was a dog-ate-my-homework tale that infuriated his parents and other times a humorous in-class exchange or mundane conflict with his older sister, who prided herself on her punctuality, work ethic, and ambition. He would regularly offer commentary on what he considered the absurdities of life, like joking about certain parents' jockeying for position in the after-school pickup line. "It's like they're all fighting for a perfect attendance record, but in the pickup line," he once observed wryly.

Charismatic, tall, and funny, Joseph was highly social and an inventive salesperson. With his high emotional intelligence, he could communicate and empathize with his peers and teachers in a way that felt welcoming. As a result, people trusted him instantly, which allowed him to make a connection with nearly everyone he met. He also loved entrepreneurial challenges. During the summer between his sophomore and junior years of high school, he and two childhood friends capitalized on their love of cars by starting a detailing service. After learning the steps required to detail a car, purchasing supplies, and soliciting his parents' friends to be customers, they spent a few hours scheduling appointments before driving from home to home, completing the work in driveways. In the process, they made more money than many of their friends working traditional summer jobs, and the extra time spent figuring out the logistical details seemed fun to them and a great way to practice developing systems.

The thoroughness and hyper-focus that led to success in his small side business didn't translate to success in the classroom, where he was expected to sit quietly and pay attention for ninety-minute intervals throughout the day. That rigid structure lacked the movement, freedom, and social interaction he craved and left him feeling disengaged and exhausted. To the outside world, he was an extrovert who was highly social and didn't care about school; however, his reality was far from that. In classes where teachers lectured for fifty minutes before giving students the rest of the elongated class period to do work, he lost focus within the first twenty minutes, cracking the occasional joke for nearby classmates. During the time designated for classwork, Joseph would become distracted and leave class without understanding the lesson or spending sufficient time on completing the work. In class, his primary motivation was social, but he also didn't like looking and feeling like a failure. School stress would lead to acute stomach pains, especially when he anticipated his parents being angry about his academic performance. Outside of class, his main outlet in school was sports, especially basketball, a year-round endeavor and one of three sports he played. He was a solid athlete but it was unlikely he would have a formal playing career beyond high school.

Over the two years we worked together, we often did triage. Even with time, structure, and support, there were emergencies, missing assignments, an exam the next day that needed to be studied for, or a paper that hadn't been started, despite numerous reminders and attempts. Joseph would start the semester with the best of intentions and show six or seven weeks of steady work and progress. Then there would be an inevitable dip, usually during a time when he had a few weekends in a row of basketball tournaments, when the missing assignments would start to pile up. At each session, we would come up with a list of to-dos, and he would schedule the week. Typically he would complete 70 to 80 percent of his scheduled work. Then at the end of nearly every marking period, he would scramble to make up his missing assignments. While Joseph got better with the time, structure, and support, his progress felt slow and incremental.

My goal is for students to become proactive rather than reactive, able and willing to develop systems to complete assignments and navigate their schedule in a way that works best for them. In Joseph's case, it was clear that his school, which required him to sit in a classroom for six to eight hours a day listening to lectures, wasn't a setting where he thrived. He was people oriented, project oriented, and solutions focused, and for the most part, his high school wasn't set up that way. By his junior year, he had developed enough of a system that he was never in danger of failing classes, so he didn't have to go to summer school, but his parents remained frustrated with his slow progress and thought he should have internalized better habits faster.

Joseph's parents, Omar and Susan, were social, well-known, and engaged members of the community, and both were organized individuals who were used to planning and running things. They were embarrassed by the way they thought their son's late and missing assignments reflected on their parenting. Joseph, trying to avoid a conflict, spun half truths or full-out lies to postpone an inevitable argument with his parents, which was distressing to all involved whenever the truths were eventually revealed. His parents wondered whether their son was a compulsive liar, but the reality was that his short-term lies were his half-hearted attempts to defer the reality and the lectures and punishment ("I'm grounded") he knew was coming.

Beginning in puberty and until about twenty-four years old, the brain rewires itself. This experience is different for every child, but as the brain develops, people typically have an increased ability to do many of the executive functions needed for developing a system, including organizing, prioritizing, and problem solving, as well as processing complex information. Just as students begin puberty at different ages, the rate of brain development can vary within those years. Often, parents get frustrated that their children haven't gotten something, when in reality they are still in the process of growing, developing, and making connections.

In my mind, Joseph would improve his skills around developing a system as he matured outside of the classroom setting. I wasn't concerned, in the long term, that Joseph would be unable to develop his talents in the workforce, but I did think it was important for him and his parents to accept where he was in his own development process and to find "wins" outside the classroom that highlighted his gifts, talents, and abilities. By focusing his time and energy on building his executive functioning skills and finding his wins outside the classroom, he would become better able to cultivate his interests and talents, especially as they related to working with the public.

This is one of the most overlooked results of practicing acceptance, both of ourselves and our kids—**acceptance builds confidence by allowing kids to develop a sense of competence**. When kids have self-acceptance, self-compassion, and self-awareness, they feel more comfortable knowing that they are doing the best they can at any moment, given the prevailing circumstances, *and* that there is room for improvement and growth. This simple acknowledgment can decrease some of the fears associated with failure and create an underlying sense of comfort, even when an outcome is disappointing. This ability to cope with setbacks is like a muscle they can then work on and strengthen over time. They're then likely to feel less anxious in environments where they think they are being judged and criticized. The notion of being "okay just as they are" provides a critical foundation for growth, reducing fear and anxiety around doing or saying the "wrong" things, learning new skills, facing different challenges, and more. This increased feeling of competence then supports better decision making. Confident kids also tend to feel more comfortable asking for help when they need it. They're more likely to take initiative on pursuits and projects they're excited about, as Joseph did that summer in high school.

By the time he was a high school senior, he received several college acceptance letters from large state universities in California and Nevada. He was accepted to one smaller private school, which had smaller classes and a more intimate overall campus setting, but the total yearly cost was three times that of the larger public school. Finances were limited, and his parents didn't think it was worthwhile to stretch and pay for the smaller private school. I understood their rationale, though my sense was that he would respond better to smaller classes and communities. Given these factors, I scheduled a meeting with him and his parents and shared my opinion.

With the faulty finish line that college admissions has become, parents and students often assume that every student should be naturally ready to leave home and go away to college and live on their own once they graduate from high school at seventeen, eighteen, or nineteen years old. They also become entrenched in believing children are behind if they somehow aren't ready to leave home to go away to college. The messaging is everywhere—from high school counselors announcing college admissions on hallway bulletin boards, to the pomp and circumstance of college signing days when students wear sweatshirts of their fall destinations to school. It can be easy to get caught up in the hype and not step back to notice that following the pack into college immediately after senior year might not be the best choice for every child. The reality is that the timeline is arbitrary, and for some students, doing something else for a year makes sense. The rise of interesting gap-year options, which may combine travel and exploration or be as straightforward as getting a job in the local community, certainly caters to that need and in some cases can help students who could benefit from the perspective they gain from being temporarily away from school.

Though some might worry that taking a gap year would cause students to stray from the path of rigorous academics, making it more difficult for them to take their studies seriously upon returning, recent data shows that taking a gap year could be linked to higher motivation in college.[1]

Omar and Susan were initially opposed to Joseph staying home and working or attending a community college before transferring. As much as they loved their son, his last two years of high school had been challenging. After years of cheering loudly for him at every basketball game, their family dynamic was strained by ongoing arguments around schoolwork. They saw his college admissions as a culmination of all that stress and equated Joseph's college options to an ability to navigate the new school environment. It's a common misperception that reflects our misunderstanding about college as a "finish line" to kids' development both personally and academically. In a college environment, Joseph would have a clean slate, they assumed, as well as a less demanding schedule, since he wouldn't be playing basketball at the college level. Plus the big public college he was set to attend didn't seem academically rigorous. He could grow up being away from home, and all would work better than it had.

It didn't work out that way. His first and second year in college were marked by large, entry-level classes with more than a hundred students. To Joseph, class sizes that large meant attendance was optional. In one class, he was absent when the professor announced a change to the syllabus, didn't show up to the midterm, and didn't even realize he had missed the exam. He had to drop that class. Even though he still went to the school's gym and weight room regularly, he missed the community, common purpose, structure, and outlet he felt from being part of an organized school sports team. His parents wanted him to focus on school and told him to not get a job during the academic year. Instead, he became engrossed in and distracted by social opportunities, going out almost every night. Before long, Joseph had fallen so far behind on class attendance and schoolwork, there wasn't enough time remaining in the semester for him to catch up.

Always waiting for the next round of criticism from his family—and likely also himself soon afterward—Joseph, like most kids who haven't learned acceptance, put off the tasks he didn't feel capable of completing well. Over time, some kids experience a downward spiral, where procrastination plants seeds of shame that erode their confidence and sense of acceptance at a much deeper level. At other times, the lack of acceptance produces a continual degradation of result, which is what Joseph experienced. By the end of his third semester of college, he was on academic probation and withdrew from the university before being asked to leave.

Upon arriving home, he initially felt deflated but later experienced a sense of relief. Though he enjoyed the social aspect of his college experience, he had always felt behind, as if everyone else had a secret college manual that he didn't. Once away from that environment, he began to accept the fact that he could move forward and thrive through a different pathway. This ability to feel self-compassion is a critical piece of acceptance. Kristin

Neff, an associate professor in educational psychology at the University of Texas at Austin and expert on self-compassion, describes it as being "kind and understanding with personal failings,"[2] instead of overly critical or judgmental. When we come to understand that we, along with everyone else, are imperfect, it ideally lets us move forward from mistakes with less self-flagellation and self-criticism.

Once back at home, Joseph drew up an agreement with his parents that he would get a job while also taking two to three classes at a community college. He started to put the structure he had learned years earlier in place, doing all his work at the school library on days when he was on campus or at a coffee shop before work on alternate days. This redefined path proved to be the right balance of stimulation and engagement. He took business and entrepreneurship classes, many of which had real-time applications to the entry-level business marketing job he found through a family friend. He would go to class two days a week, then work four days a week, and between work, school, and the gym, he stayed busy. He joined a local basketball league through his gym and sometimes played pickup games with friends who were still in the area. He ultimately transferred to a local university and earned his bachelor's degree.

In Joseph's case, coming back home gave him time and space to develop and to focus. Because there were local community college and university options nearby, he found a pathway to graduate with a bachelor's degree in five and a half years—six months less than the national average of six years.

What initially appeared to be failure—leaving school after being on academic probation—ultimately allowed him to find the path where he thrived as a student *and* a young adult. To be successful, he'd need to stray from the prevailing societal norm in his community and find his own way—something a lot of kids need but aren't always given a fair opportunity to get. Too often, "failing" is viewed as a stain on the young person's achievements and character, when in fact that so-called failure may lead to a different path that could be a better fit given the circumstances.

Over time Joseph also hesitantly admitted that he liked being home, near his family and especially his grandfather, with whom he'd always had a close relationship. Working at a job where he earned money had always given him a greater sense of purpose and meaning—something he discovered that summer in high school when he and his friends created their car detailing service—and allowed him to find wins that he'd never found in the same way in the classroom. Those wins then translated into his being more motivated to pursue learning material that interested him and combine his love of business and sales to work in partnerships and business development. Some talents and skills that weren't readily appreciated in the classroom setting at his high school, including his ability to engage with people from different backgrounds, find creative solutions, and keep moving the ball forward despite challenges, have been critically important in his professional success. In short, his story brings to my mind the adage "He'll be fine in life, he just needs to get through school." What's often overlooked in cases like Joseph's, however, is the need to "get through school" *without* losing his spirit and his sense of self-worth. That's why those wins *outside the classroom* were so critical. He's now in his midthirties, working in business development for a billion-dollar tech-focused company.

Over the past two decades, there's been increasing research on the gaps between the college matriculation and graduation rates of young men. I first became aware of it when a college student affairs officer told me, in 2005, that we had a real crisis in boys' education and that boys weren't going to college and graduating at the same rates as their female peers. At the time, my response was something along the lines of "Have you looked at their backpacks?" That conversation planted the seed for my first book, *That Crumpled Paper Was Due Last Week.*

Nearly two decades later, we're still having the same conversation. In the fall of 2021, *Wall Street Journal* reporter Douglas Belkin highlighted how men now make up about 40 percent of the college student population.[3] Strikingly, they noted the National Student Clearinghouse data, which showed the number of collegiate male students between the spring of 2019 and the spring of 2021 fell by more than 535,000, more than triple the decline of collegiate female students.[4]

It would be easy to peg this as a boys issue, but it is not. More often than not, it is a failure of us as a society to recognize the ways in which the current school structure isn't working for a lot of young people. Once we do so, we can more effectively shift efforts to come up with alternatives that help them develop systems, connections, perspective, and acceptance of their abilities and possibilities. With those pieces in place, young people can develop their own blueprint for success and thrive, as Joseph has. Instead of sidelining students like Joseph as "failures" for struggling within the current educational landscape, we need to find ways to capitalize on their strengths and passions so that they, too, are prepared to carve out a rewarding and fulfilling path for themselves.

Much of this ties into this fundamental idea of acceptance, which is not the same as complacency, nor should it be confused with giving up. No one should accept that a high school sophomore is unable to manage his time, prioritize his schoolwork, and turn assignments in on time. Joseph clearly lacked a system he needed to get through school—and life. However, instead of viewing kids like Joseph as "failures," let's notice how they think, work, and thrive—and use that information to teach them ways to develop a system that works for them and helps them move forward.

It's also important that we, as a society and as adults, accept that teaching kids these skills around developing a system, connections, perspective, and acceptance—is a *long-term process*, not a "one-and-done" set of tasks on a to-do list. There will be stops and starts along the path to progress, as there were for Joseph. Rather than resorting to blame or shame, it's important to acknowledge these imperfections as normal and work constructively with kids and young adults as they aim to get back on track. When we're tempted to get angry and frustrated at students for not making the progress we would like on our timetable, let's also take a moment to be honest with ourselves and admit that we, as adults, aren't *perfectly* organized or *perfect* at managing our time and energy 24/7! We can't ask young people to meet a standard of perfection that doesn't factor in the reality that *we're all human—and inherently imperfect, and that's okay.* We can feel proud of our kids, even when they're making slower progress than we'd like or are experiencing a return from a setback we found stressful. As adults, we can also model greater self-acceptance and self-forgiveness by treating ourselves with more understanding and compassion around our own disappointments and shortcomings.

Acceptance at a very basic level is understanding who each child is, where they are, and focusing on their needs and opportunities for growth, irrespective of the faulty finish line of college admissions or the never-ending checklist our culture suggests we "must" complete at certain times and in a specific order. I was reminded of this once again while working on this chapter. As I sat down to write one day, I received an email from the parents of an eighth grader who asked about what their son could do to better prepare himself for the college application process (these kinds of emails arrive with predictable frequency and have for years). This student does well academically but struggles with social connection and emotional regulation. In other words, he is strong in creating an organizational system and could use extra support in connection, perspective, and ultimately acceptance. I gently guided these parents away from the traditional but myopic focus on the checklist of to-dos that was certainly winding them up around grades, scores, and extracurricular activities. Instead, I suggested that their focus be more on where their son was and what he needed: learning how to better engage socially, make authentic connections, and feel support in his school and greater community. He also needed guidance around emotional self-regulation, so when something disappointing or frustrating happened, he felt better able to cope and less prone to having an angry meltdown.

Consider this profile next to Joseph, who struggled with developing a system but was able to build an incredible sense of connection and had a strong sense of perspective. Joseph needed more support around acceptance and seeing who he was as a person in the world, not just a student faltering in a traditional classroom. Each of these students had unique, specific needs that weren't being met through traditional schooling. To be clear, I'm not suggesting that schools need to do more; they're already facing enormous hurdles. However, I am suggesting that we, as adults—teachers, parents, administrators, extended family members, public policy makers, and on and on—do need to find ways to prioritize their sense of self, which is foundational to developing their own blueprint.

CHAPTER 13
LIVING WITH HEIGHTENED UNCERTAINTY

On January 31, 2020, a Reuters world news article caught my eye. "Major U.S. Airlines Cancel China Flights as Government Steps Up Warnings," the headline read, sounding alarm bells inside my brain. Living in the Bay Area, and knowing that so many individuals traveled to China for personal and business reasons, I knew that United, Delta, and American Airlines wouldn't cancel flights unless the coronavirus was of grave concern. The news article put me on high alert. Almost immediately, I started thinking about "what if" solutions.

We typically see students recovering from winter illnesses in our office and already kept large stocks of hand sanitizer and disinfectant wipes in our supply closet. We already worked with a fair percentage of students online, and about half of our staff members felt comfortable using Zoom. Still, as I saw technology companies near my office asking employees to work from home, I started to think about potential changes.

Over the next few weeks, I made sure the remainder of my staff became comfortable using Zoom for meetings and sessions with students. We also updated our best practices and guidelines to reflect what was increasingly looking like our new reality. I had no way of predicting what was to come and look back at the small choices I made as a way of focusing on my locus of control, concentrating on micro-choices that I had control of in what would turn out to be an ever-changing situation. By the time the announcement was made on March 13, 2020, that schools across California would close the following Monday, our office was as ready as it could have been. Our incredibly small size, access to technology, and head start gave us a significant advantage, one that we would see play out at highly resourced schools across the country. Starting that Monday, March 16, 2020, all of our students began meeting with us online and continued to do so for nearly fourteen months. Santa Clara County guidelines, where our office was located, were stricter than those in many other places throughout the country, and given our cozy office size, meeting in person with students in our office wasn't feasible for much of the following 2020–2021 school year.

For many of us, the months of March, April, and May 2020 remain a blur. I remember being fully exhausted by the end of each week, feeling a swirling combination of heightened concern and uncertainty at a time when there was no real playbook.

There was no way to know the many ways our lives would inextricably change over the past few years. Routines once taken for granted were upended in a matter of hours, days, and weeks, and some of those changes would last months or even years. Not to mention the activities that were given up, the tangential friendships or "hey" in the hallways that were lost, and the heightened trauma and stress felt by students, families, and educators all along the economic spectrum.

In the early weeks and months of the pandemic, I became curious about how students around the country were reacting to school closures and all the corresponding cancellations of sports teams and school events. Some students attended schools that transitioned nearly as quickly as my office, with everyone attending class online within days. Some school districts in places with frequent snow days and inclement weather adapted quickly using procedures they already had in place. Other school districts, including several in Silicon Valley, remained closed for weeks. Even when they did reopen, classes were held asynchronously, which meant that high school students were given packets of work at the beginning of the week that they were asked to turn in by the end of the week. Some of the public high schools near my office went to pass/fail grades for the spring 2020 semester, with the belief that it would be difficult to fairly evaluate students' academic performance amid so many changes.

I started interviewing students around the country as research that would become part of pieces I wrote for the *New York Times* and the *Washington Post*. I wanted to see how students were reacting, particularly those who would have been described as overscheduled, juggling a host of athletic practices and extracurricular activities with a heightened course load. At first, many students I interviewed thought the forced break wasn't all bad—some were getting more sleep than they normally would during the school year and had more time to do things they enjoyed like baking, painting, reading, or practicing a musical instrument. A few students transferred their energy to new pursuits, including a student who organized an extensive supply drive to benefit a shelter supporting victims of domestic abuse.

Of course, many of the structural inequities shone brighter than ever. Students at schools like the one where Nicole is a counselor in rural areas lacked access to reliable Wi-Fi, which upended their ability to connect to school and with friends when schools remained closed. Students who were living with family members beset by financial concerns and mental health issues no longer had the escape and safety that the school day could provide. Some students suddenly had to play oversized roles in supporting their families emotionally and otherwise, without the consistent touch points outside of the home that might have once been lifelines.

In all my formal interviews and informal conversations with students around the country, a single conversation remained etched in my mind, and I remember feeling a lingering concern—not from a physical safety or well-being perspective but rather from an adaptable-thinking perspective. Aidan was a high-achieving student whose only activity outside of school was the sport he loved to play, lacrosse. At first, he couldn't imagine the season would be canceled. When it was, it took him several days for the shock to sink in. He was reserved and might have been labeled as shy, and most of his social interactions were through lacrosse practices, games, and tournaments.

When I asked him what he might spend time on now that playing on the lacrosse team wasn't a viable option, he had no answer. His disillusionment and inability to flex his thinking worried me. When I asked him how he liked to spend his time, his only answer was that he enjoyed playing lacrosse. Aidan was in his junior year, so his disappointment was compounded by his desire to play lacrosse in college, but he had yet to make tangible progress toward being recruited to play at the collegiate level. While his chances of getting college playing opportunities he was hoping for may have been slim, he was unable to consider any alternate activities of interest. He was a concrete thinker, unable or unwilling to envision any way to spend his time other than playing lacrosse. He became angry and didn't appear willing to consider pursuing any interests.

The ways we asked young people to adapt through the spring and fall of 2020, and often beyond, are impossible to quantify. Throughout those interviews, though, I could see how other students could bring some flexibility into their thinking and reframe disappointments in a way that made them more adaptable to the barrage of letdowns. It didn't mean that the pile-on of cancellations and disappointments didn't add up, but it did mean some students handled those changes more readily. And that's not to say much for the level of trauma some students experienced around food insecurity, mental health issues, and economic instability. In truth, it can be easy to write off the distress of this lacrosse player, whose parents didn't seem to have pressing concerns around food, shelter, or basic needs. There were far greater inequities of trauma and pain than a canceled lacrosse season. We asked kids of all ages to give up so much over that time, in ways we may never fully appreciate, and the ripple effects will extend for years to come. Still, I thought back many times to my interview with Aidan and his concrete thinking as a symptom of a much larger concern in a world that seems to have become plagued with a level of uncertainty that has trickled down to nearly all kids—even those we once thought would be largely insulated until they were older.

A few years after those initial March 2020 school closures, I ran into Aidan's mom and asked how her son was doing. Her response was tempered and slow, as if she didn't want to relive the depths of the challenges he faced. She confirmed that the pandemic seemed far tougher for him than her other children, in part because he struggled to move forward from the disappointment of his canceled lacrosse season, which was then followed by the added disappointment of watching his dream of playing lacrosse in college fizzle. Having simultaneously lost his main social outlet, he was also missing the natural conversations and engagement that came from sports practices, games, and team logistics. With his school mostly online for most of the following year, he'd also lost the hellos in the hallway at school that we take for granted but that can be grounding in their consistency in times of upheaval.

People are happier on days when they say hi to a colleague in the hallway or have a brief conversation with a neighbor at the grocery store. Researchers found that people interact with somewhere between eleven and sixteen "weak ties"—or relationships involving less frequent contact, low emotional intensity, and limited intimacy—per day, whether on the way to work, while running errands, or on a break between meetings at the office.[1] All of these seemingly insignificant interactions disappeared as students were forced to shelter in place, only to gradually return into a new social reality mandating at least six feet of space between those outside of their very select intimate "bubble." For fear of risking infection, students were often unable to come into close proximity with their grandparents or close friends, much less chat with a new student on the bus or catch up with an acquaintance on their way to class. Moments that once served as pleasant boosts in the day were eliminated, leaving frequently isolating, bare-bones social structures in their place. Although Aidan had a system in place for completing his schoolwork during the school closures, he lacked opportunities for connection and needed more perspective and acceptance to navigate a precarious and disappointing time.

We've always had uncertainty in our daily lives. The past few years have amplified levels of concern for many reasons. It is not just because we are living in a pandemic-adjusted world. For a few days during the first five months of the stay-at-home orders for the pandemic, living in San Francisco meant we had an 8 p.m. curfew because of protesting, and then a few months later our skies were dark red and orange in the middle of the day because of nearby wildfires.[2] Schools were closed not just because of the pandemic but because terrible air quality made it inadvisable to be outside.

Living with uncertainty today brings a level of stress and potential trauma that we are no longer able to fully shield kids from in the way we once might have. It has unfortunately become part of daily living for this generation of young people, who have repeatedly seen routines and norms upended with little warning and the adults in their lives struggling to regroup, assess the damage, and find their footing. Much of this upending is producing a host of long-term ripple effects that most of us are still trying to notice and integrate into our thinking and our lives. Not surprisingly, kids today are noticing how we are processing, reflecting, and moving forward, and in some cases, that may mean that the kids in the household, rather than the parents, are needing to navigate uncertainty better than the adults they rely on.

It's a challenging time, and students are having to digest change at an intense and potentially unsettling rate. Yet as this is all unfolding, students still need to know they can lean on the people, places, and communities that act as the foundation of their world. Above all, they need a core sense of safety and comfort so they can be exposed to the inherent challenges in life without feeling overwhelmed or unsupported as they try to figure it all out. At the same time, we can't protect them too much, which risks depriving them of critical opportunities to develop their sense of self and age-appropriate independence and agency.

It's a delicate balance, and there's no one-size-fits-all solution for every situation, but providing opportunities to understand and accept that life includes some struggle, which may not be fair or anyone's fault, allows young people to be more self-accepting during hard times and better able to think flexibly, process setbacks, and find ways to adapt.

Given these heightened levels of uncertainty, it's especially important to emphasize these five elements, which help students develop acceptance as we collectively navigate the many unknowns of today's world:

Taking stock of what we can control. I return to the question I often ask students who are feeling overwhelmed: *Are you doing the best you can with what you've got right now?* It is meant to be a freeing question. It promotes a sense of self-awareness and self-acceptance that there are certain times when our ability to complete tasks may be affected by outside forces beyond our control. For example, if a family member is sick or we have to take on more responsibilities because of a temporary circumstance, we may not be able to do all the things we want to do in the way we once envisioned. In these moments, stepping back and looking at what is in our control can help kids identify the parts of their lives where they do have options and can make choices. For students, I often begin this process by considering their daily habits and routines, where they generally have some measure of autonomy as they get older. Cultivating autonomy and competence in these parts of life can lead them to feel greater confidence in circumstances that might otherwise feel chaotic. For example, I may encourage a student who is worried about grades and test scores to think about their daily habits and routines around learning information, completing assignments, and reviewing work, including going back through mistakes on previous quizzes and exams. For students who are overwhelmed by the uncertainty of the college admissions process, I have them focus on how they can put together an application that showcases their talents, strengths, and abilities. For students navigating social challenges at school, I encourage them to think about the daily habits that support their well-being and ability to seek support, as well as ways they can expand their connections and sense of community outside of the school day.

Taking time to process and address fears and stressors. When students find themselves in a state of overwhelm, it is often the result of unprocessed and unaddressed fears. As adults, we can also get caught up in busyness, creating whirlwind schedules and to-do lists that keep us from acknowledging and properly digesting our most pressing fears and concerns. The first step is naming those fears: What are we afraid of? What stories are we creating for ourselves?

Once we identify our fears, the next step is to address them: Are these fears realistic? What are they rooted in? What tools or resources might help us to navigate them? For instance, when Nira, whose story was shared in Chapter 3, was so afraid of air travel that her family and friends wondered why she would think of applying to colleges far from home, she initially addressed those fears by learning the data around the safety of airline travel. Her initial analysis helped her understand her fears weren't rooted in the reality of risk. Then, when she began working with a therapist to address the root cause of her fears around flying, she learned coping strategies such as talking back to negative thoughts and taking relaxing breaths, which eventually helped her work through those fears and travel with more ease. She still uses those same strategies today.

Although we often applaud apparent fearlessness, the reality is that no one is completely fearless. In fact, true fearlessness would encourage us to take risks that could put every aspect of our health and wellness—mental, physical, emotional, financial, professional, and so on—at risk. Fear is hardwired into the brain as a self-protective mechanism that prevents us from running out in front of a speeding car or making reckless decisions that rob us of security, connection, and more. Fearlessness isn't a realistic goal—*nor should it be.* The same idea applies to stress. None of us are fully "stress-free," even though some social media messaging might have us believe otherwise. Fear and stress can be productive, forcing us to step back and evaluate our next best move, rather than rushing forward on impulse alone. Instead, our goal should be to keep fear and stress at relatively healthy levels and, when they do arise, to use them as indicators that we may need to reconsider, analyze, and strategize more effectively on an issue.

Asking for help early and often. Our culture rewards rugged individualism and "going it alone." We often encourage people by saying things like "You can do it [*by yourself!*]!" or "You've got this! [*You're on your own!*]"

> ## A simple three-step process for navigating fear and stress constructively:
>
> 1. **Identify:** What are you afraid of? What is causing you stress?
> 2. **Address:** Is this based in reality? What are the "what if" scenarios running wild in your mind? How likely is the thing you fear to occur in real life? What is the root cause of the stress? What can you control?
> 3. **Support:** How can you support yourself? Whom can you reach out to for support? What resources are available to help mitigate the fear and provide support for stress?

Think about those thirty-under-thirty or forty-under-forty lists that laud individual entrepreneurs for their achievements. We highlight stories of successful executives who emphasize *their own* talents and contributions. Far less common are stories that showcase the many people who provided guidance, support, and resources along the way. That kind of singular focus on exceptional achievement resulting from supposed fearlessness and "go-it-alone" individualism further instills the message that needing or asking for help is a form of weakness, when in reality it can indicate courage, strength, and intellect.

A few years ago, I was shadowing an elementary school classroom where the students asked for help often, with everything. Students started to reason that if they asked for help, they wouldn't have to do any work. The teacher developed a workaround model to encourage students to try things for themselves first, pinpoint how and where they needed extra support, identify where they could seek that support, and then reach out for the help they needed. Students were encouraged to provide support to peers and then also identify where they could use additional support. It became a small exercise in community building that also encouraged a sense of autonomy and competence, while making them feel as though they could contribute to the community and also receive support. It made me wonder how and why the messaging around mutual aid and support tends to decrease as students go into middle school, high school, and college—often unintentionally, as we move from a place of collaboration to competition when it comes to awards, achievements, and college admission. Community building, not rugged individualism, should be our new goal.

In both business and public-service sectors, strong leaders prioritize getting the support they need, when they need it. Leaders like Steve Jobs and President John F. Kennedy were known for being effective both because they recognized what they were good at and because they sought out people who were strong in areas where they were not. The powerful partnerships they then formed benefited the whole through collective effort. These ideas need to permeate our own lives and then trickle down to our students.

An important part of encouraging students to become more comfortable asking for help early and often, and pinpointing the right people and places to seek support, is destigmatizing the fact that none of us knows everything, can do everything, and is good at everything. Especially in moments when everything seems to be changing, evolving, and uncertain, feeling comfortable asking for help can also lead to a sense of curiosity, wonder, and engagement. When we accept that we don't know everything, we're more accepting of learning new things, trying new approaches, starting over, and being open to feedback and ideas that may streamline the process that was making us feel stuck. We're more likely to succeed when we're not trying to figure it all out ourselves.

Establishing, creating, or redefining routines. When I travel to a new city for work, even if I am only there for a few days, I focus on creating a routine that works for me. Although I may vary that routine with, say, a new walking path, coffee shop, or restaurant, I try to stick to a general schedule that allows me to do what needs to get done and feel grounded despite being in a new place. That might mean waking up early to work out before meetings or finding a local place to sit before my school visits start. Some of this will vary depending on whether I'm in a city or small town and whether I have a rental car or am relying on public transportation. Still, at the core, establishing and redefining a routine for myself when other elements of my routine are shifting—namely, because I am traveling—helps me feel grounded. Over the years, when I travel back to the same cities, I might reuse a routine that worked well for me in the past as a way of slipping back into a general schedule and making a new place feel like home, even for a few days.

Student schedules also shift often, whether because of extracurricular activities or academic time changes. I've found that the students who were the most able to ease into the transition of changing schedules were those who, either consciously or subconsciously, adapted by adjusting old routines or creating new ones that provided a sense of structure and control. For instance, when the pandemic closed schools near my office, one student now had time to take her dog for a long walk before classes started virtually, and another ate outside on her porch at lunch. Making these simple changes to their routines based on what was possible to them at that time allowed them to feel more confident.

We often don't take the time to step back and intentionally create new routines and structure—instead, our routines may be formed by default. The beginning of a new school year, new sports season, new activity, new semester or quarter can all be natural times to intentionally figure out what has worked in the past and what might need to be tweaked. When students identify new routines earlier and move between creating or redefining routines based on what is on their schedule and what needs to be done, it reduces the number of decisions they need to make certain routines feel more automatic.

Routines don't need to be boring, and they do not require that we do the same thing over and over again (although for some people, repetitiveness might be helpful). I look at routines as a way to identify and accept processes and systems that work for us, and they create an adaptable structure that can be adjusted as needed. I realize, for some neurodivergent students or students who have diagnosed learning differences, routines are critically important for their mental and emotional well-being, and that establishing, creating, and redefining routines might take a good deal of time and effort. Still, figuring out what works best for each student, and using routines as a way to identify points of concern in times of uncertainty, can be an important way to take stock of what we can control.

Becoming a generalist rather than a specialist. In a world of increasing automation, it is ever more valuable to combine knowledge and experience across a variety of fields. And yet we consistently, even obsessively, encourage students to find their one special talent or activity to specialize in starting at increasingly early ages. By high school, if not years earlier, we seem to expect students to find and declare their "passion."

This counterproductive emphasis on narrowing interests, rather than broadening exposure, often leads to reduced perspective and acceptance. In his widely acclaimed bestseller *Range: Why Generalists Triumph in a Specialized World*, David Epstein integrates research from the sports world to the music industry to counter American society's stubborn focus on hyper-specialization. Among them is a study led by John Sloboda, one of the most influential researchers in the psychology of music, who found that the amount of lessons or practice time did not correlate with skill level; rather, "those children identified as exceptional by [the school] turn out to be those children who distributed their effort more evenly across three instruments." The most common path to excellence, as it turned out, consisted of a lightly structured sampling period followed by a narrowing of focus and heavy increase in practice volume. This progression from sampling and broadened exposure to narrowing focus *over time* is reflected in the journeys of some of the most talented professionals in the world. In the book, Epstein cites tennis great Roger Federer and Japanese video game designer Gunpei Yokoi, among many others.[3]

Developing a sense of acceptance can be challenging to students—and adults!—even when everything seems relatively standard and routine; and it requires even more intentionality at times of uncertainty.

CHAPTER 14
THE NEVER-ENDING CHECKLIST OF TO-DOS

A FEW WEEKS BEFORE THE START OF A NEW SCHOOL YEAR, I received an email from Charles, a father whose four children I had worked with over the years. He shared how much better Avery, his youngest, was doing and mentioned how much they were working out, participating in theater, and seemingly driven to excel at school as examples of Avery's progress. Charles wondered whether Avery should redo their sophomore year given their GPA and mentioned that his child was open to it. Charles was somewhat on the fence and wanted to chat.

I was relieved to see that email in my inbox a few weeks before the start of a new school year. Six months earlier, Avery's parents were forced to confront heightened concerns around their child's mental health and well-being. At the time, Avery was struggling through their sophomore year of high school. Avery's parents each had different approaches to their child's lack of interest in school. Avery had consistently vacillated between angry belligerence and apathy, and it seemed that some of their academic struggles were a symptom of their emotional/mental state. I communicated my concerns several times but didn't seem to be gaining traction; one parent thought Avery wasn't working hard enough while the other believed

Avery was being a rebellious teenager, making choices that would have consequences down the line. The turning point came one afternoon when Charles dropped Avery off outside our office, and Avery never made it up the stairs to their appointment. Instead, they wandered to a nearby park, where their father found them a few hours later, sitting quietly on a bench listening to music.

Avery started working with a therapist and then later consulted with a psychiatrist whose practice specializes in working with adolescents. After a few stressful months, Avery seemed to start reengaging with school, activities, and friends in a way that felt promising and meaningful. Despite all the turmoil, Avery ended the previous semester with a 3.2 GPA, which I considered a triumph given the circumstances. (*Are you doing the best with what you've got at this moment?*) Their parents were concerned that the grades didn't reflect Avery's overall abilities and wondered whether redoing sophomore year would allow the opportunity to regroup after a stressful year and improve college admission options.

There were a host of reasons why having Avery repeat sophomore year didn't make sense. Avery loved high school, had good friends, and participated in activities they enjoyed. The connection and sense of community experienced through those activities acted as an important lifeline. Avery's high school also had a policy of not allowing students to repeat grade levels—and there was no academic reason to redo sophomore year. As a result, repeating sophomore year would mean transferring to another school, which was not something they wanted to do and something we all agreed wouldn't be in their best interest. I suggested instead that Avery continue at the current high school, where they felt a strong sense of community, and that we reevaluate options at the start of Avery's senior year.

I have conversations like this with well-meaning parents more often than I'd like, and each time, I get more concerned about the culture of perfectionism that's distorting our values, warping our sense of self, and keeping us from creating the meaningful lives we all ultimately crave. Collectively, we've been sold on the idea that achievement and status must precede, even supersede, our well-being, authentic self-expression, and sense of purpose. As a result of this perceived need to continually tick off more and more of the "right" accomplishments and to connect with more and more of the "right" people, we have become hyper-focused on a never-ending list of to-dos that rarely, if ever, deliver the validation and approval they're intended to provide. Even when our achievements do win us applause, we too often find that those moments are frustratingly brief blips in an otherwise burdensome slog toward the next goal we're "supposed to" claim. Too often, adults wake up decades into their careers and lives wondering how they've worked so hard yet experience so little true fulfillment. Is this the path we intend to carve for today's young people? Perhaps it's time to pause and reassess.

Rather than doggedly pursuing the never-ending list of "must-dos" and "should-dos," we need to accept that there is not one "perfect" way to find success. Acceptance is about realizing there are generally many paths forward and there is power in any potential choice. There are so many times when the opinions of others consciously and unconsciously cloud thinking and judgment, which then tends to degrade decision making. Helping each student be comfortable with who they are in the moment can also allow kids to develop small-talk skills, or the ability to introduce and make casual conversation in a way that invites new friendships and strengthens weaker ties. In many ways acceptance is a natural and often necessary extension of gaining an expanded perspective; once we have experiences that reshape our goals and potentially reorient our life paths, we can feel better about pursuing new options.

Undoubtedly, this culture of achievement-based perfectionism is so pervasive that it can feel like a nonnegotiable truth—a "just how life is" kind of reality. In that frame of mind, some may wonder why the conversation about Avery repeating their sophomore year worried me in the first place. Let me explain, based on what I see in the students I work with. By suggesting that Avery repeat their sophomore year, their parents were effectively, if unintentionally, conveying that their academic results during a mental health crisis required a redo. That can send the message that Avery's GPA—and the college choices/life path it will supposedly deliver—are *the* highest priority. Some might argue that their parents just want Avery to have the best opportunities possible, and that sometimes in life we just need a redo. That could certainly be true, but going back to prioritizing grades, test scores, and achievements as soon as mental health concerns begin to be addressed tends to work against the goal of encouraging kids to succeed. When the prevailing priority continues to be accomplishment-centric, kids tend to resort to indifference, or they work so hard that they burn out prematurely or risk becoming crushingly insecure, or both. In time, kids inevitably end up feeling like failures, destined to disappoint no matter how hard they try. Rather than dig in, young people like Avery are more likely to give up when pressure to perform and produce measurable outcomes is continually piled on them. Why bother trying so hard, they reason, when nothing ever feels good enough and failure feels virtually guaranteed?

To be clear, this culture of perfectionism is so pervasive and convincing, it inevitably impacts all of us, especially as we are barraged with social media posts and advertisements that promote idyllic pictures of what true "self-acceptance" and "self-love" look and feel like. These adeptly curated "perfect lives" that are so prominently featured online further delude us into thinking that perfection, as defined by our accomplishments, *is* our North Star—and worse, that we need to add "perfect mental health" to our list of achievements.

As I mentioned, this list of must-dos is only growing longer and more exhausting—and to what end? As humans, we inherently seek meaning and belonging through authentic self-expression—which first requires some degree of *self-acceptance*. When we're in constant pursuit of "becoming [good] enough," we live in an amplified state of stress, burnout, fear, overwhelm, and shame that we should be doing more, and doing better, *all the time*. This thinking convinces us that what other people think of us and our lives matters more than how we feel about ourselves and our lives. That is a recipe for the perpetual anxiety and chronic depression that we, as a society, are experiencing from increasingly young ages all the way through adulthood.

By allowing ourselves to lose sight of the importance of acceptance, we also risk burnout. Put simply, trying to navigate the forces of outside

judgment and criticism is exhausting. Practicing greater self-acceptance—
of who we are, what we need, and how our prevailing circumstances can
affect us—gives us permission to pause and approach life differently.

Even as adults and kids alike face persistent, even debilitating, mental
health challenges and burnout, a simple conversation with other adults
on the sideline of any high-pressure sports match makes it clear that
this achievement-based definition of "success" is as widespread among
parents, teachers, coaches, and administrators as it is among students.
Indeed, whether we realize it or not, we model our own insecurities for
children.

What's behind all these must-dos? For adults, there's the promotion of
empowerment (*Of course you can do it all!*). Then there's the encouragement of calculated and persistent ambition along with the need for health
and wellness (*Are you doing yoga? What about CrossFit? Pilates? Meditation?
Drinking green juice? While doing handstands?*). And we're supposed to capture our glorious lives online all the while (*Vacations! Notable nonfailures!
Failures with witty commentary that really make them nonfailures!*).

For kids and teens, the must-dos rooted in our culture of perfectionism
run parallel to adult experiences. Encouragement is used to fuel calculated
and persistent ambition in all areas of life (*Are you taking all honors? APs?
First string in orchestra? Starting on the varsity team? Wait, are you getting
enough sleep? Eating healthy? Meditating? Managing stress?*). And they're supposed to capture glorious lives online all the while (*Look at me hanging out
with my friends! We do fun things! In big groups! Here's a video of my big vulnerable confession!*).

After the release of my book *The Myth of the Perfect Girl*, I interviewed
several teen girls and young adults about their experiences with the culture
of perfectionism. The first young woman I interviewed responded to my
question "Do you think girls today have a pressure to be perfect?" with a
resounding yes. She then went on to explain the pressure she feels:

The best way I can describe it is the idea of a Renaissance man. I
think that's what, that's what girls try to be. The perfect girl has to do

everything. You have to excel in school, and athletics and extracurriculars, and then you have to be perfect—you have to look perfect, you have to speak well, you have to have all the best friends. You just have to have the perfect life.

After that book came out, I received notes from numerous mothers who saw themselves throughout the book, in a way that felt uncomfortable. These notions of empowerment, calculated and persistent ambition, and health and wellness overload are now being aimed at boys and men, too. In recent years I've had countless conversations with men, many of whom are now husbands and fathers who have dutifully ticked off the boxes they were taught to value—*the* career, *the* paycheck, *the* marriage, *the* house, all while being more involved, attentive, and caring—who wake up at some point feeling utterly unmotivated. The laundry list of external and internal expectations can feel so burdensome that there's little time or energy left for enjoyment, authentic connection, exploration, self-expression, or community building.

In recent years I've been hearing more stories like these, each one tinged with wistfulness, from adults who took a preset life path without reflecting on their own interests, abilities, options, and choices. Instead of noticing what energized them and what drained them, they created résumés filled with achievements and experiences that left them feeling exhausted and unfulfilled. Some adults changed careers entirely, and others found themselves compensating in negative ways after feeling stuck—drinking, spending too much money or too much time online, avoiding friends and family, and feeling endlessly overwhelmed.

This isn't to suggest that life should be a never-ending joy fest. To be sure, certain parts of adult life are unfulfilling, even disappointing, and at times we may have to make compromises that are less than ideal. Still, as adults, we don't have to make this a permanent way of life. We can model ways outside of work to experience authentic self-expression that brings us fulfillment. By doing this, we model for our kids—*through our actions,* which will always have more weight than empty words—that we can and do claim our sense of agency, even when that means *not* ticking off some boxes on our broader culture's must-do list.

Admittedly, bucking these societal norms is more challenging than it sounds. I see the aftereffects all the time with parents and caregivers who experience heightened concern after seeing or hearing something online. The pressure to meet the rigorous demands of the "perfect life" we're supposed to be living—the college and graduate school acceptance posts, athletic recruitment, glorious vacation photos, dinners with friends at top restaurants, forced family fun, ski trips, beach weeks, weekend getaways, and exclusive opportunities—is real and none of us are immune to it. Within the pack mentality of wanting to belong, we can quickly succumb to the pressures of wanting our lives to look and feel like others'—even when we know that what we're seeing online is a distorted version of "reality." Still, the pressure to conform often leads to increased feelings of stress, burnout, and overwhelm. Even when we are happy for others, we may think we're not doing enough, leading to this shame spiral—*It's me, I should be doing more, doing it better. Why am I so behind?*

At its core, overcoming the culture of perfectionism is about accepting who we are, what our needs are, and what we each identify as energizing and draining experiences. It is also about accepting where and how we need additional support and, in doing so, how we can model the benefits of time, structure, and support so that kids, too, learn how to optimize those aspects as their lives change. It is also about how we can help kids—and ourselves—reframe draining experiences and address needs in a way that encourages the development of systems, connection, and perspective.

THE OVERSCHEDULING TRAP

One of the more obvious by-products of the never-ending checklist of to-dos is persistent overscheduling of kids from a young age. According to a 2016 study, parents in the top decile of tax brackets in the United States spent $9,000 on childcare and enrichment activities in 2010, which is a 300 percent increase since 1970 (adjusted for inflation). These statistics account only for children under the age of six.[1] With this as our norm, many kids end up with days filled with transactional experiences and too little time and energy for rest, reflection, and open-ended (non-goal-oriented) exploration. Think about it this way: a full-time job is generally around forty hours a week. I realize many Americans may work more or less and that other countries may have different cultural norms, but let's use the forty-hour workweek as a baseline for now.[2] And yet I regularly see students who are in school from 8:30 a.m. to 3 p.m., and then have an activity from 3:30 to 6 p.m., and then need to commute home and complete one to three hours of homework. More than a few students have activities that go until 8 p.m. on certain days, and their parents and caregivers are frustrated as to why homework isn't getting done effectively. On weekends, there are family events or an extracurricular activity—say, a sports tournament, dance recital, play practice, or robotics competition. When we add it all up, it can lead to sixty to seventy hours or more per week of being "on" or working in some way.

I've previously described breaking our lives into buckets of work, movement, and rest. When we think about kids who are overscheduled, I recommend double-counting activities as movement *and* work, especially if there are outside obligations, travel to and from games or tournaments, or stressful decisions week to week on who makes the starting lineup, lands the lead in the performance, or makes it to the regional semifinals. Put simply, many students are working too many hours a week, and it affects their energy, mood, motivation, and ability to navigate disappointment. For many students, this lack of *energy*, whether to pursue other interests or just to be, can lower self-esteem—after all, there's the constant nagging feeling of never doing enough and always needing to be and do more. As schedules become increasingly packed, students frequently lose valuable sleep time. A 2018 study examined physical activity, sleep, and screen-time data for 4,520 children across the United States, finding that nearly a third didn't meet any of the recommendations for exercise, sleep duration, or screen-time limits. Those who did meet these recommendations scored higher on a cognition test, after controlling for factors such as household income and parental education.[3]

IDENTIFYING ENERGY PROFILES

What is the antidote to the never-ending checklist of to-dos for kids and teens? It comes down to a focus on energy management. Right now, our focus on student well-being defaults to time management, scheduling activities, and appointments like a game of Tetris, encouraging rest but really trying to figure out ways to squeeze one more thing into an already jam-packed agenda. We send signals to teens to keep going until we see the impacts of burnout, and even then, we reach for Band-Aid fixes for the symptoms rather than getting to the root of the issues with a closer look at energy management. And, for some teens, time that would be spent on rest is spent socializing in front of a screen, which makes parents feel as though overscheduling with activities might be a better alternative than having endless hours of free time spent online playing video games or navigating social media. It's not an easy balance to strike, and the discussions and negotiations around technology time and usage become exhausting for adults and stressful for kids, too.

We've discussed and highlighted moving from time management to energy management as a means to motivation and productivity in corporate circles for years. It may seem odd to overlay a corporate consulting framework onto the development and well-being of kids, teens, and young adults. Still, a focus on energy management encourages us to accept each individual for who they are, identify energizing and draining experiences, reframe socialization, and discover our individual energetic profile.

In the *Harvard Business Review* piece "Manage Your Energy, Not Your Time," Tony Schwartz and Catherine McCarthy describe how many adults respond to increasing demands by working more hours.[4] They then argue that organizations need to shift their emphasis away from getting more out of people and toward investing in them so they are more motivated and productive.[5] The article highlights the impact of our physical well-being, emotions, mind, and spirit on our energy levels and finds that we're better able to complete tasks when we feel positive energy. As a result, it's important to encourage consistent self-awareness around the quality and nature of our energy.

How can we shift our perspective from the never-ending checklist of to-dos to focus on energy management? Here are a few strategies:

Identify and accept your child's energy profile—and what impacts their energy levels. When children are infants and toddlers, we pay attention to their energy levels because it quickly affects us. For instance, toddlers on the verge of energy depletion may melt down into a tantrum because they need a snack, quiet time, or a nap (or all three). As kids get older and become tweens and teens, we underestimate the importance of accepting and understanding their energy profile, especially as it relates to how they learn, socialize, and engage with the world.

I think of an energy profile as being made up of three components:

1. Which activities, experiences, daily happenings are energizing
2. Which activities, experiences, daily happenings are draining
3. Ways we can best recharge our energy on a daily/weekly basis and the best ways to do so after a particularly trying experience

Energy levels—and how we recharge—are important individual considerations. What is energizing for one person may be draining for another, and within families and among friends, this can lead to frustration and misunderstandings. You may recall Andrew's mother, from early in this book, who recognized that her youngest son, unlike her other children, quickly became depleted going from one activity to the next and benefited from a solid amount of buffer time between the end of the school day and appointments or activities. Was it always possible? No, but identifying that her son benefited from even a few days of simply coming home after school and having quiet time to rest allowed him to recharge and feel seen, thanks to his mother's keen awareness and acceptance of his needs.

One of the biggest disconnects happens when individual family members, particularly a parent and a child, have very different energy profiles. Recently, one of my friends planned an adventurous mother-son trip to New York City with her eleven-year-old son. She is extroverted and energetic and was excited to create a highlight-reel itinerary filled with restaurants, museums, and a Broadway show she thought he would love. She could easily spend a full day bopping from one thing to the next. Her son, however, would likely fit into the category of what author and pediatrician Thomas Boyce calls "orchid children," who "are both endowed and burdened with an exquisite sensitivity to the inhabited, living world." Boyce's research suggests that through early adaptive interactions between genetic and environmental influences, orchid children often experience stressful situations drastically differently than do their less reactive counterparts, "dandelions," even within the same family.[6] After less than a day in New York, my friend's son seemed overwhelmed and perpetually on the verge of a meltdown. *That kid needs lots of breaks, downtime and quiet to counteract the stimulation of NYC,* I texted her. A-ha! She knows her child very well, of course, but in her excitement about their trip, she'd forgotten to factor in his energy profile. She adjusted their schedule to include lots of time hanging out in her aunt's apartment, which she would never have done otherwise. Almost instantly, his mood transformed, and he began having a great time. One of his personal highlights was spending hours playing with his great aunt's family dog.

Being aware of kids' energy profiles also means paying attention to how they may change. A child who dislikes group sports, for instance, may later find one sport that they love and sincerely enjoy being on a team. Circumstances can also impact our energy profile, whether temporarily or more permanently. I recently had three back-to-back appointments with three students in different situations that were impacting their energy profile. The first had broken her leg and was in a full cast. The next student thought she needed additional support for depression and anxiety. The third was mourning the end of his first romantic relationship. Each student was navigating a circumstance that was temporarily shifting their energy profile; yet still, our world of never-ending to-dos tells us to "power through" and continue running on all cylinders. Pausing long enough to acknowledge this preprogramming, notice what's happening, and shift priorities accordingly is critically important but rarely easy.

Our goals around kids' socialization should be reframed to focus on connection and belonging, and that also takes their own energy profile within current circumstances into account. Understanding that there is no one-size-fits-all socialization experience leads to feeling a sense of competence and confidence—an idea that I am okay just as I am, and if reading quietly on a Saturday night is how I recharge best and I have friends at school I enjoy sitting with at lunch or seeing regularly at a youth group meeting, then that is okay.

Socialization is also often impacted by children's overall development—and since students begin puberty at different times, it helps to take that into consideration, too. I've known so many students who were less likely to have plans with friends on weekends during their first and second years of high school, with parents who were overly concerned that their children had no friends. Their kids did have friends, but they felt more comfortable hanging out with their family on weekend evenings, especially because they needed rest. As they got older, they began to make more plans on weekends with friends. Again, accepting these differing rhythms supports kids' self-esteem. They're more likely to feel, *I am okay just as I am, and if I want to have more meaningful and authentic friendships, or I want to have plans on weekends with friends, there are things I can do to support that.*

By understanding and accepting children's energy profiles, including shifts that might occur over time, we can support them in discovering multiple people, places, and situations where they feel a sense of connection and belonging. We need to move away from thinking there is something "wrong" with an introverted child who doesn't socialize in a way more suited to their extroverted siblings or parents. As adults, we are given far more leeway with how we socialize, and yet we often expect children to bend to a one-size-fits-all socialization experience.

Support the development of small-talk skills. One of the main areas for growth for so many young people, particularly those who were most socially impacted by our pandemic-adjusted world as well as the proliferation of technology, is small-talk skills. Essential not only for building community but for workforce development, small-talk skills help students connect with others during conversation through making eye contact, reading nonverbal cues, starting a conversation, asking questions, and wrapping up a conversation.[7] I see this most in two places: introducing themselves to others, particularly classmates at the beginning of a new school year or in a new school environment, and calling people using the "actual" telephone. One of the reasons to lament the disappearance of the home landline is that we no longer have a brief conversation with whoever picks up the household phone. It may seem trivial, but I can't tell you how many times a student has tried to call my office to say they will be late for an appointment or they need something and struggle to have a basic conversation expressing their needs.

There's another reason for small-talk skills—they can improve confidence in new social situations. Students can feel more comfortable in new and dynamic situations, which might otherwise feel overwhelming. This can be especially helpful as students get older and start to work in environments with people from different backgrounds. Being pleasant and welcoming, and feeling comfortable doing so, forges potential connections to new people, places, and ideas, which can provide expanded perspective that counteracts the never-ending checklist of to-dos.

Encourage Taking the B—and model it in your own life. When I was in graduate school, I had a professor who shared how she had gone back to school in her midforties to get her master's and then later her PhD while raising four kids. One day, when one of my classmates was feeling particularly stressed out around school and home demands, the professor proclaimed, "Why are you so worried about this project? *Take the B!*" She went on to explain how there were times when she was in school that she had to weigh the trade-offs, and she actively decided to be okay with Taking the B when the time and energy it would take to do the amount of work needed for an A wasn't feasible. If she was focused on getting all As, all the time, she knew she would never be able to move forward. "Taking the B" meant she accepted she couldn't realistically do A-quality work in all aspects of her life, all the time, and she had to make trade-offs to keep moving forward.

To me, Taking the B is not about grades. Instead, it is a metaphor for living a life of acceptance and, in the process, overcoming the culture of perfectionism and the never-ending list of to-dos. The verb "taking" is empowering—it clearly indicates that we have a choice and that we are deciding to take it. The B signifies the back seat—as in, what have you decided is Taking the Back seat in your life, at this moment, given the circumstances? For some of us, it might be a way of putting ruthless prioritization into practice. Taking the B is more empowering than telling people to just say yes or no, because there might be a time when "Yes, and I am Taking the B on this . . . " allows us to engage at the level we feel is appropriate. In my own life, there are some experiences and events at which I am happy to show up and participate and no longer feel any obligation to actively help organize or volunteer for a steering committee. At other times, I might assume a more active role. Whatever I decide, I act and react from a place of acceptance around the limits of my interest, energy, and time. Instead of feeling obligated to do it all, I intentionally and consciously choose where, how, and with whom I invest my energy. As a result, I end up feeling happier, better rested, and exponentially less vulnerable to the burnout that inevitably occurs when we perpetually overextend ourselves.

For students, the notion of Taking the B shouldn't be about grades or test scores but rather daily and weekly allocation of energy. The things that Take the Back seat could change based on sports or activity season, family obligations, or other outside forces that may be temporary. Taking the B offers a flexible mind-set that identifies where and how we can prioritize. Like so many things, the prioritization of our energy requires an ebb and flow; what is a priority in September might not be as important in December, and that's okay.

One example of Taking the B is students who opt to participate in recreational sports that might have one or two short practices a week and a game on weekends, instead of a high-pressure travel team that might have two or three longer weekday practices (or more) and then weekends filled with traveling and tournaments. Sometimes a kid just wants to participate, and playing at a recreational level is the right decision for them and their family. It keeps them active and engaged and provides a sense of belonging that has the time commitment appropriate to the amount of energy they want to commit to the activity. Taking the B is about actively deciding what Takes the Back seat. It is also about not ditching something that feels enjoyable when they could participate at a less energy-intense level.

There's such a competitive edge to every element of living right now, and it affects us as adults as much as it affects the young people in our lives. A key element to figuring out our own path forward is accepting who we are and identifying our own interests and opportunities for growth and leaning into daily and weekly experiences that are energizing while letting go, reframing, or filtering out opportunities that make us feel tethered to the never-ending checklist of to-dos.

On a far larger scale than usual, the pandemic underscored how viewing acceptance from an equity lens is critically important to overall well-being. Kids' backgrounds and home and school environments can have a profound effect on their sense of self. We need to accept that some children face additional hurdles that may range from limited resources at home to less emotional or academic support and more. Students who struggle to feel acceptance from peers, teachers, coaches, and parents or experience bias, meanness, and discrimination feel less competent and confident. One frequent example that I mentioned earlier is that students from historically marginalized and excluded communities can sometimes avoid asking for help, often fearing it will be seen as a sign of weakness or low potential. In reality, preventatively seeking resources can thwart a small issue from becoming a much bigger one. By helping them feel confident and comfortable asking for help, we can support them in becoming better able to bounce back from setbacks and disappointment.

PART FIVE

DEVELOP A BLUEPRINT

SHORTLY AFTER MY FIRST BOOK, *THAT CRUMPLED PAPER WAS DUE Last Week*, came out, I met Lisa Belkin, a journalist who at the time was the editor of the *New York Times* Motherlode column.

"I've interviewed thousands of people about their careers," Belkin explained over coffee one cold winter morning. "The people who have been the happiest about their work had one thing in common: it often started out as something they liked to do in middle school or high school."

Belkin's words stuck with me, and I knew them inherently to be true from my own experience.

I believe wholeheartedly in students' interests, pursuits, curiosity, and exploration, knowing that dreams may shift and change. I've also seen how much my attitude and approach to them and their experience matters. I see my role as helping them make the connection between their dreams and the fundamental skills and mindset they need to begin that journey and to change course when/as appropriate. If we are skeptical at every turn and don't allow ideas, skills, and principles to rightfully percolate, well, we're not allowing planted seeds to flourish properly. I see skills and experiences as fundamental building blocks to developing students' own paths forward, which also means eliminating the counterproductive false finish lines imposed upon them by external expectations, which can feel misguided and even oppressive. In doing so, we allow children and young adults to chart their own course buoyed by the internal and external support they need to flourish.

Here are some simple but effective strategies I use to help students develop a blueprint grounded in the previous four fundamentals that reflects their desires, interests, and inclinations:

1. Ask open-ended questions without judgment.
2. Tie their answers to those questions to the underlying foundational skills highlighted throughout this book.
3. Act as a resource, connector, and sponsor as applicable.
4. Suspend notions of disbelief, negativity, and judgment.
5. Convey compassion and empathy while having high expectations.

Another important aspect of students building their own blueprint is embracing what I call an **entrepreneurial model of success**. This approach isn't necessarily focused on having students start their own business, though that can certainly be an outcome. In this context, "entrepreneurial" does not inherently suggest venture-capital-backed scalable solutions that are part of the common lexicon in Silicon Valley. Rather, the entrepreneurial model of success is about cultivating curious, creative, and innovative problem-solving skills that students can benefit from in all parts of life and throughout their tween, teen, and young adult years. The goal is for students to use these skills for themselves, not just when they face decisions around college but throughout their adult lives.

The entrepreneurial model of success encourages flexibility and healthy risk taking, as well as an ability to see possibility, think through new problems with no guaranteed solution, and work toward goals that feel in alignment with who students are, what they feel drawn toward, and where they are in their own process. The hope, of course, is that kids of all backgrounds can realize that they, too, have the power to be leaders in their own lives in a way that plants the seeds of confidence and paves the way for more meaningful school and community engagement, and also allows students to think beyond a world where their sense of purpose or passion needs to also be their means for financial stability. I think back to Henry, who went to Berklee College of Music and plays the drums, and how he realized that he didn't necessarily have to make his career in music, even if music brings him immense joy. There are many ways to put a life together. Henry has a job he likes that is interesting to him. He believed that given his personality and given his ADHD profile, he would find the financial instability and overall lifestyle of a music career difficult. He's a great example of how a person can have multiple ways of thriving in career choices.

By harnessing the skills we've explored up to this point—developing a system, cultivating connection, expanding perspective, practicing acceptance—we can then layer in entrepreneurial skills such as critical thinking, problem solving, adaptability (especially in the face of disappointments and setbacks), and healthy risk taking as core components of developing a blueprint. All these skills are valuable in a world that seems to be changing in extraordinary ways and faster than ever.

Here's the ending promise: when you work through the concepts in this book with young people, in a manner that is curious, positive, skills-focused, and enthusiastic, the paths created will surprise you—and all of us—in the most glorious of ways.

CHAPTER 15

THE BLUEPRINT CAN PIVOT

"BUT I AM REALIZING I AM NEVER GOING TO BE READY. NONE OF us are . . ." A young woman's familiar voice echoes into my living room, and my head snaps up to look at the television screen. I had every intention of getting a few stretches in during the commercial break, but in reality I am just lying on the yoga mat.

"So you gotta dive in headfirst and . . . go for it!" The actress has a warm energy that radiates through the screen, and I am dumbfounded at the resemblance to my former student.

It takes me another second to realize that the young woman in the commercial *is* my former student Amanda, now an actress, model, and MBA student in New York City. I feel like I have just watched the game-winning shot in overtime, and I have no one to share my excitement with. I grab my phone to send her an email:

Subject line: Amanda!!!!! Just saw you in a commercial!!

I was binge watching a show I didn't know existed until today and I SAW YOU in a commercial.
WHAT?!!! You go, Amanda!!!!!

My enthusiasm was conveyed in my exclamation marks. The next morning Amanda replies: "Too funny, right?! Definitely a memorable moment of this year."

I had just seen Amanda a few months earlier in New York, when we met for coffee near Washington Square Park right before her graduate school class. It had been more than a decade since she had put the finishing touches on her college personal statement in my office, a statement she used to declare her love for both dance and writing, a thread she would carry through school and beyond as she worked to develop her own blueprint in her twenties and early thirties.

When we met that afternoon, she explained how she started putting together modeling photos and a portfolio in the early days of the pandemic, when she and many fellow New Yorkers were paralyzed with fear as the city shut down.

"It was a dark time," Amanda said, looking down solemnly, not wanting to offer more.

Amanda had never planned to model, and in the beginning she was told by industry folks that she might have a harder time getting placed because she had what agents deemed to be an "all-American" look—her dancer stature, strawberry blonde hair, and warm smile conveying a mixture of anxiety, enthusiasm, and excitement. She persevered, took harsh feedback, redid her photos, and began getting auditions and callbacks and doing print and television spots, a decade after initially moving to New York to pursue her dreams as a dancer.

When Amanda first walked into my office, her first dream school was Washington University in St. Louis. She was a straight-A student in mostly all honors classes, and she spent "eight days a week" at the dance studio around the corner from my office. She was a varsity cheerleader, president of a local community service organization, and loved to read and write. But she felt an internal conflict, envisioning herself as a critical thinker and intellectual who acts as a change maker, a cheerleader who hated the politics of high school. An introvert and a self-described old soul, she used her personal statement to identify these different sides of herself and to begin navigating the world in her own way over the next twelve years, including college and the choices she made after graduation. "I remember wanting to go to Wash U and really feeling grounded in the sense of knowing where I wanted to go," she recalls as we talk over coffee. "Just making a decision that felt right was reassuring." She had craved certainty, a natural impulse most of us have at times of major transition.

After applying to Washington University through Early Decision, she, like Lauren, whose story I shared in Chapter 1, was deferred. By the time she was accepted to other schools later in the spring, she had a gut reaction that she was meant to go elsewhere, which happened to be a place that checked boxes of everything she initially thought she *didn't* want.

"I did not want to go to school in California," she explains plainly, given she had lived in the Golden State her entire life. "I did not want to go to a women's college. I did not want any of that."

By the time she visited Scripps College in Southern California that spring, she was open to changing her mind. She felt energized speaking to college students who were excited to talk about their studies, their professors, and the clubs they were involved in. Their enthusiasm was contagious.

"I felt it in my gut," she now proclaims, thinking back to her first visit to the Scripps campus. She knew she wanted to be in a community like that. It was the same comfortable feeling I'd had when I arrived on Duke's campus in spring of my senior year.

"I get excited by people who are excited about what they are doing because I feel that same way," Amanda continues with a shrug. "As a kid, when I would watch an ice-skating performance, I'd be like, 'They are having so much fun. I want to do that.' I didn't want to do that, but it was their passion coming through that made me want to have the same feeling."

Years later, she recalls how a dean at Scripps College during first-year orientation said in a speech that the most important gift or skill a person has is the capacity to change their mind. "That just stuck with me so much," she reflects, "because I think it's human nature to be like, 'This is my goal and this is how I am going to get there,' but it rarely goes that way," Amanda adds, reflecting on her past experiences, some more painful than others. "And it seems like a weakness to change direction, but what a gift it is when we can do that. It seems like a weakness to change your mind. It's not."

⁂

By the time Amanda reached the second semester of her sophomore year at Scripps College in Claremont, California, she was "very much a Scrippsie," she says, referencing the affectionate term women who attend the college use to describe themselves. She nurtured her love of writing, honing her critical thinking in an environment that supported intellectual rigor in ways her high school had not. Like her college classmates, she would sometimes take the opposite stance on an issue just to have a discussion. Being able to engage in that kind of intellectual dialogue felt inspiring and energizing.

In her sophomore year, Amanda began struggling with where to study abroad. Most juniors at Scripps study abroad, and Amanda wanted to go somewhere that worked with her major and excited her. Her self-designed double major in dance and writing for education and social change was approved after she'd taken the initiative to write a proposal that was reviewed by administrators. This is a great example of one way individuals can apply the entrepreneurial model of success to their lives. It took a lot of self-awareness, self-confidence, and initiative to pursue her own path. By taking charge of her academic experience, Amanda demonstrated several important skills that continued to help her thrive, even if it meant taking extra steps to create a path that was not preset or predesigned.

Given how attached we've all become to narrowed definitions of success, including how we get from high school to college and then into working adulthood, young people like Amanda who do take the initiative to pursue their own blueprint often encounter doubt, both within themselves and from parents, teachers, and peers. Instead of increasing pressure to stay on the "straight and narrow," it's critical to encourage students—and ourselves as parents and educators—to reframe our exploration of workforce development and life.

In truth, it can feel nerve-racking when students are in the middle of potentially pivoting, reframing, and exploring. Here are some suggestions to support students as they pivot/reframe/explore potential options:

- Come from a place of curiosity—it can be as simple as encouraging students to attend an event or lecture per month or school quarter on a topic they know little about. At many schools, there are half-credit course options that are pass/fail or intensive courses that are held during winter and spring break. Online classes could work, too.
- Encourage ways to volunteer, even short-term, around a field where they have little experience to see whether it generates interest.
- Have students practice reaching out and asking for twenty- to thirty-minute informational interviews, which can be conversations with people who have had different life paths or who pursued a career in a field they may be interested in.
- Identify multiple ways of pursuing a career tied to a specific major—for example, nursing, engineering, or marketing—to highlight that there is not just one way to be a nurse or engineer.
- Promote the use of high school or college career centers early and often—many times, they offer resources including résumé review, interview preparation, and formal interest inventory assessment.

There are many ways to develop an individualized blueprint, and some veer outside the norms most of us have known. Truly pursuing our own blueprint involves much more than conventional ideas around what we're supposed to do or how things are done. As guides and mentors to young people like Amanda, we benefit from opening our own minds so that they can feel safe doing the same. When students are thinking about transferring schools or changing a field of study, allowing them the time and space to step back, reflect on their reasons, and think through multiple options, and providing a nonjudgmental opportunity for evaluating different outcomes, allows them the ability to grow as critical thinkers, problem solvers, and architects of their own future. There is no success without failure, but by supporting them in expressing their individuality through their blueprint, we can steer young people in ways that build self-confidence and connection, including when they pivot.

As her sophomore year unfolded and she considered where to go to study abroad, Amanda realized that she was yearning to spend the semester doing what she'd always loved most since she was three years old: dance. What she lacked in technique and talent as a dancer—"Honestly, I was not good," she says, thinking back—she made up for in enthusiasm.

I've always believed we all inherently know what we enjoy doing from an early age, and that there are a number of reasons our interests can be deferred, sidetracked, and thwarted—including not developing the underlying understanding and skills to move forward and not being exposed to a plethora of options to develop and pursue certain interests in different ways. I've also seen, time and time again, how young adults like Amanda develop their own blueprint by focusing on interests, skills, and experiences from their younger years. Often, developing those early life interests can lead to a professional life that feels more interesting, meaningful, and fulfilling.

Unfortunately, given how many students are overscheduled with a preprogrammed set of activities, many never figure out which activities they naturally gravitate toward and find fulfilling. Identifying and honing skills, traits, and experiences that bring enjoyment is an organic, sometimes circuitous process that takes time, exposure, and casual exploration. It's entirely different from the anxiety-inducing and often unhelpful advice to "find your passion" or do a variety of activities in order to "be well rounded."

Feeling comfortable with moving beyond a prescribed path is fundamental to creating your own blueprint, which can sometimes be messy and unpredictable, as Amanda discovered as she tried to balance what seemed like the next step (studying abroad) with her underlying interest (dance).

Amanda was in the middle of figuring out which study-abroad program she would participate in when she met a director-choreographer who had performed on Broadway and at Scripps for the semester as a visiting artist. The director-choreographer had grown up in nearby Claremont and had returned to her hometown to teach on campus and work on a few pieces.

Amanda signed up for several classes and immediately connected with her, asking her about New York and about dancing on Broadway.

With her signature problem-solver determination, Amanda quickly figured out her ideal study-away program: going to New York City, taking the kinds of dance classes she loved, and learning about the industry. There was only one problem: there wasn't a study abroad program like that offered through her school—or any other college or university. She also didn't have any idea how this might fit into the life she'd imagined after going to a school like Scripps. Instead, she convinced herself that going to New York could allow her to learn more about the arts industry in hopes of one day working in arts administration.

Looking back, Amanda doesn't fully remember what the director-choreographer said or how exactly she felt encouraged to create her own study-away experience. However, Amanda does remember learning about the place that would change the course of her life—the Broadway Dance Center, located in the Theater District in Manhattan.

"The Broadway Dance Center has a program called the Professional Semester, which is a four-month program," Amanda explains, outlining how she created her own study-away program—a first major step in creating her own blueprint in life—by taking a semester-long leave of absence from Scripps and moving into spartan dorm-like accommodations near Penn Station. "You take twelve dance classes a week. You do mock auditions, learn about headshots and résumés and agents. At the end, there was a showcase and we auditioned in front of agents. One handed me a card." She ended up being represented by that agent for over a decade.

When Amanda arrived in New York City in August of what would have been her junior year in college, she had no plans to stay there beyond her four-month commitment. Amanda's goal was to spend that time in the intensive program, to get her love of dance out of her system, and go back to Scripps to finish her degree. "I came into the program with my Scripps mind-set," she says with a decisive smile. "I wasn't going to be a dancer, especially because I didn't think I was going to be in New York forever."

By the time Thanksgiving rolled around, Amanda started looking at school programs in New York. To her (and her parents!), landing an agent who believed in her validated her potential to work in the industry. Her parents also saw how much she loved it, how excited and energized she was, and how much it felt like the ideal next step for her self-designed blueprint.

Within six months, Amanda transferred to the Gallatin School at New York University, where she could design her own major and attend college part time. She moved into a third-floor walk-up studio apartment with its own outdoor space on the Upper West Side, taking over the place from a friend she met at the Broadway Dance Center who was moving to Los Angeles.

Once she'd finished settling into her new school life, Amanda started working and going on auditions. While her classmates were finishing up their senior year in college and starting full-time jobs in different fields, Amanda was balancing two to three different jobs—including writing, babysitting, and working the front desk at a fitness studio—while attending college part time and auditioning. In keeping with the personal statement she'd written years earlier, she found a new way to combine her love of dance and writing by becoming a reviewer, which entitled her to free tickets to dance performances.

Having the freedom to change her mind, even when things were going reasonably well, allowed Amanda to carve out a new and unique pathway that she'd initially seen as experimental and temporary but that soon became integral to her life and work. By bucking societal norms around achieving certain milestones in certain ways and in a certain order, she experienced a more personally fulfilling brand of success that was based on her authentic interests, skills, and dreams.

All of this would have been much harder, if not impossible, without her parents' support, both emotionally and financially. Moving across the country, transferring schools, pursuing dance, and moving into a studio apartment all benefit from a certain level of support, which often includes the people who show up and help move boxes of essentials up three narrow flights of stairs.

After being in New York for more than a decade, Amanda views the traditional college experience of dorms, classes, study abroad, majors, and graduation as an interesting sociological experiment that may one day become obsolete. "We ship these brand-new young adults off to a compound to decide what they want to do with their life," Amanda concludes, looking back on the twists and turns she's taken in developing her own blueprint. "You're on this island with other young adults figuring out a lot of things together. It's just a mess."

Amanda was certainly able to obtain needed resources to support her along different steps of her journey, but it also brings up an important question: What could today's young people achieve if they, like Amanda, could follow dreams of their own making, in their own way? What if we could blur, then erase, the faulty finish line that being admitted to a "good" college has become and instead empower young people to carve out their own path to a brand of success they define for themselves, which could include a traditional college experience or something that includes an expanded opportunity for self-design and self-inquiry? What might become possible then?

CHAPTER 16
NEURODIVERSITY

Caroline and I started working together during her senior year at a public high school in the Bay Area and then continued throughout her first year at the community college near her home. She had been diagnosed with ADHD, and our weekly sessions were a balance of adaptable yet predictable structure and support as she transitioned from high school to college while still living at home.

Our sessions have always been online, and she normally meets me from the desk in her room, in a cozy office space she has created by raising her bed to be the top bunk, with the desk and chair underneath, somewhat like a dorm-room space. Living with her mom, stepdad, and two younger sisters, she considers her room to be a sanctuary where she can replenish her energy after feelings of sensory overload.

About a month into her new school semester, Caroline joined our meeting a bit agitated. Her room had become messy with stuff—books, clothes, craft projects she hadn't put away, and empty wrappers. I intuitively knew that even if we went through our prescribed plans for the session—going through her school schedule for the week; mapping out what we define as a forty-hour workweek between class, tasks, and personal and academic responsibilities; creating a to-do list; breaking down tasks into manageable chunks; and helping her identify "do now tasks" she could get done in three minutes or fewer—she would still end the session sitting in a room that felt stifling and overwhelming, and that would more than likely prevent her from moving forward.

"Tell you what," I said, adapting to the moment. "I am getting the sense your room is overwhelming you a bit right now. How about I set a timer for ten minutes, and during that time, you keep moving and see how much you can put away, throw away, or organize?"

Her face softened and then brightened. "Okay!" And she was off.

Ten minutes later, she had gotten more done to move forward, and having me sit there and act as a body double or accountability partner made her get far more done than if she was trying to get started on her own. She wouldn't have been receptive to the same message if it came from her parents—it would have quickly gone to a place of shame and blame, and anger and tears might have followed.

"Can I have five more minutes?" she called out when the initial timer rang. Within fifteen minutes, I saw a sense of relief fall across her face and instinctively knew that the rest of the session and her upcoming week would be more productive than they might have been otherwise.

The next few weeks, we started our sessions in the same way. She would race around the room for ten minutes, and then we would settle into the rest of our appointment. In doing so, I was trying to create a predictable routine and do something I refer to as "lowering the activation energy" required to get a task—in this case, cleaning up—initiated and completed.

In scientific terms, activation energy is the amount of energy needed to energize molecules or atoms as they prepare to undergo some form of transformation.[1] The higher the activation energy, the more perceived effort is needed for the transformation to move forward. I use the phrase "lowering the activation energy" to represent ways to make initiating a once-insurmountable task less overwhelming. In this case, the amount of energy Caroline thought she needed to clean her room—something that might seem simple to many people who are neurotypical or who didn't have Caroline's built-up barriers to initiating that task—was high. In doing it together, I was trying to create a predictable routine that didn't seem so difficult. Lowering the activation energy can be seen as a form of behavioral activation, a key component of cognitive behavioral therapy where a therapist might work with a client to identify ways to reduce avoidance, set achievable goals, and build motivation and energy by reaching incremental goals.[2]

Within six weeks, something started to shift. Caroline used less and less time at the beginning of our sessions to get her physical space organized. She felt comfortable asking for the time when she needed it and felt relieved and more focused both during our sessions and throughout the week. I introduced it without judgment or shame, knowing she might experience additional distress if she felt like she was wasting our session time with something I felt she should have been able to do on her own. By the end of the semester, she joined our meeting beaming, excited to share that she didn't need the timer that day. "I cleaned everything up before our call, and my parents said this is the cleanest they've ever seen my room!" She then went on to explain that she had been able to keep her room cleaner over the course of the week as well, which gave her a sense of pride and accomplishment. What once felt insurmountable—and thus created a sense of shame and overwhelm—had slowly become more manageable. Together, we reframed her thinking and helped her see if an accountability buddy in that moment meant she completed the task, felt satisfied, and moved forward—well, that was a success.

For years, I have worked with students with diagnosed (and undiagnosed) learning differences, including students with neurodiversity who may have different ways of learning, thinking, processing, and behaving. The term "neurodiversity," coined by American sociologist Judy Singer in her 1998 thesis, is intended to dismantle and dissolve "even our most taken-for-granted assumptions: that we all more or less see, feel, touch, hear, smell, and sort information, in more or less the same way."[3] Educational psychologists and neuropsychologists often consult with me when assessing a student for learning differences and refer students to our office after a diagnosis, particularly students with ADHD or processing speed or executive-function disorders. I consult with school counselors and families when thinking about an appropriate course load given a student's unique profile. Students with ADHD (inattentive, hyperactive-impulsive, or both), autism, dyslexia, dyscalculia and dysgraphia, along with language-based learning disorders and processing-speed issues, often find that it can take longer—and require more energy—to manage a typical day at school. Some neurodivergent students are adversely affected by sounds, sights, smells, and textures in a way that others might not fully appreciate or be aware of.

A few years ago, I began consulting with schools piloting and implementing the Life Navigator Advisory Program that my team and I had designed over several years after that initial needs assessment in Charlotte. Completing the needs assessment allowed me to thoughtfully evaluate what I believed was needed, and missing, in the current school experience and find a way to provide training for teachers, instruction for students, and guidance for parents and caregivers. Even though I had visited schools around the world as a speaker and visiting author, implementing the Life Navigator Advisory Program with a new school partner meant that my team and I had the chance to visit and closely observe the rhythms and routines of the schools we were working with regularly, with the hopes of looking at the school experience—especially as it related to systems and connection—through the eyes of a student.

Toward the end of one of my first classroom and school observation visits with a new K–8 school partner, I turned to the administrator and asked offhandedly, "Where are the spaces of silence for students throughout the day?"

By that point, I had visited multiple classrooms that were engaging—and also loud and frenetic. I am sensitive to noise, to the point where attending a loud concert or an event in a large stadium can be unappealing. I had a heightened awareness that the lunchroom was a well-orchestrated cacophony of conversation and laughter familiar to anyone who has worked with the squirmy collective energy of elementary and middle school students. While the teachers and administrators had spaces of silence during prep periods or times they were alone in their classroom, I saw students shuttling between spaces in a way that created the potential for sensory overload.

The administrator, whom I knew to be student centered and solutions oriented, was at first perplexed. In her own classes, she used mindfulness techniques but admitted that not all students had that experience, and the study halls and resource labs we saw didn't all provide consistent quiet time for regrouping, reflection, and task initiation. The principal met with us after having a parent-child conference for a student who had a meltdown after becoming overwhelmed. I wasn't necessarily saying that spaces of silence would have prevented that, but I did know that for many children, getting through a typical school day takes far more energy than we recognize or appreciate, leading to a decreased ability to tolerate frustration.

For Dr. Courtney Murphy, a neuropsychologist and clinical psychologist, much of her work is providing assessments and supporting families as they navigate a new diagnosis. "People usually come see me when everything else is not working," she explains. "The point where I see them is putting together a treatment plan and launching them forward with providers and helping to rework a treatment plan if something is not working."

Here are some strategies for supporting students with neurodiversity as they create their own blueprint:

Acknowledgment and validation can be healing. Dr. Murphy works with students of all ages, as well as adults, many of whom were never diagnosed with learning differences as children. "One of the consistent messages that I find to be important, particularly for those who have experienced some level of trauma, is some level of authentic validation." She goes on to explain how it is often something along the lines of, "I hear you and I see you. I know you're bright and you have been working hard to mask these areas of difficulty. I also understand that the message you have received has been to 'work harder' because others didn't see how much effort you were giving. You've been working so hard to mask and compensate for these difficulties and now you are exhausted."

More structure up front is likely needed. One of the issues I see pop up in my work with neurodivergent students and their families is that parents will say, *Oh, I feel like it is better to let my child fail and figure it out.* And yet, particularly for neurodivergent students and those with learning differences, it may be that more support is essential initially, with the goal of having the student work toward greater independence. In occupational therapy and psychological terms, this is referred to as frontloading and is also a bit of scaffolding, providing extra support in the beginning that can then be readjusted as a student makes progress.

Dr. Murphy often explains to parents how it is easier to have more structure up front initially and then to sort of taper back with time as students start to make progress. In the beginning, though, the structure has to be very organized and strategically placed, because adding support later is actually more difficult and can backfire with regard to student confidence and feelings around competence. She admits this can be incredibly challenging for many parents and caregivers, particularly those who are exhausted and overwhelmed themselves. "For parents who've also been overburdened or stressed out, they may not have the tools that they need in terms of parenting," she admits. What works for one child, in one scenario, may no longer be effective. "When we are diagnosing difficulties, and that might mean the formal diagnosis, or just recognizing that a student is experiencing a challenge in one area, having more support up front is essential." For teens who may push back and want to have a level of independence, she surmises that honesty is the best policy. "Teens may want to prove that they can be independent, and they might say how they need space or need their parents to back off a bit." It can be helpful to have a conversation with the student about the shared goal of independence. For instance, I've often recommended parents and caregivers work with their child to identify areas the child can start to "own" in their desire for independence— perhaps getting themselves up in the morning, or completing certain tasks without reminders.

Self-advocacy can start small and provide opportunities for personal growth. All students benefit from having self-awareness and an ability to self-advocate. When students receive a diagnosis and have a 504 or IEP (individualized education plan), Dr. Murphy suggests that students who are able write their teachers a letter putting the words of their 504 or IEP into their own voice, something to the effect of, "When you see me put my head on my hands, or when you see me turn red, or when you see me not looking at you, just know that I'm experiencing X, Y, and Z. And in that situation, A, B, and C are helpful for me." She encourages students to end the note with gratitude and acknowledgment that their teacher is likely juggling many competing demands. "It is such a nice way for a student to learn to self-advocate and take charge of their own learning needs, and it builds a sense of empowerment."

Taking it one step further, by the time a student reaches seventh or eighth grade, if they are able to compose an email around an issue in class, they should start to take that over from parents and then just include the parents in their email to the teacher. That way, they get practice self-advocating, and the parent or caregiver can offer support as needed.

Parental modeling and psychoeducation can be just as important as student support. In Dr. Murphy's experience, students who see that their parents have activities, interests, and social relationships outside of work and in their community, whether it is through a house of religious worship or a place where they are of service, tend to be the most adaptable. Seeing parents engage in activities that fill their cup in another way, especially around connection and perspective, allows students the opportunity to reflect without being told—a classic case of showing being more powerful than telling. Another way parents can support their children is by pursuing their own psychoeducation around their child's diagnosis and therapeutic needs. Much of Dr. Murphy's time with parents post-assessment is spent talking about parent coaching. Sometimes that means parents being self-aware and monitoring their own moments of anger, frustration, and anxiety. Other times, Dr. Murphy notes, it may mean more intensive psychotherapeutic work. "I think it's really, really hard to be an effective parent unless you can kind of dig up your own stuff that you're carrying around with you," she concludes.

Parents and caregivers may need to check themselves on measuring progress. I sometimes see parents, particularly of students recently diagnosed with ADHD, who are frustrated at what they perceive to be a lack of progress. Not long ago, I fielded a call from the parents of a sixth-grader with extraordinary challenges with distraction. The child hadn't been completing work in class and was spending hours at home on evenings and weekends trying to finish classwork. It was going to take time to help the student build predictable routines in a way that worked for him, and we spent the first four sessions on the most basic of organizational fundamentals. In frustration, one of his parents began trying to micromanage sessions, telling us what to do even though everything they had been doing at home wasn't working. Their involvement was counterproductive, given their son's perfectionist tendencies and processing speed challenges. The parents discontinued sessions after four weeks, complaining they were not seeing fast enough progress. On some level, I felt bad the parents couldn't celebrate their son's incremental progress.

I juxtaposed that situation to that of several students that same week, all of whom reached significant milestones that would have seemed impossible when we had first started working together years earlier. Progress can feel slow, and there can be leaps forward and steps back. Consistent time, structure, and support is key. As I watched another student get herself situated in a way that would have been unfathomable when we started working together two years earlier, I was reminded that there is often no acceptable timetable for those wanting immediate results.

Remember: there can be many effective approaches to mindfulness. I encourage students to identify their opportunities for silence and stillness throughout the day. Many students with ADHD struggle to fall asleep, in part because it can be the first time that they are still, and the whole day catches up with them. Finding ways to help students build moments of silence that don't necessarily require complete stillness can help students build their own figurative muscle around mindfulness techniques. It could be guided visual imagery, a quick body scan, or a progressive muscle relaxation. Growth around mindfulness techniques may feel uncomfortable at first, but it builds those neural connections.

For some students, the idea of sitting still and closing their eyes might feel wholly uncomfortable, and that is okay. One technique Dr. Murphy suggests is the self-instructional training model, where a student talks to themselves about completing a task. "It could be as simple as, 'I am putting the pasta in the pot and putting the lid on the pasta, and setting the heat, you know, the stove to, like, a high heat, I'm going to set the timer to five minutes'—literally just narrating step by step." So many of us are thinking about a conversation we had earlier and how that other person reacted to us, and what we need to get done by tomorrow, or *Did I forget my keys?* Much of the work around creating systems and community building and outreach to others and self-awareness starts with being present in the moment. And that means paying attention, especially for kids who have executive functioning issues, because they're always thinking, *What next? What now?* Especially in high-pressure, achievement-oriented communities, creating spaces for them to slow down in the context of an ordinary day acts as a preventative to protect their energy and encourage them to be present with others and themselves.

For students with neurodiversity, focusing on some of the skills in the earlier sections of this book can be at once enormously helpful and enormously challenging. Developing practical systems that work and receiving the support needed to be consistent may reduce some of the challenges that come from navigating a world designed for neurotypical brains. For instance, the everyday school experience—filled with uncertainty, a jumble of routines mixed with changes and potential sensory overload of sights, sounds, and smells—can leave students feeling exhausted at the end of a typical day, much less when something doesn't go as planned. Children (and adults) with ADHD are highly likely to manifest deficient emotional self-regulation, which has been shown to uniquely predict social rejection and greater stress in family conflict.[4] And because students can be undiagnosed, or diagnosed but not yet have the accommodations necessary to help them thrive, we want to be intentional about creating spaces of silence within the daily school experience for all students, as a way to proactively address the time and energy needed to navigate school and life. At the same time, meeting each student where they are and collaborating to find strategies that work for incremental progress are especially important for neurodivergent students.

During a recent Q&A after a talk for parents and caregivers, I was asked about my main takeaways from neurodivergent youth and how my approach differs when working with young people with diagnoses like ADHD or autism, as examples. My response was simple and related to the work in schools: We need to focus more on energy management as a way to help students understand their own triggers for exhaustion. In doing so, we can better empower students to identify and advocate for their needs for quiet time, a night off, or an accommodation as a proactive preventative rather than reaction after a figurative meltdown.

I think about this a lot, especially when parents and caregivers get frustrated that a student is taking more time to complete work or to get basic tasks done during the day, and yet the student experiences a slew of school-day rituals and after-school activities that leave them completely spent. By focusing on energy management and making adjustments, we can help students recognize the signs that they need to take time to recalibrate and identify what the recalibration tools might be for them. We often overlook that it is easier to offer support up front, before a student is in a situation where their brain is dysregulated and they are in a sort of "survival mode" and not taking in new tools or skills.

Mark was a ninth grader who had recently started attending a new high school and also had a recent diagnosis of mild autism, or autism level 1. His parents explained the doctors had diagnosed their son with "high-functioning autism," which is a quick way to convey that Mark was able to complete tasks independently but also needed a good deal of structure and support around initiating tasks and implementing systems and routines. When Mark first started working with us, his parents' main underlying concern was the transition to high school, especially socially. Within a few months, they felt more at ease, and Mark met classmates he engaged with and who engaged with him regularly and supportively—a big win that came from years of additional support around social skills and hygiene. The next concern Mark's parents had was how long it took to start and complete daily assignments and recurring tasks. I asked questions about his activities after school and on weekends, and they started to tick through lists of groups—Boy Scouts, fencing, martial arts, and baseball—and admitted he usually didn't get home until 7 or 8 p.m. after a long school day. Still, the different activities represented the nonoverlapping circles of connection that provided him with needed socialization and connection that his parents believed were beneficial to his well-being. The daily intense physical activity also improved his mood and concentration. Their thoughtful approach made sense and also addressed how Mark could use time and resources available to him during the school day to start getting work done so that he wasn't trying to begin work in the midst of mental and physical exhaustion after he got home. I also noted that the sense of connection that his parents, especially his mom, were concerned about—she fretted that he didn't have close friends—was more *her* concern than *her son's*. Mark felt connected and supported among classmates and wasn't feeling social exclusion or isolation—and quieter weekends were needed, given all the demands on his energy during the school week. Meeting students where they are and helping them identify strategies that work isn't just about systems—it is also about what connection looks like and how connected the student feels to others. In this case, it was also about parents needing to unpack their own fears and triggers, which were affecting them and their relationship with their son.

Ultimately, the goal is to help students with neurodiversity identify the support and accommodations needed for them to thrive and to understand that success in that realm may look very different for students depending on their needs and developmental process. One of the frequent questions I field when parents first call my office, often with a new diagnosis of ADHD or something similar, is "How many sessions is this going to take?" I empathize with wanting to know some variation of "How long till this works and we can stop doing it?" but I gently respond by honestly admitting that I don't know their child and there's no one-size-fits-all solution.

However, meeting students where they are, finding strategies that work, and optimizing what works for each student means understanding that a student who needs ongoing or consistent outside support isn't a failure. Asking for and receiving appropriate support that helps us move forward should be a sign of success. More recently, I've seen several students start to thrive with a combination of emotional support and executive function support, and then parents rush to discontinue the structures that are working. "They're doing much better, so they can do it on their own," the adults reason, not fully appreciating that the outward support has allowed the student to feel a sense of autonomy and competence that spilled over to all aspects of their lives. Instead, these structures need to be strategically and intentionally tapered—not cut off cold turkey. To be sure, too much support can become a crutch or prevent a child from experiencing their own growth. Systems, connection, perspective, and acceptance may look different for neurodivergent individuals, but when a child (or adult!) can identify the time, structure, and support they need in that moment to thrive, that is success. Progress may (and likely will!) ebb and flow, and what is needed could change over time, depending on circumstances. Even as adults, many people with ADHD figure out that there are certain kinds of structures and support they need on an ongoing basis. An outside support system may include daily routines and checkpoints, an accountability partner who checks in weekly, a time-blocked calendar that provides guidance and structure, or a weekly check-in with a therapist to navigate and thrive. There is no "right" or "wrong" support, only what we each need at different times to create and support our own unique blueprints.

CONCLUSION

NOTEBOOK CHECKS

"IN HIGH SCHOOL, MY GRADES WOULD REALLY FLUCTUATE," LUIS SAYS with a disapproving grin, shaking his head at his past mistakes. "There would be a number of classes where I would get As and Bs, and then some where I would get Cs."

At four years old Luis had immigrated to the United States from South America. His family's income was meager, and, like many newcomers, his parents juggled a variety of low-paying jobs to make ends meet. Luis attended a public school where he was placed in a program for students who were in the process of learning English. In a few short months, he tested out of his school's program for English language learners, and by third grade, his test scores had him singled out for the Gifted and Talented Program, which he hated.

By the time Luis and I first met over Zoom, he was in his midthirties, with a wife and two children he adored. In the time we worked together, he would be promoted twice and buy his family home—in all aspects, his life looked a lot like the American Dream. Only after two years of working together did I learn how he spent three years in community college, followed by three years at his local state university, living at home with his parents and paying for school while working. He ultimately majored in accounting, the class he dropped four times while floundering in his early days at community college. After graduating from college, he then worked at a big accounting firm before landing a job at his current organization, where he was a finance manager with considerable potential.

Thinking back on his schooling, he has mixed memories. He performed exceptionally well on standardized tests from an early age, though he would miss points from easier assignments. "It would be homework. And I would fail the notebook checks." He chuckles, recalling how he would shove papers into his backpack and how other students' notebooks seemed to be more pristine.

"No one was guiding me. Other than, like, the very broad strokes of school being important, there was no one sitting with me telling me how to manage my time, telling me how you can do whatever. It wasn't coming from home, and it wasn't specifically coming from teachers. It was mostly, *Why aren't you doing your work?* or *I wish you would do your work; you're so good when you try.*" Decades later this lack of organizational and other core skills was still affecting him, preventing him from being promoted and frustrating his career ambitions.

Working with Luis would ultimately confirm what I already knew—that these skills have a significant impact on career trajectory throughout adulthood. Luis has a distinctly personable nature—he's warm, upbeat, easy to talk to, with a calm demeanor that puts others at ease. His superpower is connecting easily with people with different backgrounds and perspectives. Before we started working together, his peer reviews were mostly focused on what a nice person he was to work with; no one mentioned that he lacked some of the fundamental underlying skills he needed to reach his own career goals. At first Luis and I met twice a week—initially for an hour each time, and then for forty-five minutes on Tuesdays, followed by thirty minutes on Friday. Consistency was key, and we would triage issues that came up and then build short- and longer-term strategies around managing email, time, and tasks, including breaking larger tasks into a series of smaller ones that felt easier to navigate. Before long, the system I helped him to think through and develop became automatic, allowing him to create higher-order strategy.

Within weeks, he and his colleagues noticed a marked difference, and within a year, Luis was promoted. His boss was thrilled, and the global head of talent at his organization was floored. He was working on high-impact projects and received consistently high marks from people in his organization and elsewhere. In addition to helping him develop a system for managing day-to-day tasks and more complicated month- and year-long projects, we worked on identifying how and when to ask for help; how to streamline his messaging into concise, direct statements; and when to proactively lean on his boss when her clout could move something along faster. As Luis saw the results of these little tweaks, he bought into our work together. A few months later, his boss shared that Luis had caught a nuanced error—something he would never have done before.

These changes didn't result purely from developing a system. He also learned how to reach out for help proactively and how to press on to find solutions even when he needed to be more forceful than agreeable. His perspective as a young newcomer to America who spent years navigating the trenches of the immigration system to eventually become a US citizen meant he took little for granted. "Once I got all the paperwork sorted, nothing in the world can ever stress me out again," he reflects. "I think that's why people always tell me, 'Oh, you're so calm, you're so collected. You're never frazzled. You're never stressed.' And I'm like, you're right. I'm never stressed. There is nothing I can't handle. At the end of the day, I know I am okay, and I can bounce back."

For much of our first year of meetings, he worked from home, where his virtual-office backdrop featured the artwork of his elementary-school-aged children. Like many others, he loved not commuting, in part because it made balancing his children's school drop-off and pickup easier. Still, Luis is extroverted and needed to figure out how to manage his energy so he could stay focused. The solution? He realized he was far more productive when he had a long, intense outdoor workout early in the morning, before starting his work for the day. Sometimes that wasn't possible, given early morning meetings across different time zones, but he prioritized an intense workout nearly every day.

By all accounts, Luis achieved the social and economic mobility touted in academic papers and research studies. Earlier exposure and shared experiences from working full-time at a law firm while attending community college helped him develop his perspective and feel comfortable navigating rooms where others had incredible wealth and resources and be confident that he could effectively engage with people from all backgrounds. Today, he continues an upward professional trajectory, buoyed by supporters and clarifiers, some of whom are mentors and others who act as sponsors.

For me, our work together served to answer essential questions—yes, all students need this, and yes, lack of these skills has a direct impact on workforce development. A younger Luis was exactly who I was hoping to reach with the Life Navigator Advisory Program I started to design in hopes of giving all students access to skill building that can and will change their lives. An older Luis saw his professional ambitions, once on the verge of being thwarted, realized with the help of his supervisor, who acted as a sponsor by reaching out and providing him access to the skill building he needed to move forward. In doing so, the ripple effects to his family, to his community, to his coworkers, and to his organization are endless.

My hope has always been that all individuals can build and develop the skills they need to support them over a lifetime. In my ideal world, students wouldn't need to move from lower-opportunity spaces to those seen as higher-opportunity and more resourced to improve their chances of changing their life trajectory in remarkable ways. If our hope is to empower our next generation, our old rigid standards and faulty finish lines and assumptions need to be reframed and transformed. The earlier we encourage students to focus on the underlying skills around systems, connection, perspective, and acceptance, the more we allow students to move beyond an emphasis on any one arbitrary moment in time. In doing so, we better prepare them for a rapidly changing world in a way that is adaptive, nourishing, and life affirming. In these momentous times, our students are our greatest reflection of growth and inspiration. It is to our benefit to serve them well.

ACKNOWLEDGMENTS

THIS BOOK WAS A COLLABORATION THAT EVOLVED FROM A COMBINA-tion of systems, connection, perspectives, and acceptance. I have tremendous gratitude for the help and encouragement from the individuals who supported every stage of the process.

First and foremost, I would like to thank the students—those who have walked into my office over the past twenty years and those I've met at schools throughout the world. Your curiosity, generosity, authenticity, and humor make me believe that my work is a gift. And to their families, thank you for the opportunity to work with your children.

I recognize the enormous privilege of working with an editor as thoughtful, patient, and reasonable as Dan Ambrosio (being reasonable is so underrated!). Thank you, truly, to Dan and the entire team at Hachette Go for being open to the vision of this book and for supporting its transformation through various stages. And thank you, Michael Barrs and Kindall Gant, for your support in getting this book out into the world.

As always, thank you to my incredible agent, Rebecca Gradinger, for everything you do, and to Kelly Karczewski, for taking care of so many details, both little and big.

In this book, I talk a great deal about the power of connection, and I would be remiss not to mention the many webs of connection that brought this book to life.

I am forever grateful to Alan Finder, a longtime *New York Times* reporter who was a kind, generous, and unintentional sponsor. Alan visited my office for a piece on disorganized boys in the fall of 2007, which ended up on the first page of the National section on January 1, 2008. Alan later forwarded an email that resulted in an introduction to my literary agent and ultimately led to my first book deal. He passed away in March 2020, and I've thought about Alan and his family throughout my work on this book.

Thank you to Lauren Sandler, whom I originally met through Katie Orenstein and the OpEd Project, for her brainstorming brilliance and for encouraging me through the early stages. I am indebted to Farnoosh Torabi's Instagram story about Richelle Fredson, who will forever be known as the book proposal fairy godmother as well as a phenomenal cheerleader and friend.

Through Richelle, I met Wyndham Wood, without whom this book would not exist. Wyndham, thank you for your enduring support, for seeing the bigger picture, and for making sure that my ideas made sense on paper. A big thanks to Emma Tapscott, an extraordinary research assistant whose thoughtful insights were integral to the development of this book. And to Christina Mazza, who became an essential part of my get-the-book-done team, I offer my sincerest gratitude.

My work in Charlotte, North Carolina, provided the opportunity for the initial stages of development of the Life Navigator Advisory Program. That work exists thanks to a fortuitous conversation at Saint Frank Coffee on Polk Street in San Francisco in February 2016. Thank you to Mark Reed, Laura Wellman, Brian Collier, and LaTarzja Henry, who each played an important role in making the vision a reality. And Amy Poag and Court Young, your initial connections played pivotal roles that you probably don't even realize! Thank you to those in Charlotte who acted as connectors and supporters of the Life Navigator Advisory Program, including Lauren Batten, Kathy Capps, Michelle Icard, Anne Dunton Lam, LaToya Pousa, Danielle Squires, and Danyae Thomas.

I would like to thank LinkedIn's search engine for the timely introduction to Kristi Ransick, whose invaluable guidance, support, and friendship meant we were able to create the first iteration of the Life Navigator Advisory curriculum on a less-than-shoestring budget. It would never have happened without you, Kristi—thank you so much.

We should all be lucky enough to have deeply dedicated champions like Margaret Miller, who has read nearly every page of every draft of every book I have written and has offered real-world commentary, often with very tight turnaround times. My thanks, also, to Alice Kleeman, who read early drafts of this book and provided helpful feedback. Thank you as well to Susan Marquess: this book is a tribute to the time when I walked into your office nearly thirty years ago and you asked whether I could help a classmate with chemistry.

To the amazing people who took time out of their busy schedules to discuss the topics in this book, I am so appreciative of your time and effort—especially because some of you were simply friends allowing me to bounce ideas off you: Kwad Acheampong, Jeanmarie Cahill, Carliss Chatman, Abby Davisson, Josh Jackson, Saidah Jones, Bill Kuhn, Lauren Linder, Courtney Monk, Dan-el Padilla Peralta, Elise Van Middelem, and Shannon Wardlow.

Thank you to Dr. Courtney Murphy for your professional expertise and empathetic, child-centered insight. I am grateful to have you as a colleague working in the best interests of children.

Thank you to Lorri Hamilton Durbin, Peggy Laurent, Kimberly Paton, and the wonderful staff and administrators at Town School for being such incredible educational partners.

A special thanks to the staff at Green Ivy Educational Consulting, who supported my writing of this book: Brandon Williams, Alyssa Vincent, and Morgan Wright. Much of the initial proposal for this book, and later the manuscript, were written in the early morning hours at my favorite back corner table at Behind the Bookstore in Edgartown. I am so grateful for that magical time and space.

Finally, thanks always to my family, including my supportive parents, Amir Homayoun and Barbara Manning, and my brilliant sister, Dr. Allia Griffin. And a special thanks to my nephew Cameron, to whom this book is dedicated. May you always let your light shine bright and create your own blueprint. With love from Auntie Ana.

REFERENCES

Arain, Mariam, Maliha Haque, Lina Johal, Puja Mathur, Wynand Nel, Afsha Rais, Ranbir Sandhu, and Sushil Sharma. "Maturation of the Adolescent Brain." *Neuropsychiatric Disease and Treatment* 9 (2013): 449–461. doi:10.2147/NDT.S39776.

Barkley, Russel. "DESR: Why Deficient Emotional Self-Regulation Is Central to ADHD (and Largely Overlooked)." *ADDitude*, July 11, 2022. www.additudemag.com/desr-adhd-emotional-regulation/.

Barret, Paul M., Justin Hendrix, and J. Grant Sims. *Fueling the Fire: How Social Media Intensifies U.S. Political Polarization—and What Can Be Done About It.* New York: NYU Stern Center for Business and Human Rights, 2021. https://static1.squarespace.com/static/5b6df958f8370af3217d4178/t/613a4d4cc86b9d3810eb35aa/1631210832122/NYU+CBHR+Fueling+The+Fire_FINAL+ONLINE+REVISED+Sep7.pdf.

Belkin, Douglas. "A Generation of American Men Give Up on College: 'I Just Feel Lost.'" *Wall Street Journal*, September 7, 2021. www.wsj.com/articles/college-university-fall-higher-education-men-women-enrollment-admissions-back-to-school-11630948233?mod=article_inline.

Bowker, Julie C., and Sarah V. Spencer. "Friendship and Adjustment: A Focus on Mixed-Grade Friendships." *Journal of Youth and Adolescence* 39, no. 11 (2010): 1318–1329. https://doi.org/10.1007/s10964-009-9474-0.

Boyce, W. Thomas. *The Orchid and the Dandelion: Why Some Children Struggle and How All Can Thrive.* Ontario: Penguin Canada, 2019.

Bruni, Frank. *Where You Go Is Not Who You'll Be: An Antidote to the College Admissions Mania.* New York: Grand Central, 2015.

Bureau of Labor Statistics. *Number of Jobs, Labor Market Experience, Marital Status, and Health: Results from a National Longitudinal Survey.* Washington, DC: US Department of Labor, 2021. www.bls.gov/news.release/pdf/nlsoy.pdf.

Cain, Susan. *Quiet: The Power of Introverts in a World That Can't Stop Talking.* New York: Crown, 2012.

Center for Behavioral Health Statistics and Quality. *2020 National Survey on Drug Use and Health (NSDUH): Methodological Summary and Definitions.* Rockville, MD: Substance Abuse and Mental Health Services Administration, 2021. www.samhsa.gov/data/sites/default/files/reports/rpt35330/2020NSDUHMethodSummDefs092421/2020NSDUHMethodsSummDefs092421.htm.

Charlotte Country Day School. *Philanthropy 101*. Charlotte, NC, 2021, https://resources
.finalsite.net/images/v1629735533/charlottecds/a1jskfqetbuqibyx7mdb/CDF
Philanthropy101.pdf.

Chetty, Raj. "Where Is the Land of Opportunity?: The Geography of Intergenerational
Mobility in the United States." *Quarterly Journal of Economics* 129, no. 4 (2014).
doi:10.1093/qje/qju022.

Chetty, Raj, John N. Friedman, Emmanuel Saez, Nicholas Turner, and Danny Yagan.
Mobility Report Cards: The Role of Colleges in Intergenerational Mobility. Cambridge:
National Bureau of Economic Research, 2017.

Chetty, Raj, and Nathaniel Hendren. "The Impacts of Neighborhoods on Intergenerational Mobility: Childhood Exposure Effects and County-Level Estimates." *Quarterly
Journal of Economics* 133, no. 3 (2018): 1107–1162. https://doi.org/10.1093/qje/qjy007.

Chetty, Raj, Nathaniel Hendren, Maggie R. Jones, and Sonya R. Porter. "Race and
Economic Opportunity in the United States: An Intergenerational Perspective."
Quarterly Journal of Economics 135, no. 2 (2020): 711–783. https://doi.org/10.1093/qje
/qjz042.

Chetty, Raj, Matthew O. Jackson, Theresa Kuchler, Johannes Stroebel, Nathaniel Hendren, Robert B. Fluegge, Sara Gong, et al. "Social Capital II: Determinants of Economic Connectedness." *Nature News* 608 (2022): 122–134. www.nature.com/articles
/s41586-022-04997-3.

Cillessen, Antonius H. N., and Lara Mayeaux. "From Censure to Reinforcement: Developmental Changes in the Association Between Aggression and Social Status." *Child
Development* 75 (2004): 147–163. https://doi.org/10.1111/j.1467-8624.2004.00660.x.

Claret, Bob. "Middlebury and UNC-Chapel Hill Over/Under-Performance Study."
Gap Year Research Consortium at Colorado College. Accessed September 2, 2022.
https://sites.coloradocollege.edu/gapyearresearchconsortium/gap-year-research
-outcomes/academic-outcomes/.

Cox, Daniel A. "Men's Social Circles Are Shrinking." The Survey Center on American Life, June 29, 2021. www.americansurveycenter.org/why-mens-social
-circles-are-shrinking/.

——— "The State of American Friendship: Change, Challenges, and Loss." The Survey
Center on American Life, June 8, 2021. www.americansurveycenter.org/research
/the-state-of-american-friendship-change-challenges-and-loss/.

Cristofori, Irene, Shira Cohen-Zimerman, and Jordan Grafman. "Executive Functions." *Handbook of Clinical Neurology* 163 (2019): 197–219. doi:10.1016/B978-0-12
-804281-6.00011-2.

de Bono, Edward. *Lateral Thinking: Creativity Step by Step*. New York: Harper &
Row, 1970.

Diamond, Adele. "Executive Functions." *Annual Review of Psychology* 64 (2013): 135–168.
doi:10.1146/annurev-psych-113011-143750.

——— "How to Sharpen Executive Functions: Activities to Hone Brain Skills."
ADDitude Magazine. Last modified December 13, 2022. https://www.additudemag.
com/how-to-improve-executive-function-adhd/.

Diamond, Adele, and Daphne S. Ling. "Conclusions About Interventions, Programs,
and Approaches for Improving Executive Functions That Appear Justified and

Those That, Despite Much Hype, Do Not." *Developmental Cognitive Neuroscience* 18 (2015): 34–38. https://doi.org/10.1016/j.dcn.2015.11.005.

Duffy, John. *Parenting the New Teen in the Age of Anxiety: A Complete Guide to Your Child's Stressed, Depressed, Expanded, Amazing Adolescence (Parenting Tips from a Clinical Psychologist and Relationships Expert)*. Miami: Mango, 2019.

"EA Deferred FAQS." MIT Admissions. Accessed September 2, 2022. https://mit admissions.org/pages/ea-deferred-faq/.

Easton, John Q., Esperanza Johnson, and Lauren Sartain. *The Predictive Power of Ninth-Grade GPA*. Chicago: University of Chicago Consortium on School Research, 2017. https://consortium.uchicago.edu/sites/default/files/2018-10/Predictive %20Power%20of%20Ninth-Grade-Sept%202017-Consortium.pdf.

Elbogen, Eric, Megan Lanier, Shannon M. Blakey, H. Ryan Wagner, and Jack Tsai. "Suicidal Ideation and Thoughts of Self-Harm During the COVID-19 Pandemic: The Role of COVID-19-Related Stress, Social Isolation, and Financial Strain." *Depression and Anxiety* 38, no. 7 (2021): 739–748. doi:10.1002/da.23162.

Endo, Kaori, Shuntaro Ando, Shinji Shimodera, Marcus Richards, Stephani Hatch, and Atsushi Nishida. "Preference for Solitude, Social Isolation, Suicidal Ideation, and Self-Harm in Adolescents." *Journal of Adolescent Health* 61, no. 2 (2017): 187–191. http://dx.doi.org/10.1016/j.jadohealth.2017.02.018.

Epstein, David. *Range: Why Generalists Triumph in a Specialized World*. New York: Riverhead Books, 2019.

FAIR Health. *The Impact of COVID-19 on Pediatric Mental Health: A Study of Private Healthcare Claims*. New York: FAIR Health, 2021. https://s3.amazonaws.com/media2 .fairhealth.org/whitepaper/asset/The%20Impact%20of%20COVID-19%20on%20 Pediatric%20Mental%20Health%20-%20A%20Study%20of%20Private%20Health care%20Claims%20-%20A%20FAIR%20Health%20White%20Paper.pdf.

Fisher, Julia Freeland. *Who You Know: Unlocking Innovations That Expand Students' Networks*. San Francisco: Jossey-Bass, 2018.

Fracassa, Dominic. "San Francisco to End Nightly Curfew After Wednesday." *San Francisco Chronicle*, June 4, 2020. www.sfchronicle.com/bayarea/article/San-Francisco -to-end-nightly-curfew-after-15314823.php.

Freeman, Mark, Brian H. Kim, Preston Magouirk, and Trent Kajikawa. *Deadline Update: First-Year Application Trends Through March 15*. Common App, 2022. https://s3.us-west-2.amazonaws.com/ca.research.publish/Research+briefs +2020/20211123_Deadline_Update_FY.pdf.

Gallup. *Great Jobs, Great Lives: The 2014 Gallup-Purdue Index Report*. Gallup, 2014, 2016. www.gallup.com/file/services/176768/The_2014_Gallup-Purdue_Index_Report .pdf.

Goldstone, Aimeé, Harold S. Javitz, Stephanie A. Claudatos, Devin E. Prouty, Ian M. Colrain, and Fiona C. Baker. "Sleep Disturbance Predicts Depression Symptoms in Early Adolescence: Initial Findings from the Adolescent Brain Cognitive Development Study." *Journal of Adolescent Health* 66, no. 5 (2020). https://doi.org/10.1016/j .jadohealth.2019.12.005.

Grygiel, Pawel, Slawomir Rebisz, Anna Gawel, Barbara Ostafińska-Molik, Malgorzata Michel, Julia Łosiak-Pilch, and Roman Dolata. "The Inclusion of Other-Sex Peers in Peer Networks and Sense of Peer Integration in Early Adolescence: A Two-Wave Longitudinal Study." *International Journal of Environmental Research and Public Health* 19, no. 22 (2022). https://doi.org/10.3390/ijerph192214971.

Harris, Adam. "Parents Gone Wild: High Drama Inside D.C.'s Most Elite Private School." *Atlantic*, June 5, 2019. www.theatlantic.com/education/archive/2019/06/sidwell-friends-college-admissions-varsity-blues/591124/.

Haskell, Will. "A Gossip App Brought My High School to a Halt." *Cut*, April 28, 2014. www.thecut.com/2014/04/gossip-app-brought-my-high-school-to-a-halt.html.

Hewlett, Sylvia Ann. *The Sponsor Effect: How to Be a Better Leader by Investing in Others.* Brighton: Harvard Business Review Press, 2019.

Hiatt, Cody, Brett Laursen, Karen S. Mooney, and Kenneth H. Rubin. "Forms of Friendship: A Person-Centered Assessment of the Quality, Stability, and Outcomes of Different Types of Adolescent Friends." *Personality and Individual Differences* 77 (2015): 149–155. https://doi.org/10.1016/j.paid.2014.12.051.

Holt-Lunstad, Julianne, Timothy B. Smith, and J. Bradley Layton. "Social Relationships and Mortality Risk: A Meta-analytic Review." *PLOS Medicine* 7, no. 7 (2010). https://doi.org/10.1371/journal.pmed.1000316.

Homayoun, Ana. "Back-to-School Lesson in Kindness." *HuffPost*, October 19, 2013. www.huffpost.com/entry/back-to-school-lesson-in-kindness_b_3776626.

Icard, Michelle. *Middle School Makeover: Improving the Way You and Your Child Experience the Middle School Years.* London: Routledge, 2014.

Kasakove, Sophie. "The College Admissions Scandal: Where Some of the Defendants Are Now." *New York Times*, October 9, 2021. www.nytimes.com/2021/10/09/us/varsity-blues-scandal-verdict.html.

Kim, Simon, Frances Palin, Page Anderson, Shannan Edwards, Gretchen Lidner, and Barbara Olisov Rothbaum. "Use of Skills Learned in CBT for Fear of Flying: Managing Flying Anxiety After September 11th." *Journal of Anxiety Disorders* 22, no. 2 (2008): 301–309. doi:10.1016/j.janxdis.2007.02.006.

Kitagawa, N. "Practice of Behavioral Activation in Cognitive-Behavioral Therapy." *Seishin Shinkeigaku Zasshi* 117, no. 1 (2015): 26–33 (in Japanese). PMID: 26514043.

Kornrich, Sabino. "Inequalities in Parental Spending on Young Children: 1972 to 2010." *American Educational Research Association* 2, no. 2 (2016): 1–12. doi:10.1177/2332858416644180.

Luminaria Learning Solutions. "Lesson 22: Skills for Small Talk." Life Navigator Sixth Grade Curriculum, 2022.

Lund, Jessie I., Elaine Toombs, Abbey Radford, Kara Boles, and Christopher Mushquash. "Adverse Childhood Experiences and Executive Function Difficulties in Children: A Systematic Review." *Child Abuse & Neglect* 106 (2020). https://doi.org/10.1016/j.chiabu.2020.104485.

Luthar, Suniya S., and Lucia Ciciolla. "What It Feels Like to Be a Mother: Variations by Children's Developmental Stages." *Developmental Psychology* 52, no. 1 (2016): 143–154. https://doi.org/10.1037/dev0000062.

Martin, Andrew J. "Should Students Have a Gap Year? Motivation and Performance Factors Relevant to Time Out After Completing School." *Journal of Educational Psychology* 102, no. 3 (2010): 561–576. https://doi.org/10.1037/a0019321.

Mason, Kenneth A., Jonathan B. Losos, Tod Duncan, Peter H. Raven, and George B. Johnson. *Biology.* 12th ed. New York: McGraw-Hill Education, 2020.

Metha, Clare M., and JoNell Strough. "Sex Segregation in Friendships and Normative Contexts Across the Life Span." *Developmental Review* 29, no. 3 (2009): 201–220. https://doi.org/10.1016/j.dr.2009.06.001.

National Student Clearinghouse Research Center. *Overview: Spring 2022 Enrollment Estimates.* May 26, 2022. https://nscresearchcenter.org/wp-content/uploads/CTEE _Report_Spring_2022.pdf.

Navarro, Raúl, Elisa Larrañaga, and Santiago Yubero. "Gender Identity, Gender-Typed Personality Traits and School Bullying: Victims, Bullies and Bully-Victims." *Child Indicators Research* 9, no. 1 (2016): 1–20. https://doi.org/10.1007/s12187-015-9300-z.

Neff, Kristin. "Definition and Three Elements of Self-Compassion," *Self-Compassion,* July 9, 2020. https://self-compassion.org/the-three-elements-of-self-compassion-2/.

Newcomb, Alyssa. "Why These Apps Can Make High School a Nightmare." *ABC News,* May 5, 2014. https://abcnews.go.com/Technology/secret-messaging-apps-make -high-school-nightmare/story?id=23597535.

"Next Steps for Deferred Students: Undergraduate Admission." Georgia Tech Undergraduate Admission. Accessed September 2, 2022. https://admission.gatech.edu /first-year/defer.

Nietzel, Michael T. "Ivy League Colleges Reveal Acceptance Numbers for Class of 2026." *Forbes,* April 5, 2022. www.forbes.com/sites/michaeltnietzel/2022/04/04/ivy-league -colleges-announce-acceptance-numbers-for-class-of-2026/?sh=312484f0625d.

Niño, Michael, Gabe Ignatow, and Tianji Cai. "Social Isolation, Strain, and Youth Violence." *Youth Violence and Juvenile Justice* 15, no. 3 (2017): 299–313. doi:10.1177/1541204016636435.

Ozcelik, Hakan, and Sigal Barsade. *Work, Loneliness, and Employee Performance.* Academy of Management Annual Meeting Proceedings, 2011. https://faculty.wharton .upenn.edu/wp-content/uploads/2012/05/Work_Loneliness_Performance _Study.pdf.

Pew Research Center. *How Teens and Parents Navigate Screen Time and Device Distractions.* August 2018. www.pewresearch.org/internet/wp-content/uploads /sites/9/2018/08/PI_2018.08.22_teens-screentime_FINAL.pdf.

Prinstein, Mitch. *Popular: The Power of Likability in a Status-Obsessed World.* New York: Viking, 2017.

Redfin. "Los Altos Hills Housing Market." Accessed November 17, 2022. www.redfin .com/city/11022/CA/Los-Altos-Hills/housing-market.

Reeves, Richard V., and Kimberly Howard. "Vague Hopes and Active Aspirations, Part 1." *Brookings* (blog), July 29, 2016. www.brookings.edu/blog /social-mobility-memos/2014/04/15/vague-hopes-and-active-aspirations-part-1/.

Rideout, Victoria, and Michael B. Robb. *Common Sense Census: Media Use by Tweens and Teens, 2019.* Common Sense Media, 2019. www.commonsensemedia.org/sites /default/files/research/report/2019-census-8-to-18-full-report-updated.pdf.

Ryan, Richard M., and Edward L. Deci. "Self-Determination Theory and the Facilitation of Intrinsic Motivation, Social Development, and Well-Being." *American Psychologist* 55, no. 1 (2000): 68–78. https://doi.org/10.1037/0003-066X.55.1.68.

Sandstrom, Gillian M., and Elizabeth W. Dunn. "Social Interactions and Well-Being: The Surprising Power of Weak Ties." *Personality and Social Psychology Bulletin* 40, no. 7 (2014): 910–922. doi:10.1177/0146167214529799.

Sandstrom, Marlene, and Antonius H. N. Cillessen. "Likable Versus Popular: Distinct Implications for Adolescent Adjustment." *International Journal of Behavioral Development* 30, no. 4 (2006): 305–314. doi:10.1177/0165025406072789.

Santomauro, Damian F., Ana M. Mantilla Herrera, Jamileh Shadid, Peng Zheng, Charlie Ashbaugh, David M. Pigott, Cristiana Abbafati, et al. "Global Prevalence and Burden of Depressive and Anxiety Disorders in 204 Countries and Territories in 2020 due to the COVID-19 Pandemic." *Lancet* 398, no. 10312 (2021): 1700–1712. https://doi.org/10.1016/S0140-6736(21)02143-7.

Savidge, Nico, and Rick Hurd. "'It's Kind of Like Nuclear Winter': Unprecedented Smoke Layer Darkens Bay Area Skies as West Coast Burns." *Mercury News*, September 16, 2020. www.mercurynews.com/2020/09/09/complete-smoke-out-in-bay-area-darkens-the-daytime/.

Schwartz, Tony, and Catherine McCarthy. "Manage Your Energy, Not Your Time." *Harvard Business Review*, October 3, 2019. https://hbr.org/2007/10/manage-your-energy-not-your-time.

Sheridan, David C., Sara Grusing, Rebecca Marshall, Amber Lin, Adrienne R. Hughes, Robert G. Hendrickson, and B. Zane Horowitz. "Changes in Suicidal Ingestion Among Preadolescent Children from 2000 to 2020." *JAMA Pediatrics* 176, no. 6 (2022). doi:10.1001/jamapediatrics.2022.0069.

Singer, Judy. "Odd People In: The Birth of Community Amongst People on the 'Autistic Spectrum': A Personal Exploration of a New Social Movement Based on Neurological Diversity." University of Technology, Sydney, 1998.

Smialek, Jeanna, Lydia DePillis, and Ben Casselman. "Why Are Middle-Aged Men Missing from the Labor Market?" *New York Times*, December 2, 2022. www.nytimes.com/2022/12/02/business/economy/job-market-middle-aged-men.html.

Swarns, Rachel L. "Obamas Pick Sidwell School, Ending a Washington Guessing Game." *New York Times*, November 21, 2008. www.nytimes.com/2008/11/22/us/politics/22sidwell.html?_r=1&em.

Starecheski, Laura. "Take the ACE Quiz—and Learn What It Does and Doesn't Mean." *National Public Radio*, March 2, 2015. www.npr.org/sections/health-shots/2015/03/02/387007941/take-the-ace-quiz-and-learn-what-it-does-and-doesnt-mean.

Tuominen-Soini, Heta, Katariina Salmela-Aro, and Markku Niemivirta. "Achievement Goal Orientations and Subjective Well-Being: A Person-Centred Analysis." *Learning and Instruction* 18, no. 3 (2008): 251–266. doi:10.1016/j.learninstruc.2007.05.003.

Victor, Christina, Pamela Qualter, and Manuela Barreto. "What Is Loneliness: Insights from the BBC Loneliness Experiment." *Innovation in Aging* 3, no. 1 (2019). https://doi.org/10.1093/geroni/igz038.1366.

Wadekar, Adway S. "Duke Admits 4.6% of Regular Decision Applicants to Class of 2026." *Chronicle*, March 31, 2022. www.dukechronicle.com/article/2022/03/duke-regular-decision-acceptance-rate-class-of-2026-admissions.

Walsh, Jeremy J., Joel D. Barnes, Jameason D. Cameron, Gary S. Goldfield, Jean-Philippe Chaput, Katie E. Gunnel, Andrée-Anne Ledoux, Roger L. Zemek, and Mark S.

Tremblay. "Associations Between 24 Hour Movement Behaviours and Global Cognition in US Children: A Cross-Sectional Observational Study." *Lancet* 2, no. 11 (2018). https://doi.org/10.1016/S2352-4642(18)30278-5.

Weaver, Caity. "Typing These Two Letters Will Scare Your Young Co-workers: Everything Was O.K. Until You Wrote 'O.K.'" *New York Times*, November 21, 2019. www.nytimes.com/2019/11/21/business/kk.html.

Wray, Bridget, Amanda Grimes, Katlyn Eighmy, and Joseph Lightner. "The Relationship Between Social Integration and Physical Activity, Diet, and Sleep Among Youths: Cross-Sectional Survey Study." *JMIR Pediatrics and Parenting* 5, no. 4 (2022). doi:10.2196/40354.

NOTES

INTRODUCTION

1. Sophie Kasakove, "The College Admissions Scandal: Where Some of the Defendants Are Now," *New York Times*, October 9, 2021, www.nytimes.com/2021/10/09/us/varsity-blues-scandal-verdict.html.

2. Michael T. Nietzel, "Ivy League Colleges Reveal Acceptance Numbers for Class of 2026," *Forbes*, April 5, 2022, www.forbes.com/sites/michaeltnietzel/2022/04/04/ivy-league-colleges-announce-acceptance-numbers-for-class-of-2026/?sh=312484f0625d.

3. Mark Freeman et al., *Deadline Update: First-Year Application Trends Through March 15*, Common App, 2022, https://s3.us-west-2.amazonaws.com/ca.research.publish/Research+briefs+2020/20211123_Deadline_Update_FY.pdf.

4. Frank Bruni, *Where You Go Is Not Who You'll Be: An Antidote to the College Admissions Mania* (New York: Grand Central, 2015).

5. Drew DeSilver, "A Majority of U.S. Colleges Admit Most Students Who Apply," Pew Research Center, May 30, 2020, www.pewresearch.org/fact-tank/2019/04/09/a-majority-of-u-s-colleges-admit-most-students-who-apply/.

6. Gallup, *Great Jobs, Great Lives: The 2014 Gallup-Purdue Index Report* (Gallup, 2014, 2016), www.gallup.com/file/services/176768/The_2014_Gallup-Purdue_Index_Report.pdf.

7. Gallup, *Great Jobs, Great Lives.*

8. John Duffy, *Parenting the New Teen in the Age of Anxiety: A Complete Guide to Your Child's Stressed, Depressed, Expanded, Amazing Adolescence (Parenting Tips from a Clinical Psychologist and Relationships Expert)* (Miami: Mango, 2019), 73.

9. Gallup, *Great Jobs, Great Lives.*

10. FAIR Health, *The Impact of COVID-19 on Pediatric Mental Health: A Study of Private Healthcare Claims* (New York: FAIR Health, 2021), https://s3.amazonaws.com/media2.fairhealth.org/whitepaper/asset/The%20Impact%20of%20COVID-19%20on%20Pediatric%20Mental%20Health%20-%20A%20Study%20of%20Private%20Healthcare%20Claims%20-%20A%20FAIR%20Health%20White%20Paper.pdf.

11. Centers for Disease Control and Prevention, *Youth Risk Behavior Survey: Data Summary & Trends Report 2011–2021*, www.cdc.gov/healthyyouth/data/yrbs/pdf /YRBS_Data-Summary-Trends_Report2023_508.pdf.

CHAPTER 1

1. Adway S. Wadekar, "Duke Admits 4.6% of Regular Decision Applicants to Class of 2026," *Chronicle*, March 31, 2022, www.dukechronicle.com/article/2022/03 /duke-regular-decision-acceptance-rate-class-of-2026-admissions.

2. "Next Steps for Deferred Students: Undergraduate Admission," Georgia Tech Undergraduate Admission, accessed September 2, 2022, https://admission.gatech.edu /first-year/defer.

CHAPTER 2

1. Charlotte Country Day School, *Philanthropy 101* (Charlotte, 2021), https:// resources.finalsite.net/images/v1629735533/charlottecds/a1jskfqetbuqibyx7mdb/CDF Philanthropy101.pdf.

2. Raj Chetty et al., *Mobility Report Cards: The Role of Colleges in Intergenerational Mobility* (Cambridge: National Bureau of Economic Research, 2017), https://opportunity insights.org/wp-content/uploads/2018/03/coll_mrc_paper.pdf.

3. Raj Chetty and Nathaniel Hendren, "The Impacts of Neighborhoods on Inter-generational Mobility: Childhood Exposure Effects and County-Level Estimates," *Quarterly Journal of Economics* 133, no. 3 (2018): 1107–1162, https://doi.org/10.1093/qje /qjy007.

4. Chetty and Hendren, "The Impacts of Neighborhoods on Intergenerational Mobility."

5. Richard V. Reeves and Kimberly Howard, "Vague Hopes and Active Aspi-rations, Part 1," *Brookings* (blog), July 29, 2016, www.brookings.edu/blog /social-mobility-memos/2014/04/15/vague-hopes-and-active-aspirations-part-1/.

6. Reeves and Howard, "Vague Hopes and Active Aspirations, Part 1."

PART ONE

1. Adele Diamond and Daphne S. Ling, "Conclusions About Interventions, Pro-grams, and Approaches for Improving Executive Functions That Appear Justified and Those That, Despite Much Hype, Do Not," *Developmental Cognitive Neuroscience* 18 (2015): 34–38, https://doi.org/10.1016/j.dcn.2015.11.005.

2. Jessie I. Lund et al., "Adverse Childhood Experiences and Executive Func-tion Difficulties in Children: A Systematic Review," *Child Abuse & Neglect* 106 (2020), https://doi.org/10.1016/j.chiabu.2020.104485; Laura Starecheski, "Take the ACE Quiz—and Learn What It Does and Doesn't Mean," *National Public Radio*, March 2, 2015, www.npr.org/sections/health-shots/2015/03/02/387007941 /take-the-ace-quiz-and-learn-what-it-does-and-doesnt-mean.

CHAPTER 3

1. Adele Diamond, "Executive Functions," *Annual Review of Psychology* 64 (2013): 135–168, doi:10.1146/annurev-psych-113011-143750; Adele Diamond, "How to Sharpen

Executive Functions: Activities to Hone Brain Skills," *ADDitude Magazine*, last modified December 13, 2022, www.additudemag.com/how-to-improve-executive -function-adhd/.

2. Irene Cristofori, Shira Cohen-Zimerman, and Jordan Grafman, "Executive Functions," *Handbook of Clinical Neurology* 163 (2019): 197–219, doi:10.1016 /B978-0-12-804281-6.00011-2.

3. Richard M. Ryan and Edward L. Deci, "Self-Determination Theory and the Facilitation of Intrinsic Motivation, Social Development, and Well-Being," *American Psychologist* 55, no. 1 (2000): 68–78, https://doi.org/10.1037/0003-066X.55.1.68.

4. Edward de Bono, *Lateral Thinking: Creativity Step by Step* (New York: Harper & Row, 1970).

5. Mariam Arain et al., "Maturation of the Adolescent Brain," *Neuropsychiatric Disease and Treatment* 9 (2013): 449–461, doi: 10.2147/NDT.S39776. In this instance, I am defining gender biologically, as of birth.

6. Jessie I. Lund et al., "Adverse Childhood Experiences and Executive Function Difficulties in Children."

CHAPTER 4

1. John Q. Easton, Esperanza Johnson, and Lauren Sartain, *The Predictive Power of Ninth-Grade GPA* (Chicago: University of Chicago Consortium on School Research, 2017), https://consortium.uchicago.edu/sites/default/files/2018-10/Predictive %20Power%20of%20Ninth-Grade-Sept%202017-Consortium.pdf.

2. Aimée Goldstone et al., "Sleep Disturbance Predicts Depression Symptoms in Early Adolescence: Initial Findings from the Adolescent Brain Cognitive Development Study," *Journal of Adolescent Health* 66, no. 5 (2020), https://doi.org/10.1016 /j.jadohealth.2019.12.005.

CHAPTER 5

1. Jeanna Smialek, Lydia DePillis, and Ben Casselman, "Why Are Middle-Aged Men Missing from the Labor Market?," *New York Times*, December 2, 2022, www.nytimes .com/2022/12/02/business/economy/job-market-middle-aged-men.html.

2. Daniel A Cox, "Men's Social Circles Are Shrinking," The Survey Center on American Life, July 29, 2021, www.americansurveycenter.org/why-mens -social-circles-are-shrinking/.

PART TWO

1. Michael Niño, Gabe Ignatow, and Tianji Cai, "Social Isolation, Strain, and Youth Violence," *Youth Violence and Juvenile Justice* 15, no. 3 (2017): 299–313, doi:10.1177/1541204016636435; Kaori Endo et al., "Preference for Solitude, Social Isolation, Suicidal Ideation, and Self-Harm in Adolescents," *Journal of Adolescent Health* 61, no. 2 (2017), 187–191, http://dx.doi.org/10.1016/j.jadohealth.2017.02.018.

2. Eric B. Elbogen et al., "Suicidal Ideation and Thoughts of Self-Harm During the COVID-19 Pandemic: The Role of COVID-19-Related Stress, Social Isolation, and Financial Strain," *Depression and Anxiety* 38, no. 7 (2021): 739–748, doi:10.1002 /da.23162.

3. Caity Weaver, "Typing These Two Letters Will Scare Your Young Co-workers: Everything Was O.K. Until You Wrote 'O.K.,'" *New York Times*, November 21, 2019, www.nytimes.com/2019/11/21/business/kk.html.

CHAPTER 6

1. Raj Chetty et al., "Social Capital II: Determinants of Economic Connectedness," *Nature News* 608 (2022): 122–134, www.nature.com/articles/s41586-022-04997-3.

2. Daniel A. Cox, "The State of American Friendship: Change, Challenges, and Loss," The Survey Center on American Life, June 8, 2022, https://www.american surveycenter.org/research/the-state-of-american-friendship-change-challenges -and-loss/.

3. Clare M. Metha and JoNell Strough, "Sex Segregation in Friendships and Normative Contexts Across the Life Span," *Developmental Review* 29, no. 3 (2009): 201–220, https://doi.org/10.1016/j.dr.2009.06.001.

4. Raúl Navarro, Elisa Larrañaga, and Santiago Yubero, "Gender Identity, Gender-Typed Personality Traits and School Bullying: Victims, Bullies and Bully-Victims," *Child Indicators Research* 9, no. 1 (2016): 1–20, https://doi.org/10.1007 /s12187-015-9300-z.

5. Pawel Grygiel et al., "The Inclusion of Other-Sex Peers in Peer Networks and Sense of Peer Integration in Early Adolescence: A Two-Wave Longitudinal Study," *International Journal of Environmental Research and Public Health* 19, no. 22 (2022), https://doi.org/10.3390/ijerph192214971.

6. Marlene Sandstrom and Antonius H. N. Cillessen, "Likable Versus Popular: Distinct Implications for Adolescent Adjustment," *International Journal of Behavioral Development* 30, no. 4 (2006): 305–314, doi:10.1177/0165025406072789.

7. Antonius H. N. Cillessen and Lara Mayeaux, "From Censure to Reinforcement: Developmental Changes in the Association Between Aggression and Social Status," *Child Development* 75 (2004): 147–163, https://doi.org/10.1111/j.1467-8624.2004 .00660.x.

8. Mitch Prinstein, *Popular: The Power of Likability in a Status-Obsessed World* (New York: Viking, 2017).

9. Raj Chetty et al., "Social Capital II."

10. Raj Chetty et al., "Social Capital II."

11. Sylvia Ann Hewlett, *The Sponsor Effect: How to Be a Better Leader by Investing in Others* (Brighton: Harvard Business Review Press, 2019).

12. Cox, "The State of American Friendship."

13. Julia Freeland Fisher, *Who You Know: Unlocking Innovations That Expand Students' Networks* (San Francisco: Jossey-Bass, 2018).

14. Bridget Wray et al., "The Relationship Between Social Integration and Physical Activity, Diet, and Sleep Among Youths: Cross-Sectional Survey Study," *JMIR Pediatrics and Parenting* 5, no. 4 (2022), doi:10.2196/40354.

15. Paul M. Barret, Justin Hendrix, and J. Grant Sims, *Fueling the Fire: How Social Media Intensifies U.S. Political Polarization—and What Can Be Done About It* (New York: NYU Stern Center for Business and Human Rights, 2021), https://static1.squarespace

.com/static/5b6df958f8370af3217d4178/t/613a4d4cc86b9d3810eb35aa/1631210832122
/NYU+CBHR+Fueling+The+Fire_FINAL+ONLINE+REVISED+Sep7.pdf.

16. Suniya S. Luthar and Lucia Ciciolla, "What It Feels Like to Be a Mother: Variations by Children's Developmental Stages," *Developmental Psychology* 52, no. 1 (2016): 143–154, https://doi.org/10.1037/dev0000062.

17. Cody Hiatt et al., "Forms of Friendship: A Person-Centered Assessment of the Quality, Stability, and Outcomes of Different Types of Adolescent Friends," *Personality and Individual Differences* 77 (2015): 149–155, https://doi.org/10.1016/j.paid.2014.12.051.

18. Julie C. Bowker and Sarah V. Spencer, "Friendship and Adjustment: A Focus on Mixed-Grade Friendships," *Journal of Youth and Adolescence* 39, no. 11 (2010): 1318–1329, https://doi.org/10.1007/s10964-009-9474-0.

19. Bowker and Spencer, "Friendship and Adjustment."

CHAPTER 8

1. Bureau of Labor Statistics, *Number of Jobs, Labor Market Experience, Marital Status, and Health: Results from a National Longitudinal Survey* (Washington, DC: US Department of Labor, 2021), www.bls.gov/news.release/pdf/nlsoy.pdf.

2. Bureau of Labor Statistics, *Number of Jobs, Labor Market Experience, Marital Status, and Health.*

3. Raj Chetty et al., "Race and Economic Opportunity in the United States: An Intergenerational Perspective," *Quarterly Journal of Economics* 135, no. 2 (2020): 711–783, https://doi.org/10.1093/qje/qjz042.

CHAPTER 9

1. Bureau of Labor Statistics, *Number of Jobs, Labor Market Experience, Marital Status, and Health.*

CHAPTER 10

1. Raj Chetty, "Where Is the Land of Opportunity?: The Geography of Intergenerational Mobility in the United States," *Quarterly Journal of Economics* 129, no. 4 (2014), doi:10.1093/qje/qju022.

CHAPTER 11

1. Will Haskell, "A Gossip App Brought My High School to a Halt," *Cut*, April 28, 2014, www.thecut.com/2014/04/gossip-app-brought-my-high-school-to-a-halt.html; Alyssa Newcomb, "Why These Apps Can Make High School a Nightmare," *ABC News*, May 5, 2014, https://abcnews.go.com/Technology/secret-messaging-apps-make-high-school-nightmare/story?id=23597535.

2. Pew Research Center, *How Teens and Parents Navigate Screen Time and Device Distractions*, August 2018, www.pewresearch.org/internet/wp-content/uploads/sites/9/2018/08/PI_2018.08.22_teens-screentime_FINAL.pdf.

3. Victoria Rideout and Michael B. Robb, *Common Sense Census: Media Use by Tweens and Teens, 2019* (Common Sense Media, 2019), www.commonsensemedia.org/sites/default/files/research/report/2019-census-8-to-18-full-report-updated.pdf.

CHAPTER 12

1. Andrew J. Martin, "Should Students Have a Gap Year? Motivation and Performance Factors Relevant to Time Out After Completing School," *Journal of Educational Psychology* 102, no. 3 (2010): 561–576, https://doi.org/10.1037/a0019321.

2. Kristin Neff, "Definition and Three Elements of Self-Compassion," *Self-Compassion*, July 9, 2020, https://self-compassion.org/the-three-elements-of-self-compassion-2/.

3. Douglas Belkin, "A Generation of American Men Give Up on College: 'I Just Feel Lost,'" *Wall Street Journal*, September 7, 2021, www.wsj.com/articles/college-university-fall-higher-education-men-women-enrollment-admissions-back-to-school-11630948233?mod=article_inline.

4. National Student Clearinghouse Research Center, *Overview: Spring 2022 Enrollment Estimates* (May 26, 2022), https://nscresearchcenter.org/wp-content/uploads/CTEE_Report_Spring_2022.pdf.

CHAPTER 13

1. Gillian M. Sandstrom and Elizabeth W. Dunn, "Social Interactions and Well-Being: The Surprising Power of Weak Ties," *Personality and Social Psychology Bulletin* 40, no. 7 (2014): 910–922, doi:10.1177/0146167214529799.

2. Nico Savidge and Rick Hurd, "'It's Kind of Like Nuclear Winter': Unprecedented Smoke Layer Darkens Bay Area Skies as West Coast Burns," *Mercury News*, September 16, 2020, www.mercurynews.com/2020/09/09/complete-smoke-out-in-bay-area-darkens-the-daytime/; Dominic Fracassa, "San Francisco to End Nightly Curfew After Wednesday," *San Francisco Chronicle*, June 4, 2020, www.sfchronicle.com/bayarea/article/San-Francisco-to-end-nightly-curfew-after-15314823.php.

3. David Epstein, *Range: Why Generalists Triumph in a Specialized World* (New York: Riverhead Books, 2019).

CHAPTER 14

1. Sabino Kornrich, "Inequalities in Parental Spending on Young Children: 1972 to 2010," *American Educational Research Association* 2, no. 2 (2016): 1–12, doi: 10.1177/2332858416644180.

2. US Bureau of Labor Statistics, "Labor Force Statistics from the Current Population Survey."

3. Jeremy J. Walsh et al., "Associations Between 24 Hour Movement Behaviours and Global Cognition in US Children: A Cross-Sectional Observational Study," *Lancet* 2, no. 11 (2018), https://doi.org/10.1016/S2352-4642(18)30278-5.

4. Tony Schwartz and Catherine McCarthy, "Manage Your Energy, Not Your Time," *Harvard Business Review*, October 3, 2019, https://hbr.org/2007/10/manage-your-energy-not-your-time.

5. Schwartz and McCarthy, "Manage Your Energy, Not Your Time."

6. W. Thomas Boyce, *The Orchid and the Dandelion: Why Some Children Struggle and How All Can Thrive* (Ontario: Penguin Canada, 2019), 15.

7. Luminaria Learning Solutions, "Lesson 22: Skills for Small Talk," Life Navigator Sixth Grade Curriculum, 2022.

CHAPTER 16

1. Kenneth A. Mason et al., *Biology*, 12th ed. (New York: McGraw-Hill Education, 2020).

2. N. Kitagawa, "Practice of Behavioral Activation in Cognitive-Behavioral Therapy," *Seishin Shinkeigaku Zasshi* 117, no. 1 (2015): 26–33 (in Japanese), PMID: 265 14043.

3. Judy Singer, "Odd People In: The Birth of Community Amongst People on the 'Autistic Spectrum': A Personal Exploration of a New Social Movement Based on Neurological Diversity" (University of Technology, Sydney, 1998).

4. Russell Barkley, "DESR: Why Deficient Emotional Self-Regulation Is Central to ADHD (and Largely Overlooked)," *ADDitude*, July 11, 2022, www.additudemag.com /desr-adhd-emotional-regulation/.

INDEX

Aaron, 85–93
academic performance
  evaluating, 19–22, 38–39
  impacts on, 19–55, 57–64, 97–100,
    126–128, 131–163
  stress and, 19–35, 97–100, 127–128, 131–163
acceptance
  developing, xxi, 131–171
  practicing, 132–144, 175, 177–182
  self-acceptance, 28, 96–99, 132–144,
    150–151, 160–161
  uncertainty and, 145–156
  see also college acceptance
access
  exposure and, xvii, xviii, 14–16
  opportunity and, xix–xx, 6–8, 14–16,
    27, 61–73, 79–87, 93, 97–107, 146–147,
    201–202
  to skill building, 201–202
  to support, 58–60, 67–75, 89–93,
    128–130, 202
accountability, 33, 38–40, 105, 188–189, 198
acknowledgment, 123, 138, 143, 191–193
activation energy, 188–189
adaptable perspective, 147–148
adaptable structure, 155–156
adaptable thinking, 2, 20–22, 26–28, 80, 175
ADHD, 47–48, 55, 175, 187–190, 193–198
Advanced Placement (AP) courses, 1, 4–5,
  40, 78–81, 133, 161
Aidan, 147–149
Amanda, 177–185
American Airlines, 145
American Dream, 199
American River College, 103

Andrew, 37–46, 166
anxiety
  causes of, xiii–xvii, 19–29, 32–34, 66, 86,
    96–100, 160
  impact of, 32–35, 99–100, 138
  levels of, xiii–xvii, 21, 123, 160
  managing, 7–9, 35, 41, 138–139
  for parents, xiii–xvii, 5, 73, 123, 133, 193
  reducing, 7–9, 35, 41, 138
  see also stress
Apple, xvii
athletics, 20, 131–133, 136, 147, 162–163. See
  also sports
Austen, Jane, 47–48
autism, 190, 195–196
autonomy, 7, 38, 151–154, 197
Avery, 157–160

Belkin, Douglas, 142
Belkin, Lisa, 173
Berklee College of Music, 52–55, 175
blueprint
  developing, xv–xxii, 6–9, 17–18, 45–55,
    82–84, 95–100, 132–134, 142–144,
    173–175, 177–185, 187–198
  neurodiversity and, 187–198
  pivoting, 177–185
  for success, xv–xxii, 6–9, 17–18, 45–55,
    82–84, 95–100, 132–134, 142–144,
    173–175, 177–185, 187–198
Boyce, Thomas, 167
Broadway Dance Center, 183–184
Brookings Institution, 12, 16
Bruni, Frank, xiv
burnout, 160–165, 170

California State Summer School for Science and Mathematics, 78
career trajectory, xviii, 177–185, 200–202. *See also* life trajectory
Caroline, 187–189
Center for Health Sciences, 41
Charles, 157–158
Charlotte Country Day School, 11–16
Chetty, Raj, 12, 66
Christopher, 109–115, 129
Cindy, 110–112, 114–115
Clara, 90–91, 93
clarifiers, 60, 67–69, 128–129, 202
cognitive behavioral therapy, 188–189
cognitive flexibility, 25–27
college acceptance
    dreams of, xi–xvii, 2–5, 152, 178–179
    grades and, xvi–xvii, 20, 39–40, 48–51, 158–160
    joy of, xi–xiv, 23–35, 62–63
    overemphasis on, xiii–xvii, 16, 35–40, 77–78, 88–89, 98–99, 132–139
    pandemic and, xiv–xvi, xix–xxii
    pressure for, xiii–xvii, 2–3
    test scores and, xvii, 6–9, 20, 48–51
    videos of, xi, xiii–xiv
college admissions
    anxiety over, xiii–xvii, 2–3
    competitive impacts of, xv–xvii, 154
    Early Decision process, xiii, 3–5, 179
    faulty finish line and, xvi, 88–89, 101–102, 132–144
    scandal about, xiv
    uncertainty of, 96–99, 102, 151
college application process
    deferrals and, 2–5, 179, 182
    enrollment strategies, xiii, 3–5, 179
    managing, 2–9, 17, 41, 81, 112–114
    navigating, xii–xiii, 2–9, 41, 67–68, 77–78, 112–114, 144
college costs, xiv–xv, 42, 86, 103–104, 138–139
college enrollment strategy, xiii, 3–5, 179
Common Sense Media, 121
community building, 153–154, 162, 195
competence, sense of, 27, 138, 151–154, 168, 192, 197
competitive edge, xii–xv, 50, 78, 83, 99, 133, 170–171

connection
    casual connections, 70–71, 149, 159
    developing, xviii, xix–xx, 57–93, 113–122, 128–169, 173–175, 182, 190–198
    family time and, 70–72
    importance of, 13–18, 39–44, 57–93, 190–202
    in-real-life connection, 60–65, 117–130
    multiple circles of, 60, 69–79, 128, 196–197
    need for, xvii, 13–18, 39–44, 57–93, 113–122, 128–169, 190–198
    networks, xix, 16–17, 37–43, 58–60, 72–74, 79–93, 95–99
    online connections, 60–65, 117–130
    relationship building, xix–xxii, 58–60, 70–72, 79–80, 111
    sense of, 35–36, 67–68, 118–122, 130, 144, 168, 197
    social capital and, xix, 16, 60, 79–88, 91–93, 95–99
    social media and, 58–65, 117–130
    transactional socializing, 57–58, 66–67, 79
    see also friendships
control
    attentional control, 25
    developing, xxiii, 6, 146–156
    inhibitory control, 25–28, 59
    self-control, 25, 59
    taking stock of, 151–156
COSMOS, 78
COVID-19 pandemic
    adjusting to, xiv–xvi, 20–21, 37, 44, 123, 128–130, 178
    impact of, xiv–xvi, xix–xxii, 20–21, 29, 48, 123, 128–130, 145–156, 168, 171, 178
    uncertainty and, 145–156
critical-thinking skills, xix, 2, 96, 175, 177–183. *See also* skills
curiosity
    discovering, 115, 124
    focusing on, xix, xxii, 27, 60–75, 77–84, 96–97, 173–175, 181
    importance of, 2–6
    openness and, 60–75, 77–84, 154

Dana-Farber Cancer Institute, 82
"dandelion children," 167
Day Worker Center, 32

De Bono, Edward, 28
Deci, Edward, 27
deferrals, 2–5, 179, 182
deliverables, 37–46
Delta Airlines, 145
Diamond, Adele, 25–26
disappointment, xiii, xvii, 3, 45, 80, 96–126, 138–164, 171, 175
diversity, 17, 64, 69–74, 87, 102, 113, 187–198
downward mobility, 87. *See also* economic mobility
"dream school," xiii, 3–5, 178–179
Duffy, John, xv
Duke University, xi–xiii, 3, 179

Early Decision process, xiii, 3–5, 179
economic mobility
    achieving, 15–17, 201–202
    analysis of, xviii–xxi, 11–17, 114
    barriers to, xviii–xxi, 11–16, 68, 84–87, 92–93
    downward mobility and, 87
    opportunities for, 67–73
    social mobility and, xvii, xxi, 15–16, 68, 92, 201–202
    upward mobility and, 12–15, 72–73, 85, 114, 202
Effective Self-regulation, 120, 126
Ellie, 117–118
energy
    activation energy, 188–189
    level of, 41, 57–58, 132–133, 165–170, 187–197
    managing, 119, 165–166, 187–197
    profile of, 165–168
    recharging, 41, 132–133, 166–168
entrepreneurs
    challenges of, 135–136
    models of success, 174–175, 180
    side businesses, 135–137
Epstein, David, 156
Equality of Opportunity Project, 11–15, 114
exclusion, 96, 105, 117–118, 127, 197
executive functioning skills, xviii–xxi, 5, 20–45, 137–138, 189–197. *See also* skills
exposure
    access and, xvii, xviii, 14–16
    benefits of, xvii–xxii, 62, 71–74, 81–93, 95–107, 109–115, 130, 156, 182, 201–202

immersive exposure, 104–107, 113–115
opportunity and, xviii, 71–72, 102–103
see also shared experiences

extracurricular activities, xvii, 20–24, 144–147, 155, 161–164. *See also specific activities*

Facebook, 73, 83, 119
false finish lines, xv–xvi, 1–2, 173–174
family time, 70–72
faulty finish line
    college admissions and, xvi, 88–89, 101–102, 132–144
    erasing, x–xxiii, 16–17, 185, 202
    expanding vision beyond, 1–9, 88, 132–144, 148–151, 202
    false finish lines, xv–xvi, 1–2, 173–174
    impact of, xix, 1–9, 101–102, 132–144
    levers and, 88–89
    limitations of, xix, 1–9, 101–102, 132–144
fear
    causes of, xv, 133, 152–153, 160, 178
    impact of, 123, 133, 138, 152, 160
    levels of, xv, 123, 160
    managing, 26, 138–139, 151–153
    for parents, 123, 133
    processing, 151–153
    reducing, 7, 26, 138–139, 151–153
    see also stress
Federer, Roger, 156
financial aid, 103–104
finish line
    erasing, x–xxiii, 16–17, 185, 202
    expanding vision beyond, 1–9, 88, 132–144, 148–151, 202
    false finish lines, xv–xvi, 1–2, 173–174
    faulty finish line, x–xxiii, 1–9, 16–17, 88–89, 101–102, 132–144, 173–174, 185, 202
floaters, 35, 61–75
foundational skills, xix–xxiii, 7, 11–18, 20, 45, 98, 174. *See also* skills
friendships
    acceptance and, 131–171
    authentic friendships, xvii, 24, 35, 42, 57–66, 71–72, 144, 168
    close friendships, 58, 63–72, 86, 149, 197–198
    community of, xvii–xviii, xxii, 5, 15–17, 32–48, 52–75, 103–107, 109–115, 118–119

friendships (*cont.*)
  genuine friendships, xvii, 42, 57–72, 79, 168
  in-real-life friends, 60–65, 117–130
  intergenerational friendships, 105, 127–128
  networks and, xix, 16–17, 37–43, 58–60, 72–74, 79–93, 95–99
  new friendships, 62–63, 117, 158–163
  online friends, 60–65, 117–130
  social needs and, 60, 67–75
  supportive friends, xvii, 37–43, 57–75, 122, 127–128, 196
  uncertainty and, 145–156
fulfillment
  blueprint for, xv–xvii, 83–84, 142–143, 181–184
  focusing on, 2–3, 83–84
  lack of, 159, 162
  success and, xv–xvii, 2–3, 35–36, 83–84, 142–143, 159–162, 181–184
fundamental skills, xiv–xvii, 1–9, 18, 50, 118–119, 173–174, 193–194. *See also* skills

Gallatin School, 184
generalists/specialists, 156
Georgia Tech University, 3
Gifted and Talented Program, 199
Google, xvii, 4, 7
GPA, 47, 50–51, 157–160
grades
  challenging classes and, 19–21
  college acceptance and, xvi–xvii, 20, 39–40, 48–51, 158–160
  focus on, 1–9, 14–16, 47, 50–51, 157–160
  GPA, 47, 50–51, 157–160
  learning differences and, 30–32
  overemphasis on, xvii, xix–xxi, 1–9, 48–51, 60, 97–98, 112, 131–133, 144, 151, 158–160, 199–200
  "Taking the B" and, 169–171

Harvard Business Review (magazine), 165
Harvard Business School, 82
Harvard University, xiv, 11–12, 77, 81–83, 114
Healthy Socialization, 120, 126
help, seeking, 15–17, 129–138, 153–154, 171, 201
Henry, 47–55, 175
Hewlett, Sylvia Ann, 68
Holy Cross Leadership Conference, 110

Holy Cross School, 110
honors classes, 40, 117, 161, 178
"how to learn," 28, 54–55
Humboldt State, 104
Hurricane Katrina, 110, 114–115

immersive exposure, 104–107, 113–115. *See also* exposure
inclusion, 71, 87
individualized education plan (IEP), 192–193
inhibitory control, 25–28, 59
Instagram, xi, 119, 121, 126, 128
Intel International Science and Engineering Fair, 80
internships, xv, 11, 44, 68, 80–93, 101–102, 181
IRL (in real life) connection, 60–65, 117–130. *See also* connection
Ivy League schools, xiv, 133

Jasmin, 15–18
Jobs, Steve, 154
Joseph, 135–144

Kennedy, John F., 154

Lauren, 2–9, 16, 41, 179
learning commitment, 47–55
learning differences, 29–32, 126, 155–156, 187–192
learning how to learn, 28, 54–55
levers, 60–62, 85–93
Life Navigator Advisory Program, 190–191, 202
life skills, xix–xxiii, 1–9. *See also* skills
life trajectory
  career trajectory and, xviii, 177–185, 200–202
  changing, xxi, 12–15, 60–62, 84–93, 103–104, 115
  impact on, xi, xviii, xxi, 45, 60–62, 67–68, 84–93, 115, 177–185, 200–202
  levers and, 60–62, 85–93
  supporting, 67–68
LinkedIn, 83
Luis, 38–39, 45–46, 71, 199–202

"Manage Your Energy, Not Your Time," 165
Mark, 196–197

Marvel, 97
McCarthy, Catherine, 165
McCullough, David, 97
mental health, xvi–xix, 7–9, 32–46, 57–58, 99–100, 123–132, 147–165. *See also* well-being
mentors, xv, xviii, 60, 67–72, 79–93, 113–115, 181, 202
mentorship, 67–72, 79–84, 91–93
Meta, xvii
Microsoft, 82
mindfulness, 35, 190–191, 194–197
MIT, 3
Molly, 118
Murphy, Dr. Courtney, 191–194
music, 49, 52–55, 130, 156–158, 175
"must-dos," 159–163
Myth of the Perfect Girl, The (book), 161–162

National Student Clearinghouse, 142
Neff, Kristin, 140–141
networks, xix, 16–17, 37–43, 58–60, 72–74, 79–93, 95–99. *See also* connection
neurodiversity, 187–198
New York Times (newspaper), xiv, 147, 173
New York University (NYU), 73, 184
Nicole, 102–104, 128, 147
Nira, 23–24, 31–36, 42, 62, 152
Notre Dame, 23, 33

Ollie, 97–102
Olympics, 125
Omar, 137–139
online connection, 60–65, 117–130. *See also* connection
openness, 17, 45, 60–75, 77–84, 130, 154. *See also* curiosity
Operation Varsity Blues, xiv
opportunity
    access and, xix–xx, 6–8, 14–16, 27, 61–73, 79–87, 93, 97–107, 146–147, 201–202
    expanding, xvii, xix–xx
    exposure and, xviii, 71–72, 102–103
    paths to success and, 143–144, 170–175
    shared experiences and, xviii, 71–72, 102–103
    for skill building, 45, 143–144, 201–202
Opportunity Insights, 66
optimism, xxiii, 77–84, 88–93

"orchid children," 167
organizational skills, 7–9, 12–16, 19–55, 137–147, 187–195, 200–202. *See also* skills
organizational system, 7–9, 19–55, 82–93, 97–99, 112–115, 119–147, 187–202. *See also* system
Overall Safety, 120, 126
overscheduling, 33–34, 40–42, 147, 163–165, 182, 196

Parenting the New Teen in the Age of Anxiety (book), xv
parents
    anxiety for, xiii–xvii, 5, 73, 123, 133, 193
    family time with, 70–72
    as models, 70–71, 129–133, 143, 160–169, 193–194
    stress for, xiii–xvii, 5, 73, 123, 133, 143, 165, 192–193
    supportive parents, 6, 41–43, 47, 52–54, 61–62, 67–71, 180–181
passion, 104, 143, 156, 175, 179, 182
pathways
    developing, 135–144
    following own, xv, xxi, 82–83, 135–144, 170–175, 180–185
    to success, xv, xxi–xxii, 82–83, 135–144, 155–156, 170–175, 180–185
perfectionism
    culture of, 131–134, 158–169
    idea of perfect life and, 161–163
    idea of success and, 100–101
    impact of, 8–9, 31, 119–120, 131–134, 158–169, 193–194
    social media and, 119–120
perspective
    adaptable perspective, 147–148
    developing, xvii, 5, 69–74, 80, 95–107, 109–133, 147, 159, 163, 175, 193, 198–201
    expanding, xvii, 95–104, 109–115, 159, 169, 175
    limited perspective, 99–101, 156
Philip, 77–84
pivoting process, 177–185
Placer County School District, 102
planning skills, xix, 9–36, 112–113. *See also* skills

possibilities, expanding, 68, 101–105, 109–115, 142–143
possibilities, seeing, 74–75, 96, 119, 174–175
Pride and Prejudice (book), 47–50, 54
Princeton University, 77
Prinstein, Mitch, 66
prioritizing skills, xix, 2, 20–36, 46, 98, 112–113, 137, 160, 170. *See also* skills
problem-solving skills, 26–27, 51–55, 137–138, 174–175, 177–183. *See also* skills
Professional Semester, 183
progress, measuring, 136–148, 157, 192–198
psychoeducation, 193
purpose, sense of, 45–46, 84, 104–105, 141–143, 175

Range: Why Generalists Triumph in a Specialized World (book), 156
Reeves, Richard, 16–17
Regeneron International Science and Engineering Fair, 80
relationship building
    connection and, xix–xxii, 58–60, 79–80, 111
    family and, 70–72
    networks and, xix, 16–17, 37–43, 58–60, 72–74, 79–88, 91–93, 95–99
    social capital and, xix, 16, 60, 79–88, 91–93, 95–99
    see also friendships
"résumé builders," xix
Reuters, 145
routines
    creating, 27–39, 49–55, 146–156, 188–196
    predictable routines, 21, 27–39, 49–55, 187–196
    structure and, 155, 187
Ryan, Richard, 27
Ryanne, 110–111

San Francisco State, 103
SAT, 78, 103
Saved by the Bell (television show), 112
savvy consumers, 96, 124–125
Schwartz, Tony, 165
Scripps College, 179–183
self-acceptance, 28, 96–99, 132–144, 150–151, 160–161
self-advocacy, 30, 126, 192–193, 196

self-awareness, xvii, 8, 27–45, 59, 99, 132–138, 150–165, 180, 192–195
self-compassion, 8, 132–134, 138–141
Self-Determination Theory, 27
self-expression, 158–162
setbacks, 96, 138, 143, 150–151, 171, 175
shared experiences
    benefits of, xvii–xxii, 7, 15, 69–74, 84–89, 95–96, 102–103, 115–119, 201–202
    opportunity and, xviii, 71–72, 102–103
    see also exposure
"should-dos," 159–163
skills
    adaptable-thinking skills, 2, 20–22, 26–28, 80, 175
    building, xiv–xxiii, 1–9, 20–55, 59–60, 137–147, 173–174, 195–202
    critical-thinking skills, xix, 2, 96, 175, 177–183
    executive functioning skills, xviii–xxi, 5, 20–45, 137–138, 189–197
    foundational skills, xix–xxiii, 7, 11–18, 20, 45, 98, 174
    fundamental skills, xiv–xvii, 1–9, 18, 50, 118–119, 173–174, 193–194
    lateral-thinking skills, 28
    learning how to learn, 28, 54–55
    life skills, xix–xxiii, 1–9
    organizational skills, 7–9, 12–16, 19–55, 137–147, 187–195, 200–202
    planning skills, xix, 19–36, 112–113
    prioritizing skills, xix, 2, 20–36, 46, 98, 112–113, 137, 160, 170
    problem-solving skills, 26–27, 51–55, 137–138, 174–175, 177–183
    reasoning skills, 26–28
    small-talk skills, 60, 70–71, 149, 159, 168–169
    starting/completing tasks, xvii, 9, 22–30, 44–50, 151, 164–165, 188, 196
    time-management skills, 7–9, 20, 31–33, 164–167
Sloboda, John, 156
small-talk skills, 60, 70–71, 149, 159, 168–169
Snapchat, 119
social capital, xix, 16, 60, 79–88, 91–93, 95–99
social media
    connections and, 58–65, 117–130

immersion in, 118–122

impact of, 73, 126–128

limiting time on, 82–83, 126–127

perfectionism and, 119–120

videos on, xi, xiii–xiv

Social Media Wellness (book), 58, 120, 127

social mobility, xviii, xxi, 15–16, 68, 92, 201–202. *See also* economic mobility

social needs, 60, 67–70

specialists/generalists, 156

Sponsor Effect: How to Be a Better Leader by Investing in Others (book), 68

sponsors, xviii, 60, 67–72, 79–84, 89–93, 114–115, 174, 202

sponsorship, 67–72, 79–84, 89–93

sports

  athletics, 20, 131–133, 136, 147, 162–163

  energy levels and, 167, 170

  high-pressure sports, 161–162

  overscheduling, 33–34, 40–42, 147, 163–164, 196

  pandemic and, 146–149

  sports camp, 106–107

  staying busy with, 20–23, 49–52, 61, 111–112, 136, 139–142

Stanford Law School, 100

Stanford University, 77–78, 80, 100

Stern Center for Business and Human Rights, 73

stress

  causes of, 19–35, 97–100, 127–128, 146–170, 195

  impact of, 21, 29, 98–100, 127–128, 131–163

  levels of, xvii, 5–9, 21, 146–163

  managing, 7–9, 26–35, 97–98, 138–139, 151–163, 169–171, 201–202

  for parents, xiii–xvii, 5, 73, 123, 133, 143, 165, 192–193

  processing, 151–153

  reducing, 7–9, 26–35, 97–98, 138–139, 151–163, 169–171, 201–202

structure

  accountability and, 38–40, 198

  adaptable structure, 155–156

  boundaries and, 111–112

  control and, 155

  more structure, 191–198

  predictable structure, 187

  routines and, 155, 187

support and, xix–xx, 9, 21–35, 48, 111–114, 136–140, 163, 187–198

student loans, xiv–xv, 86

success

  artificial markers of, xvi–xvii, xxi, 7–9

  blueprint for, xv–xxii, 6–9, 17–18, 45–55, 82–84, 95–100, 132–134, 142–144, 173–175, 177–185, 187–198

  defining, xix–xxii, 96–105, 119–120, 154–161, 180, 185

  fulfillment and, xv–xvii, 2–3, 35–36, 83–84, 142–143, 159–162, 181–184

  learning and, 28, 47–55

  model of, 174–175, 180

  paths to, xv, xxi–xxii, 82–83, 135–144, 155–162, 170–175, 180–185

  predictor of, xv, 20, 39

  redefining, xix–xxii, 55, 96–105, 140–142, 154–161

  system for, xv–xxii, 5–9, 12–55, 82–100, 112–115, 119–120, 131–147, 173–175, 177–185, 187–202

  vision of, 1–9, 88, 132–144, 148–151, 202

supporters

  access to, 58–60, 67–75, 89–93, 128–130, 202

  benefits of, 58–60, 67–75, 89–93, 128–130, 202

  definition of, 67

  friends, xvii, 37–43, 57–75, 122, 127–128, 196

  levers and, 89–93

  parents, 6, 41–43, 47, 52–54, 61–62, 67–71, 180–181

  social needs and, 60, 67–75

Susan, 137–139

system

  developing, xv–xxii, 5–9, 12–55, 82–93, 97–100, 112–115, 119–120, 131–147, 173–175, 177–185, 187–202

  implementing, 28–46, 187–198

  key times for developing, 21, 28–30, 37–43

  organizational system, 7–9, 12–16, 19–55, 82–93, 97–99, 112–115, 119–147, 187–202

  for success, xv–xxii, 5–9, 12–55, 82–100, 112–115, 119–120, 131–147, 173–175, 177–185, 187–202

"Taking the B," 169–171

tasks, starting/completing, xvii, 9, 22–30, 38, 44–50, 140–143, 151, 164–165, 187–188, 196

test scores
  challenging classes and, 19–21
  college acceptance and, xvii, 6–9, 20, 48–51
  learning differences and, 31–32
  overemphasis on, xvii, xix–xxi, 12–13, 60, 97–98, 131–133, 144, 151, 160, 199–200
  SAT scores, 78, 103
  "Taking the B" and, 169–171

That Crumpled Paper Was Due Last Week (book), 21, 52, 142, 173

Thomasboro Academy, 11, 15

Three Ss framework, 120, 126

TikTok, 119, 121, 126

time-management skills, 7–9, 20, 31–33, 164–167

to-dos
  checklists of, xix, 18, 50, 144, 157–171
  coping with, xix, 7–9, 18, 33–35, 133, 157–171
  managing, 7–9, 18, 33–35, 50, 82–83, 136–137, 157–171

transactional socializing, 57–58, 63–67, 79, 122, 163–164

trauma
  causes of, 21, 29, 110, 114–115, 146–150
  healing from, 115, 191
  impact of, 21, 29, 110, 114–115, 146–150
  levels of, 29, 115, 146–150, 191
  see also stress

Tulane University, 114

tutors, 67, 98, 105, 113

Twitter, 73, 119

UCLA, 85

uncertainty, xix, xxii, 4, 21–29, 96–102, 145–156, 195

United Airlines, 145

university costs, xiv–xv, 42, 86, 103–104, 138–139

University of British Columbia, 25

University of California, Berkeley, 11–12, 44, 114

University of California, Davis, 42

University of California, Los Angeles, 85

University of Connecticut, 61

University of Texas, 141

upward mobility, 12–15, 72–73, 85, 114, 202. *See also* economic mobility

validation, 23, 33, 104, 123, 133, 159, 184, 191–193

vision, expanding, 1–9, 88, 132–144, 148–151, 202

volunteering, 8–9, 15, 32, 71–73, 81–84, 101–106, 118, 170, 181

Wall Street Journal (newspaper), 142

Washington Post (newspaper), 147

Washington University, 178–179

"weak ties," 149

well-being
  emotional well-being, xiv–xviii, xxi, 7–9, 41–46, 58, 65–72, 81, 117–134, 145–171
  mental well-being, xvi–xix, 7–9, 32–46, 57–58, 99–100, 123–132, 147–165
  overall well-being, xxi, 7–9, 20, 41–42, 96, 117–119, 171
  social well-being, xv–xviii, xxi, 7–9, 46, 58, 65–72, 117–134, 171

WhatsApp, 119

Where You Go Is Not Who You'll Be (book), xiv

working memory, 20, 25–27

Yale School of Medicine, 82

Yale University, xiv, 82

Yokoi, Gunpei, 156

YouTube, 73, 119, 126

Zoom, 4, 8, 145–146, 199